JUMP Math

Book 5 Part 1 of 2

D0128443

Contents

jump math™

MULTIPLYING POTENTIAL.

JUMP Math
Toronto, Ontario
www.jumpmath.org

Writers: Dr. John Mighton, Dr. Sindi Sabourin, Dr. Anna Klebanov
Consultant: Jennifer Wyatt
Cover Design: Blakeley Words+Pictures
Special thanks to the design and layout team.
Cover Photograph: Eugene Kasimiarovich

ISBN: 978-1-897120-74-3

8th printing June 2014

ANCIENT FOREST™ FRIENDLY

970 trees were saved for our forests

Preserving our environment

Jump Math chose to print the pages of this book on recycled paper and saved these resources[1]:

energy	water	greenhouse gases	solid waste
415 million BTUs	1,650,531 L	41,182 kg	13,579 kg

Printed by **Webcom Inc.** on Legacy Brite 100%

RECYCLED
100%
RECYCLABLE
Legacy Brite 100%

Printed by **Webcom Inc.**

[1]Estimates were made using the Environmental Defense Paper Calculator.

This book was manufactured without the use of additional coatings or processes, and was assembled using the latest equipment to achieve almost zero waste. Manufacturing this book in Canada ensures compliance with strict environmental practices and eliminates the need for international freight, which is a major contributor to global air pollution.

Printed and bound in Canada

Welcome to JUMP Math

Entering the world of JUMP Math means believing that every child has the capacity to be fully numerate and to love math. Founder and mathematician John Mighton has used this premise to develop his innovative teaching method. The resulting materials isolate and describe concepts so clearly and incrementally that everyone can understand them.

JUMP Math is comprised of workbooks, teacher's guides, evaluation materials, outreach programs, tutoring support through schools and community organizations, and provincial curriculum correlations. All of this is presented on the JUMP Math website: **www.jumpmath.org**.

Teacher's guides are available on the website for free use. Read the introduction to the teacher's guides before you begin using these materials. This will ensure that you understand both the philosophy and the methodology of JUMP Math. The workbooks are designed for use by children, with adult guidance. Each child will have unique needs and it is important to provide the child with the appropriate support and encouragement as he or she works through the material.

Allow children to discover the concepts on the worksheets by themselves as much as possible. Mathematical discoveries can be made in small, incremental steps. The discovery of a new step is like untangling the parts of a puzzle. It is exciting and rewarding.

Children will need to answer the questions marked with a ▨ in a notebook. Grid paper and notebooks should always be on hand for answering extra questions or when additional room for calculation is needed. Grid paper is also available in the BLM section of the Teacher's Guide.

The ⬡ means "Stop! Assess understanding and explain new concepts before proceeding."

Contents

PART 1

Patterns & Algebra

Number Sense

Measurement

Probability & Data Management

Geometry

PART 2
Patterns & Algebra

Number Sense

Measurement

Probability & Data Management

Geometry

PA5-1: Counting

Jamie finds the **difference** between 15 and 12 by counting on her fingers.
She says "12" with her fist closed, then counts to 15, raising one finger at a time:

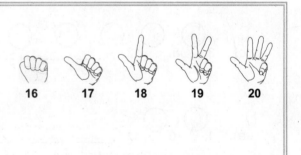

| 12 | 13 | 14 | 15 |

When she says "15", she has raised 3 fingers. So the difference or "gap" between 12 and 15 is 3.

---

1. Count the gap between the numbers. Write your answer in the circle:
   HINT: If you know your subtraction facts, you may be able to find the answer without counting.

   a) 2 ⑤ 7   b) 5 ③ 8   c) 3 ⑥ 9   d) 3 ④ 7   e) 2 ⑥ 8

   f) 11 ⑥ 17   g) 11 ⑤ 16   h) 22 ⑥ 28   i) 36 ② 38   j) 31 ⑨ 40

   k) 32 ⑤ 37   l) 43 ④ 47   m) 49 ③ 52   n) 85 ⑥ 91   o) 67 ⑤ 72

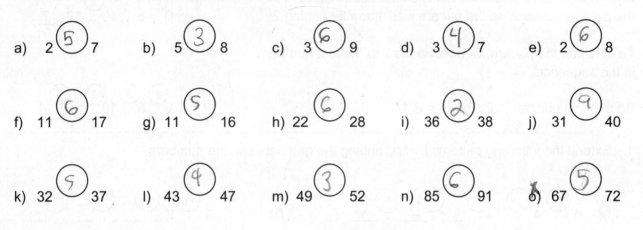

What number is 4 <u>more</u> than 16? (Or: 16 + 4 = ?)

Ravi finds the answer by counting on his fingers. He says
16 with his fist closed, then counts up from 16 until he has
raised 4 fingers:

| 16 | 17 | 18 | 19 | 20 |

The number 20 is 4 more than 16.

2. Add the number in the circle to the number beside it. Write your answer in the blank:

   a) 5 ③ 8   b) 8 ④ 12   c) 6 ⑥ 12   d) 17 ② 19   e) 12 ⑧ 20

   f) 25 ⑨ 34   g) 34 ⑦ 41   h) 62 ③ 65   i) 83 ④ 87   j) 91 ⑥ 97

3. Fill in the missing numbers:

   a) _11_ is 5 more than 6   b) _33_ is 7 more than 26   c) _25_ is 8 more than 17

   d) _34_ is 5 more than 29   e) _42_ is 4 more than 38   f) _74_ is 9 more than 65

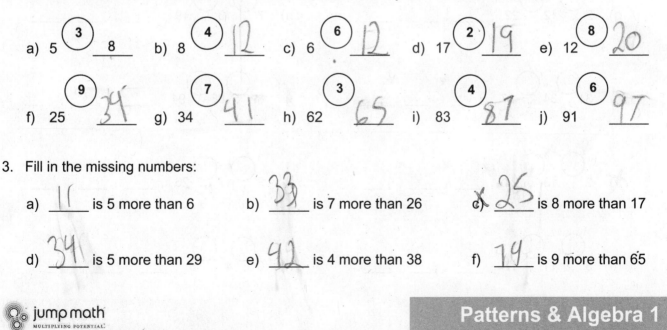

In an **increasing sequence**, each number is greater than the one before it.

Deborah wants to continue the number pattern:

6 , 8 , 10 , 12 , ?

She finds the **difference** between the first two numbers:

6   7   8

6 , 8 , 10 , 12 , ?   ②

She finds that the difference between the other numbers in the pattern is also 2, so the pattern was made by adding 2:

6 , 8 , 10 , 12 , ?   ② ② ②

To continue the pattern, Deborah adds 2 to the last number in the sequence.

So the final number in the pattern is 14:

6 , 8 , 10 , 12 , 14   ② ② ② ②

---

1. Extend the following patterns by first finding the gap between the numbers.

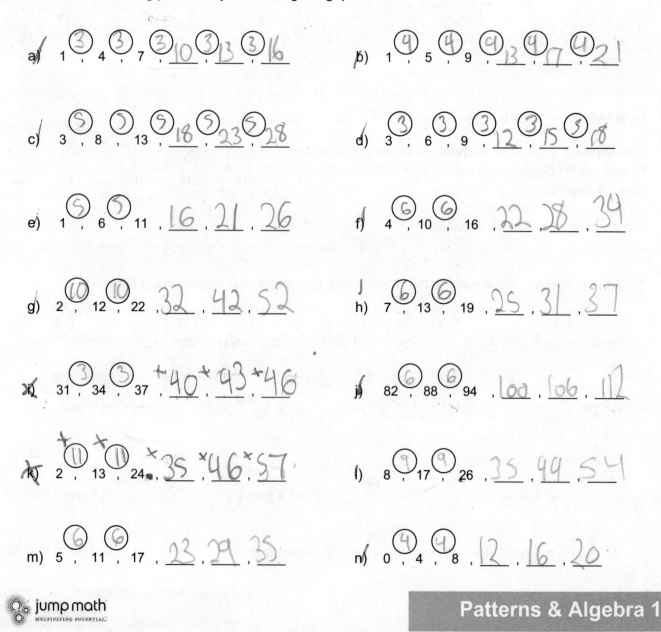

a) 1 ③, 4 ③, 7 ③, 10 ③, 13 ③, 16

b) 1 ④, 5 ④, 9 ④, 13 ④, 17 ④, 21

c) 3 ⑤, 8 ⑤, 13 ⑤, 18 ⑤, 23 ⑤, 28

d) 3 ③, 6 ③, 9 ③, 12 ③, 15 ③, 18

e) 1 ⑤, 6 ⑤, 11 , 16 , 21 , 26

f) 4 ⑥, 10 ⑥, 16 , 22 , 28 , 34

g) 2 ⑩, 12 ⑩, 22 , 32 , 42 , 52

h) 7 ⑥, 13 ⑥, 19 , 25 , 31 , 37

i) 31 ③, 34 ③, 37 , 40 , 43 , 46

j) 82 ⑥, 88 ⑥, 94 , 100 , 106 , 112

k) 2 ⑪, 13 ⑪, 24 , 35 , 46 , 57

l) 8 ⑨, 17 ⑨, 26 , 35 , 44 , 54

m) 5 ⑥, 11 ⑥, 17 , 23 , 29 , 35

n) 0 ④, 4 ④, 8 , 12 , 16 , 20

What number must you subtract from 43 to get 39? **43 – ? = 39**

Jess finds the answer by counting backwards on her fingers. She uses the number line to help:

When Jess says 39, she has raised four fingers, so 4 subtracted from 43 gives 39: **43 – 4 = 39**

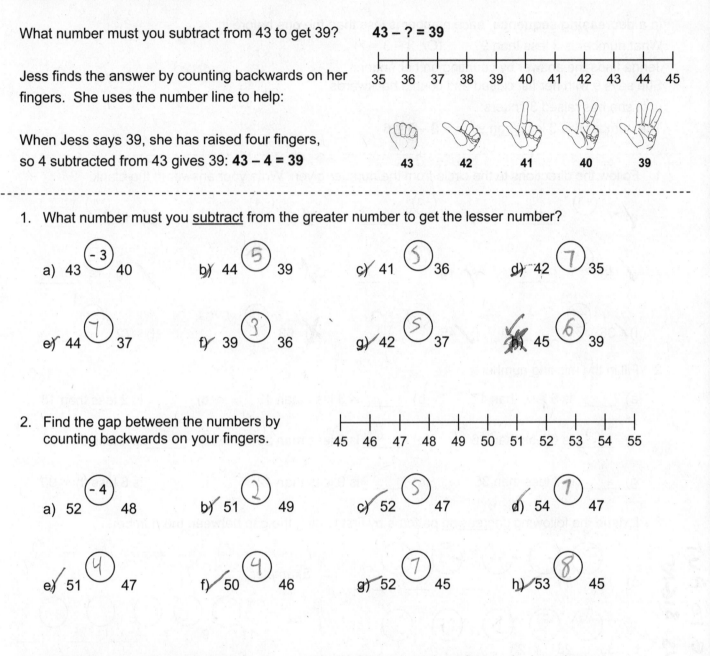

1. What number must you <u>subtract</u> from the greater number to get the lesser number?

a) 43 ⟨- 3⟩ 40   b) 44 ⟨5⟩ 39   c) 41 ⟨5⟩ 36   d) 42 ⟨7⟩ 35

e) 44 ⟨7⟩ 37   f) 39 ⟨3⟩ 36   g) 42 ⟨5⟩ 37   h) 45 ⟨6⟩ 39

2. Find the gap between the numbers by counting backwards on your fingers.

a) 52 ⟨- 4⟩ 48   b) 51 ⟨2⟩ 49   c) 52 ⟨5⟩ 47   d) 54 ⟨7⟩ 47

e) 51 ⟨4⟩ 47   f) 50 ⟨4⟩ 46   g) 52 ⟨7⟩ 45   h) 53 ⟨8⟩ 45

3. Find the gap between the numbers by counting backwards on your fingers (or by using your subtraction facts):

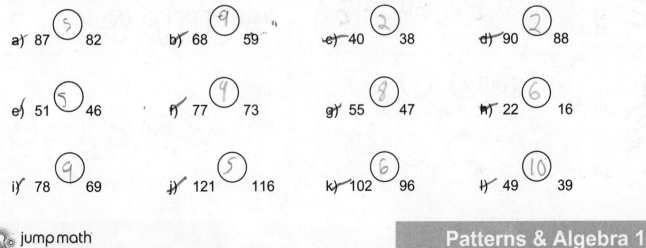

a) 87 ⟨5⟩ 82   b) 68 ⟨9⟩ 59   c) 40 ⟨2⟩ 38   d) 90 ⟨2⟩ 88

e) 51 ⟨5⟩ 46   f) 77 ⟨4⟩ 73   g) 55 ⟨8⟩ 47   h) 22 ⟨6⟩ 16

i) 78 ⟨9⟩ 69   j) 121 ⟨5⟩ 116   k) 102 ⟨6⟩ 96   l) 49 ⟨10⟩ 39

PA5-4: Decreasing Sequences

In a **decreasing sequence**, each number is less than the one before it.

What number is 3 less than 9?   (Or: 9 – 3 = ?)

Jenna finds the answer by counting on her fingers.
She says 9 with her fist closed and counts backwards
until she has raised 3 fingers:

The number 6 is 3 <u>less than</u> 9:   **9 – 3 = 6**

9   8   7   6

----

1. Follow the directions to the circle from the number given. Write your answer in the blank:

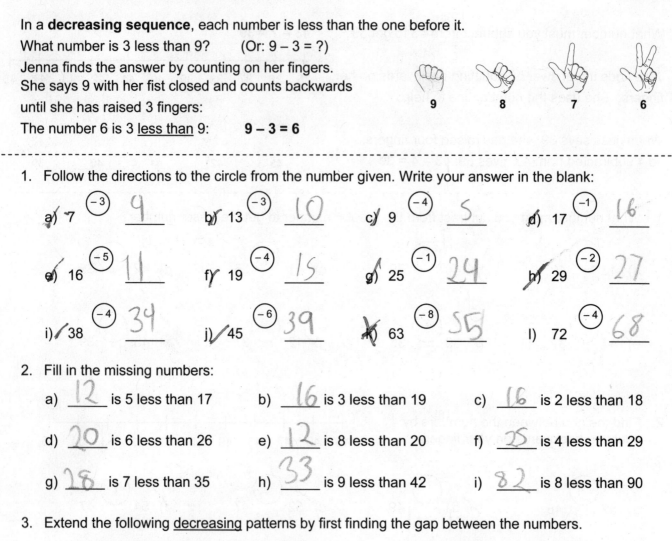

a) 7   (–3)   9   b) 13   (–3)   10   c) 9   (–4)   5   d) 17   (–1)   16

e) 16   (–5)   11   f) 19   (–4)   15   g) 25   (–1) 24   h) 29   (–2) 27

i) 38   (–4)   34   j) 45   (–6)   39   k) 63   (–8) 55   l) 72   (–4) 68

2. Fill in the missing numbers:

   a) __12__ is 5 less than 17   b) __16__ is 3 less than 19   c) __16__ is 2 less than 18

   d) __20__ is 6 less than 26   e) __12__ is 8 less than 20   f) __25__ is 4 less than 29

   g) __28__ is 7 less than 35   h) __33__ is 9 less than 42   i) __82__ is 8 less than 90

3. Extend the following <u>decreasing</u> patterns by first finding the gap between the numbers.

a) 13 , 11 , 9 , (–2) _7_ , (–2) _5_ , (–2) _3_

b) 33 , 28 , 23 , (5) _18_ , (5) _13_ , (5) _8_

c) 64 , 61 , 58 , (3) _55_ , (3) _52_ , (3) _49_

d) 55 , 46 , 37 , (9) _28_ , (9) _19_ , (9) _10_

e) 110 , 90 , 70 , (20) _50_ , (20) _30_ , (20) _10_

All good You HAVE to PUT MINUS SIGN

Example:

11 , 9 , 7 , ___ , ___ , ___

Step 1:   11 , 9 , 7 , ___ , ___ , ___
          (–2) (–2) (–2) (–2) (–2)

Step 2:   11 , 9 , 7 , _5_ , _3_ , _1_
          (–2) (–2) (–2) (–2) (–2)

PA5-5: Increasing and Decreasing Sequences

1. Extend the following patterns, using the "gap" provided:

Example 1:

(+1)

6 , 7 , __8__ , __9__

Example 2:

(−2)

8 , 6 , __4__ , __2__

a) 5 (+6) 11 , __17__ , __23__ , __29__

b) 1 (+4) 5 , __9__ , __13__ , __17__

c) 3 (+4) 7 , __11__ , __15__ , __19__

d) 6 (+3) 9 , __12__ , __15__ , __18__

e) 36 (−5) 31 , __26__ , __21__ , __16__

f) 10 (+7) 17 , __24__ , __31__ , __38__

g) 17 (−4) 13 , __9__ , __5__ , __1__

h) 19 (−4) 15 , __11__ , __7__ , __3__

2. Extend the following patterns by first finding the "gap".

a) 4 (4) 8 (4) 12 , __16__ , __20__

b) 3 (7) 10 (7) 17 , __24__ , __31__

c) 1 (3) 4 (3) 7 , __10__ , __13__

d) 21 (4) 25 (4) 29 , __33__ , __37__

f) 55 (−2) 53 (−2) 51 , __49__ , __47__

Example:

○ ○

3 , 5 , 7 , ____

Step 1:

(+2) (+2)

3 , 5 , 7 , ____

Step 2:

(+2) (+2)

3 , 5 , 7 , __9__

e) 11 (5) 16 (5) 21 , __26__ , __31__

g) 79 (6) 73 (6) 67 , __61__ , __55__

3. Jameson has a roll of 52 stamps.
   He uses 4 each day for 6 days.
   How many are left? __28__

4. Amy has saved $36. She saves $6 each day after that.
   How much money has she saved after 5 days? __66__

1. Continue the following sequences by <u>adding</u> the number given:

   a) (add 3)   41 , 44 , _47_ , _50_ , _53_

   b) (add 5)   60 , 65 , _70_ , _75_ , _80_

   c) (add 2)   74 , 76 , _78_ , _80_ , _82_

   d) (add 10)   20 , 30 , _40_ , _50_ , _60_

   e) (add 4)   61 , 65 , _69_ , _53_ , _57_

   f) (add 9)   31 , 40 , _49_ , _58_ , _67_

   g) (add 6)   20 , 26 , _32_ , _38_ , _44_

2. Continue the following sequences, <u>subtracting</u> by the number given:

   a) (subtract 2)   24 , 22 , _20_ , _18_ , _16_

   b) (subtract 3)   25 , 22 , _19_ , _16_ , _13_

   c) (subtract 5)   85 , 80 , _75_ , _70_ , _65_

   d) (subtract 10)   70 , 60 , _50_ , _40_ , _30_

   e) (subtract 4)   56 , 52 , _48_ , _44_ , _40_

   f) (subtract 7)   56 , 49 , _42_ , _35_ , _28_

   g) (subtract 11)   141 , 130 , _129_ , _119_ , _108_

BONUS

3. Create a pattern of your own. Say what number you added or subtracted each time:

   _10_ , _9_ , _8_ , _7_ , _6_   My rule: Start at 10 minus 1 each time

4. Which one of the following sequences was made by adding 4? Circle it.
   HINT: Check all the numbers in the sequence.

   a) 4, 8, 10, 14   b) (4, 8, 12, 16)   c) 3, 9, 11, 15

5. **72, 63, 54, 45, 36 ...**

   Yen says this sequence was made by subtracting 8 each time.
   Hyun says it was made by subtracting 9. Who is right?

   Hyun is right

PA5-7: Identifying Pattern Rules

1. What number was added each time to make the pattern?

   a) 2, 6, 10, 14   add __4__   b) 2, 5, 8, 11   add __3__   F

   c) 18, 24, 30, 36   add __6__   d) 40, 47, 54, 61   add __7__

   e) 81, 86, 91, 96   add __5__   f) 69, 72, 75, 78   add __3__

2. What number was subtracted each time to make each pattern?

   a) 38, 36, 34, 32   subtract __2__   b) 65, 60, 55, 50   subtract __5__

   c) 200, 199, 198, 197   subtract __1__   d) 91, 88, 85, 82   subtract __3__

   e) 67, 64, 61, 58   subtract __3__   f) 399, 397, 395, 393   subtract __2__

3. State the rule for the following patterns:

   a) 219, 212, 205, 198, 191   subtract __7__   b) 11, 19, 27, 35, 43, 51   add __8__

   c) 301, 305, 309, 313   __Add 4__   d) 210, 198, 186, 174   __Subtract 12__

   e) 633, 622, 611, 600, 589   __Subtract 11__   f) 821, 830, 839, 848, 857   __Add 9__

   g) 407, 415, 423, 431   __Add 8__   h) 731, 725, 719, 713   __Subtract 6__

4. Find the rule for the pattern. Then continue the pattern:

   a) 22, 27, 32, _37_, _42_, _47_   The rule is: __Start at 22 and add 5 each time__

   b) 38, 45, 52, _59_, _66_, _73_   The rule is: __Start at 38 and add 7 each time__

   c) 124, 136, 148, _160_, _172_, _179_   The rule is: __Start at 124 and add 12 each time__

5.   **5, 9, 13, 17, 21 ...**

   Jonah says the pattern rule is: "Start at 5 and subtract 4 each time."
   Pria says the rule is: "Start at 5 and add 5 each time."
   Genevieve says the rule is: "Start at 5 and add 4 each time."

   a) Whose rule is correct? __Genevieve__

   b) What mistakes did the others make? __Jonah's mistake was__
   __he said subtract and Pria's mistake__
   __was close but she was one ahead__

Claude makes a **growing pattern** with squares.
He records the number of squares in each figure in a chart or T-table.

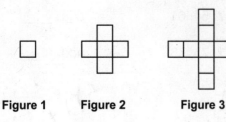

Figure 1   Figure 2   Figure 3

Figure	# of Squares
1	1
2	5
3	9

④ → Number of squares
④ → <u>added</u> each time.

The number of squares in the figures are 1, 5, 9, …
Claude writes a rule for this number pattern:

RULE: Start at 1 and add 4 each time.

----

1. Claude makes other growing patterns with squares.
   How many squares does he add to make each new figure?
   Write your answer in the circles provided. Then write a rule for the pattern:

a)

Figure	Number of Squares
1	2
2	7
3	12

⑤
⑤

Rule:
Start at 2 and
add 5 each time

b)

Figure	Number of Squares
1	2
2	9
3	16

⑦
⑦

Rule: start at
2 and add 7
each time

c)

Figure	Number of Squares
1	1
2	4
3	7

③
③

Rule:
start at 1 add
3 each time

d)

Figure	Number of Squares
1	1
2	7
3	13

⑥
⑥

Rule: Start at
1 add 6 each
time

e)

Figure	Number of Squares
1	5
2	12
3	19

⑦
⑦

Rule: Start at
5 add 7 each
time

f)

Figure	Number of Squares
1	13
2	21
3	29

⑧
⑧

Rule: Start at
13 add 8,
each time

jump math
MULTIPLYING POTENTIAL

Patterns & Algebra 1

g)

Figure	Number of Squares
1	3
2	11
3	19

⑧ ⑧

Rule: Start at 3 add 8 each time

h)

Figure	Number of Squares
1	7
2	11
3	15

④ ④

Rule: Start at 7, add 4 each time

i)

Figure	Number of Squares
1	8
2	14
3	20

⑥ ⑥

Rule: Start at 8 add 6 each time

2. Extend the number pattern. How many squares would be used in Figure 6?

a)

Figure	Number of Squares
1	2
2	9
3	16
4	23
5	30
6	37

⑦ ⑦   7 7

b)

Figure	Number of Squares
1	2
2	6
3	10
4	14
5	18
6	22

④ ④   4 4

c)

Figure	Number of Squares
1	6
2	11
3	16
4	21
5	26
6	31

⑤ ⑤   5 5

3. Trina makes the following growing patterns with squares.
After making Figure 3, she only has 16 squares left.
Does she have enough squares to complete Figure 4?

a)

Figure	Number of Squares
1	4
2	9
3	14
4	19

YES   (NO)

b)

Figure	Number of Squares
1	5
2	9
3	13
4	17

YES   (NO)

c)

Figure	Number of Squares
1	3
2	7
3	11
4	15

(YES)   NO

4. Make a chart to show how many shapes will be needed to make the fifth figure in each pattern.

a)

b)

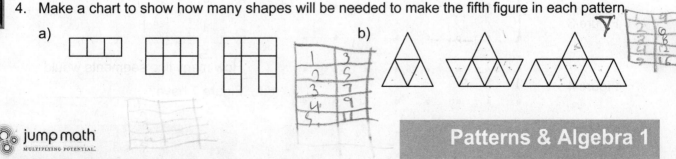

1. Count the number of line segments (lines that join pairs of dots) in each figure.
   HINT: Count around the outside of the figure first, marking line segments as you go.

Example:

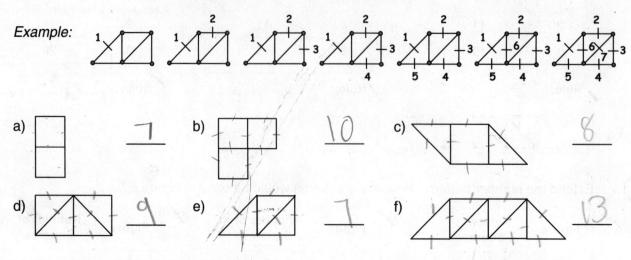

a)   7

b)   10

c)   8

d)   9

e)   7

f)   13

2. Continue the pattern below, then complete the chart:

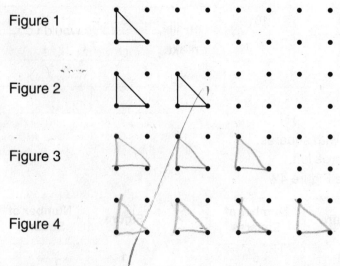

Figure 1

Figure 2

Figure 3

Figure 4

Figure	Number of Line Segments
1	3
2	6
3	9
4	12

How many line segments would Figure 5 have? _____ 15

3. Continue the pattern below, then complete the chart:

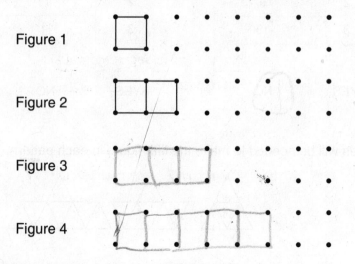

Figure 1

Figure 2

Figure 3

Figure 4

Figure	Number of Line Segments
1	4
2	8
3	12
4	16

How many line segments would Figure 7 have? _____ 28

jump math
MULTIPLYING POTENTIAL

Patterns & Algebra 1

Continue the patterns below, then complete the charts.

4.

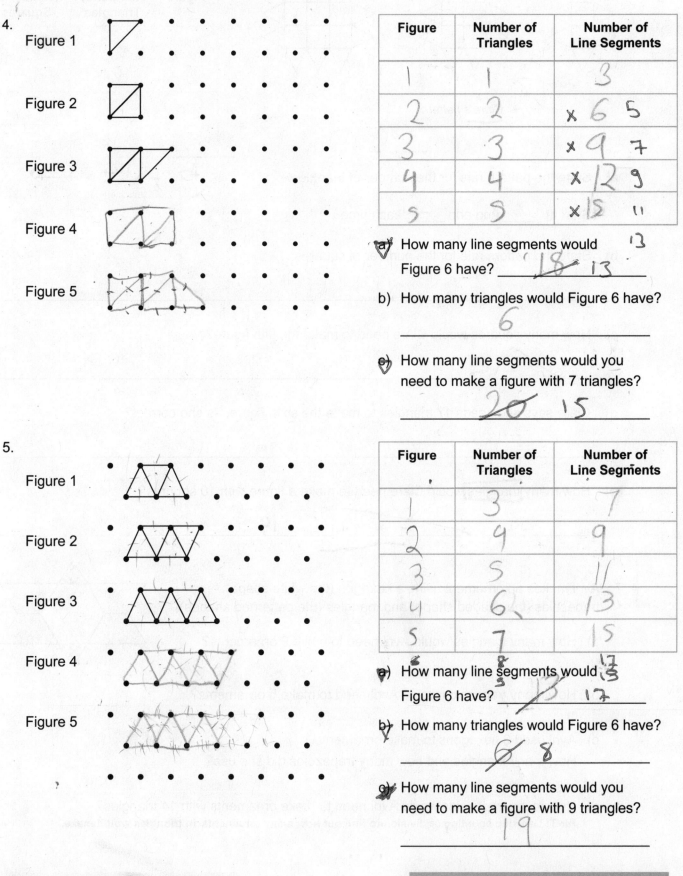

Figure 1

Figure 2

Figure 3

Figure 4

Figure 5

Figure	Number of Triangles	Number of Line Segments
1	1	3
2	2	x 6 5
3	3	x 9 7
4	4	x 12 9
5	5	x 15 11

a) How many line segments would Figure 6 have? ~~18~~ 13   13

b) How many triangles would Figure 6 have?

6

c) How many line segments would you need to make a figure with 7 triangles?

~~20~~ 15

5.

Figure 1

Figure 2

Figure 3

Figure 4

Figure 5

Figure	Number of Triangles	Number of Line Segments
1	3	7
2	4	9
3	5	11
4	6	13
5	7	15

a) How many line segments would Figure 6 have? ~~15~~ 17   17

b) How many triangles would Figure 6 have?

~~6~~ 8

c) How many line segments would you need to make a figure with 9 triangles?

19

6.

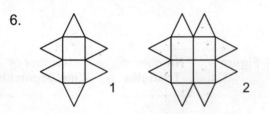 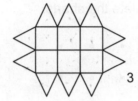

Clare's pattern

Figure	Number of Triangles	Number of Squares
1	6	2
2	8	4
3	10	6
4	12	8
5	14	10

a) State the pattern rule for the number of triangles:

Start at __6__ and add __2__ each time.

b) State the pattern rule for the number of squares:

Start at 2 and add 2 each time

c) How many squares would Clare need to make the fifth figure?

2+8 10

d) Clare says she needs 17 triangles to make the sixth figure. Is she correct?

No she

e) How many triangles would Clare need to make a figure with 10 squares?

5 Squares 14

7. Avril makes an ornament using a hexagon (the white shape), trapezoids (the shaded shape) and triangles (the patterned shapes):

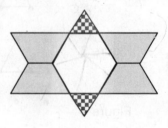

a) How many triangles would Avril need to make 9 ornaments?

b) How many trapezoids would Avril need to make 5 ornaments?

c) Avril used 6 hexagons to make ornaments.
How many triangles and how many trapezoids did she use?

d) How many trapezoids would Avril need to make ornaments with 14 triangles?
HINT: Use skip counting or division to find out how many ornaments 14 triangles would make.

1. Sarah's fish tank is leaking.

   At 6 pm, there are 21 L of water in the tank.

   At 7 pm, there are 18 L.

   At 8 pm, there are 15 L.

Hour	Amount of water in the tank
6 pm	21 L
7 pm	18 L
8 pm	15 L
9 pm	12 L
10 pm	10 L

   a) How many litres of water leak out each hour?

   3

   b) How many litres will be left in the tank at 10 pm?

   10 L 9

   c) How many hours will it take for all the water to leak out?   Means zero L

   8

2. Maral has $28 in his savings account at the end of March.

   He saves $7 each month.

   How much does he have in his account at the end of June?

Month	Savings
March	$28
June	$35
July	$42
August	$49

   where is April

3. Reema has $42 in her savings account at the end of October.

   She spends $7 each month.

   How much does she have at the end of January?

Month	Savings
October	$42
November	$35
december	$28
January	$21

4. Jane plants a 30 cm tall rose bush on May 1st.

   It grows 25 cm every month.

   What is its height on August 1st?

Date	Height
May 1st	30 cm
June 1	55 cm
July 1	80 cm
August 1	105 cm

5. A white cedar tree seedling grows about 9 cm in a year.

   How tall will it be after 3 years?

Years	Height
0	0 cm
1	9 cm
2	18 cm
3	27 cm

jump math
MULTIPLYING POTENTIAL

Patterns & Algebra 1

PA5-11: T-tables (Advanced)

The **terms** of a sequence are the numbers or items in the sequence.

A **term number** gives the position of each item.

This is **term number 4** since it is in the fourth position.

4, 7, 10, 13, 16

---

1. Extend the T-table to find the 5th term in the sequence:

    3, 5, 7, ...

Term Number	Term
1	3
2	5
3	7
4	9
5	11

2. Draw a T-table for each sequence to find the given term:

    a) Find the 6th term: 2, 5, 8, 11, ...

    b) Find the 7th term: 21, 26, 31, 36, ...

3. Travis says that the 6th term of the sequence 5, 7, 9, ... is 17. Is he correct? Explain.

4. Using blocks or other shapes, make a model of a sequence of figures that could go with each T-table:

a)

Term Number	Term
1	2
2	5
3	8
4	11

b)

Term Number	Term
1	1
2	5
3	9
4	13

5. A marina rents sailboats at $6 for the first hour and $5 for every hour after that. How much does it cost to rent a sailboat for 6 hours?

6. Zoe saves $65 in August. She saves $6 each month after that.
    Adrian saves $62 in August. He saves $7 each month after that.
    Who has saved the most money by the end of January?

7. A newborn elephant weighs about 77 kg.
    It drinks about 11 litres of milk a day and gains about 1 kg every day.

    a) How much weight does the baby gain in a week?

    b) How many litres of milk does the baby drink in a week?

    c) How many days does it take for the baby to double its weight?

PA5-12: Repeating Patterns

Marco makes a repeating pattern using blocks:

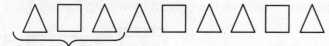

This is the **core** of Marco's pattern.

The **core** of a pattern is the part that repeats.

---

1. Circle the core of the following patterns. The first one is done for you:

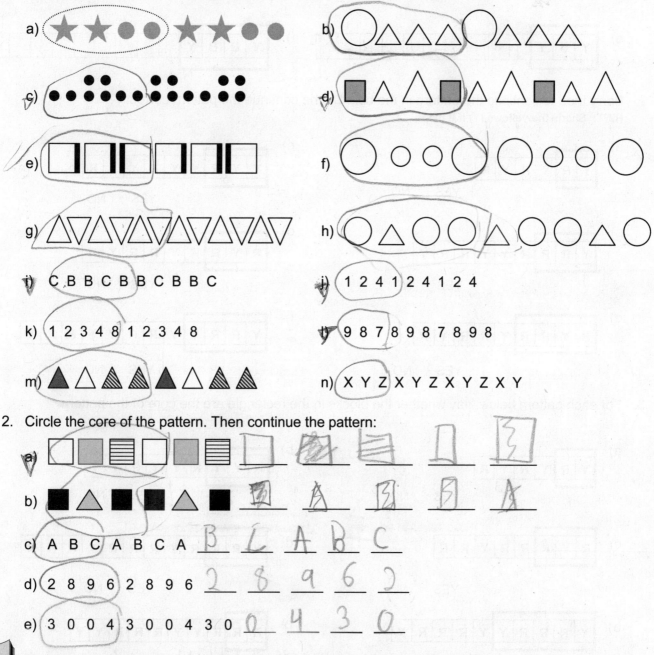

a) ★ ★ ● ● ★ ★ ● ●

b) ○ △ △ △ ○ △ △ △

c) ● ● ● ● ● ● ● ● ● ●

d) ▪ △ △ ▪ △ △ ▪ △ △

e) ▢ ▢ ▢ ▢ ▢ ▢

f) ○ ○ ○ ○ ○ ○ ○ ○

g) △▽ △▽ △▽ △▽ △▽ △▽

h) ○ △ ○ ○ △ ○ ○ △ ○

i) C B B C B B C B B B

j) 1 2 4 1 2 4 1 2 4

k) 1 2 3 4 8 1 2 3 4 8

l) 9 8 7 8 9 8 7 8 9 8

m) ▲ △ △ ▲ ▲ ▲ △ △ ▲

n) X Y Z X Y Z X Y Z X Y

2. Circle the core of the pattern. Then continue the pattern:

a) [squares pattern]

b) ■ △ ■ ■ △ ■

c) A B C A B C A   B C A B C

d) 2 8 9 6 2 8 9 6   2 8 9 6 2

e) 3 0 0 4 3 0 0 4 3 0   0 4 3 0

3. In your notebook (or using blocks) make several repeating patterns of your own. Have your teacher or another student guess the core of your pattern.

 jump math
MULTIPLYING POTENTIAL

Patterns & Algebra 1

1. Angela makes a repeating pattern using blue (**B**) and yellow (**Y**) blocks.
   The box shows the core of her pattern. Continue the pattern by writing Bs and Ys:

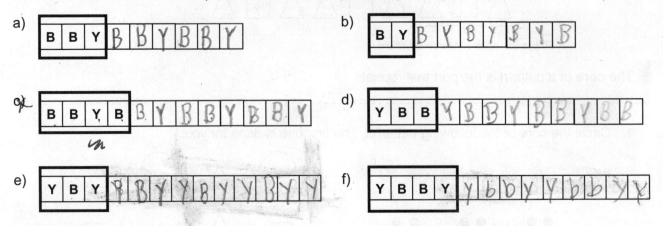

a) `B B Y` B B Y B B Y

b) `B Y` B Y B Y B Y B

c) `B B Y B` B Y B B Y B B Y

d) `Y B B` Y B B Y B B Y B B

e) `Y B Y` B B Y Y B Y Y B Y Y

f) `Y B B Y` Y B B Y Y B B Y Y

2. Barry tried to continue the pattern in the box. Did he continue the pattern correctly?
   HINT: Shade the yellows (Y) if it helps.

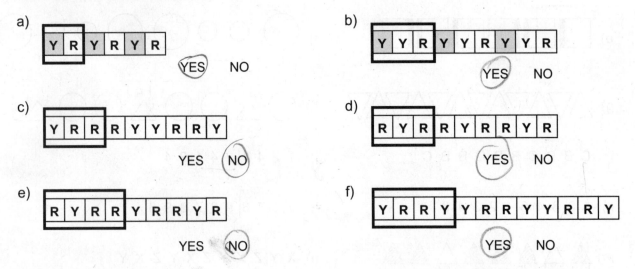

a) `Y R Y R Y R`   (YES)   NO

b) `Y Y R Y Y R Y Y R`   (YES)   NO

c) `Y R R R Y Y R R Y`   YES   (NO)

d) `R Y R R Y R R Y R`   YES   (NO)

e) `R Y R R Y R R Y R`   YES   (NO)

f) `Y R R Y Y R R Y Y R R Y`   (YES)   NO

3. For each pattern below, say whether the blocks in the rectangle are the <u>core</u> of the pattern:

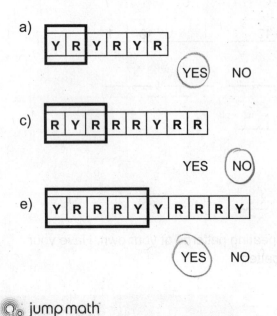
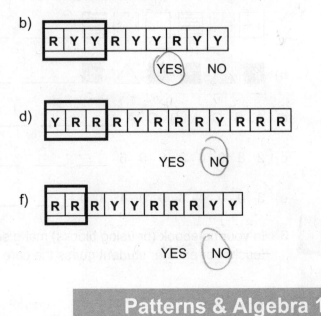

a) `Y R Y R Y R`   (YES)   NO

b) `R Y Y R Y Y R Y Y`   (YES)   NO

c) `R Y R R R Y R R`   YES   (NO)

d) `Y R R R Y R R R Y R R R`   YES   (NO)

e) `Y R R R Y Y R R R Y`   (YES)   NO

f) `R R R Y Y R R R Y Y`   YES   (NO)

Sally wants to predict the colour of the 17th block in the pattern. First she finds the core of the pattern:

The core is 3 blocks long. Sally marks every <u>third</u> number on a hundreds chart.

Each X shows the position of a block where the core ends:

1	2	~~3~~	4	5	~~6~~	7	8	~~9~~	10
11	~~12~~	13	14	~~15~~	16 R	17 R	18 Y	19	20

The core ends on the 15th block.

Sally writes the letters of the core on the chart, starting at 16.

The 17th block is red.

- -

4. In the patterns below, put a rectangle around the blocks that make up the core:

a) | Y | R | R | Y | R | R | Y | R | R |
   |---|---|---|---|---|---|---|---|---|

b) | R | Y | R | Y | R | Y | R | Y |
   |---|---|---|---|---|---|---|---|

c) | Y | Y | R | R | Y | Y | R | R | Y | Y | R | R |
   |---|---|---|---|---|---|---|---|---|---|---|---|

d) | Y | R | R | Y | Y | R | R | Y | Y |
   |---|---|---|---|---|---|---|---|---|

e) | R | Y | R | Y | Y | Y | R | Y | R | Y | Y | Y |
   |---|---|---|---|---|---|---|---|---|---|---|---|

f) | R | R | R | Y | R | R | R | Y | R | R |
   |---|---|---|---|---|---|---|---|---|---|

5. Predict the colour of the 18th block using Sally's method:

    NOTE: Start by finding the core of the pattern.

R	Y	Y	Y	R	Y	Y	Y

1	2	3	4	5	6	7	⑧	9	10
11	12	13	14	15	16	17	18	19	20

Colour: _yellow_

6. Predict the colour of the 19th block:

R	R	Y	Y	R	R	Y	Y

1	2	3	4	5	6	7	⑧	9	10
11	12	13	14	15	16	17	18	19	20

Colour: _yellow_

7. Predict the colour of the 17th block:

R	R	Y	Y	Y	R	R	Y	Y	Y

1	2	3	4	5	6	7	8	9	⑩
11	12	13	14	15	16	17	18	19	20

Colour: _Red_

Patterns & Algebra 1

8. Draw a box around the core of the pattern. Then predict the colour of the 35ᵗʰ block:

| Y | R | Y | Y | R | Y | Y | R | Y |

Colour: __yellow__

1	2	3	4	5	6	7	8	9	10
11	12	13	14	15	16	17	18	19	20
21	22	23	24	25	26	27	28	29	30
31	32	33	34	35	36	37	38	39	40

9. Carl makes a pattern with red, green, and yellow beads:

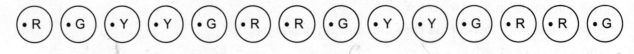

R • G • Y • Y • G • R • R • G • Y • Y • G • R • R • G

What colour will the 43ʳᵈ bead be?

10. Megan plants a row of daisies and pansies in the pattern shown:

D   P   P   D   P   P   D

Is the 37ᵗʰ flower a daisy or a pansy?

11. Explain how you could find the colour of the 48ᵗʰ block in this pattern without using a hundreds chart.

| R | R | Y | Y | Y | R | R | Y | Y | Y |

12. Design a repeating pattern that has a core that is ten squares long.
What is the colour of the 97ᵗʰ square? How do you know?

| R | O | Y | G | B | V | P | W | B | Gray |

13. a) What is the 15ᵗʰ coin in this pattern? Explain how you know.

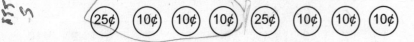

25¢ 10¢ 10¢ 10¢ 25¢ 10¢ 10¢ 10¢

BONUS
b) What is the total value of the first 20 coins?

PA5-14: Number Lines

On Monday morning, Olivia is 600 kilometres from Winnipeg.

Her solar-powered car can travel 150 km per day.

How far from Winnipeg will she be by Wednesday evening?

| | Wednesday | | Tuesday | | Monday | |

```
|----|----|----|----|----|----|----|----|----|----|----|----|
0   50  100  150  200  250  300  350  400  450  500  550  600
Winnipeg                                                  Start
```

On Wednesday evening, Olivia will be 150 km from Winnipeg.

---

1. On Thursday morning, Eduardo's campsite is 19 km from Great Bear Lake.
   He plans to hike 6 km towards the lake each day.

   How far from the lake will he be on Saturday evening? _____ 1 Km _____

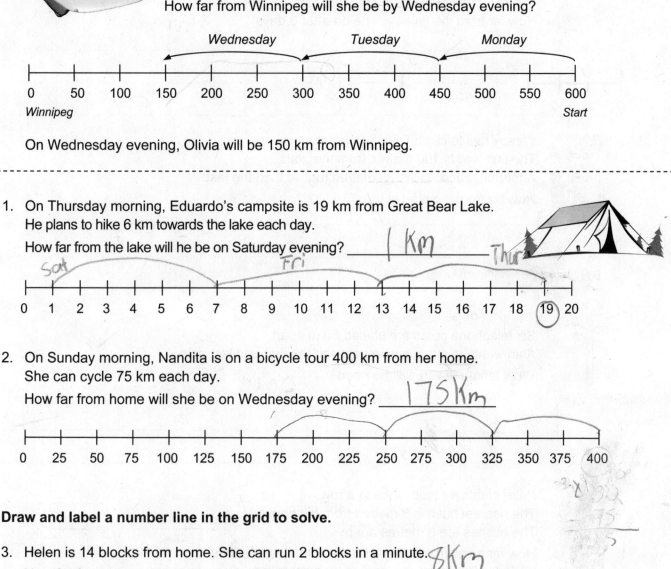

```
|--|--|--|--|--|--|--|--|--|--|--|--|--|--|--|--|--|--|--|--|
0  1  2  3  4  5  6  7  8  9  10 11 12 13 14 15 16 17 18 (19) 20
```

2. On Sunday morning, Nandita is on a bicycle tour 400 km from her home.
   She can cycle 75 km each day.

   How far from home will she be on Wednesday evening? _____ 175 Km _____

```
|----|----|----|----|----|----|----|----|----|----|----|----|----|----|----|----|
0   25   50   75  100  125  150  175  200  225  250  275  300  325  350  375  400
```

Draw and label a number line in the grid to solve.

3. Helen is 14 blocks from home. She can run 2 blocks in a minute. 8 Km
   How far from home will she be in 3 minutes?

```
0  1  2  3  4  5  6  7  8  9  10  11  12  13  14
```

4. Ravi is 15 blocks from the store. He can cycle 4 blocks in a minute.
   How far from the store will he be after 3 minutes? 3 Km

```
0  1  2  3  4  5  6  7  8  9  10  11  12  13  14  15
```

In each of the problems below you will have to decide on a scale for your number line.

1. Kristal has entered a 250 km bike race. He can cycle 75 km each day.
   How far from the finish will he be after 3 days? 25 Km

   | 0 | 25 | 50 | 75 | 100 | 125 | 150 | 175 | 200 | 225 | 250 | | | | | | | | | |

2. Wendy has to climb 5 walls in an obstacle course.
   The first wall is 100 metres from the start.
   After that, each wall is 75 metres further than the last.
   How far from the start is the 3rd wall? 250M

   | 0 | 100 | 175 | 250 | 325 | 400 | | | | | | | | | | | | | | |

   175 250 325
   75   75   75
   250 325 400

3. Six telephone poles are placed 50 m apart.
   Alan wants to string a wire between the first and last pole.
   What length of wire will he need? 300m

   | | 50 | 100 | 150 | 200 | 250 | | | | | | | | | | | | | | |

4. Peter plants 4 rosebushes in a row.
   The nearest bush is 8 metres from his house.
   The bushes are 3 metres apart.
   How far away from Peter's house is the last rosebush? 19m
   HINT: Put Peter's house at zero on the number line.

    | 8 | 9 | 10 | 11 | 12 | 13 | 14 | 15 | 16 | 17 | 18 | 14 | 15 | 16 | 17 | 18 | 14 |

5. Jill's house is 20 metres from the sidewalk.
   A dog is tied to a tree halfway between the house and the sidewalk.
   The dog's leash is 8 m long.
   How close to the sidewalk can the dog come?

   | 0 | 1 | 2 | 3 | 4 | 5 | 6 | 7 | | | | | | | | | | 18 | | 20 |

The multiples of 2 and 3 are marked with Xs on the number lines below:

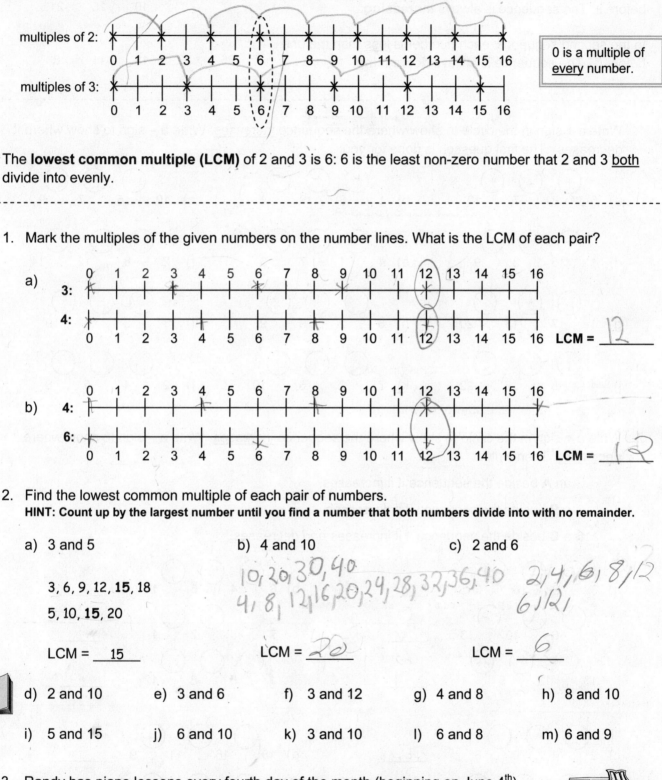

multiples of 2:

0 1 2 3 4 5 6 7 8 9 10 11 12 13 14 15 16

0 is a multiple of <u>every</u> number.

multiples of 3:

0 1 2 3 4 5 6 7 8 9 10 11 12 13 14 15 16

The **lowest common multiple (LCM)** of 2 and 3 is 6: 6 is the least non-zero number that 2 and 3 <u>both</u> divide into evenly.

---

1. Mark the multiples of the given numbers on the number lines. What is the LCM of each pair?

   a)
   3:    0 1 2 3 4 5 6 7 8 9 10 11 12 13 14 15 16

   4:    0 1 2 3 4 5 6 7 8 9 10 11 12 13 14 15 16   LCM = 12

   b)
   4:    0 1 2 3 4 5 6 7 8 9 10 11 12 13 14 15 16

   6:    0 1 2 3 4 5 6 7 8 9 10 11 12 13 14 15 16   LCM = 12

2. Find the lowest common multiple of each pair of numbers.
   HINT: Count up by the largest number until you find a number that both numbers divide into with no remainder.

   a) 3 and 5   b) 4 and 10   c) 2 and 6

   3, 6, 9, 12, **15**, 18   10, 20, 30, 40   2, 4, 6, 8, 12
   5, 10, **15**, 20   4, 8, 12, 16, 20, 24, 28, 32, 36, 40   6, 12

   LCM = ___15___   LCM = _20_   LCM = _6_

   d) 2 and 10   e) 3 and 6   f) 3 and 12   g) 4 and 8   h) 8 and 10

   i) 5 and 15   j) 6 and 10   k) 3 and 10   l) 6 and 8   m) 6 and 9

3. Randy has piano lessons every <u>fourth</u> day of the month (beginning on June 4th).
   Will has piano lessons every <u>sixth</u> day (beginning on June 6th).

   What is the first day of the month when they will have lessons on the same day?

In the first sequence, each number is <u>greater</u> than the one before it. The sequence is always **increasing**:

7   8   10   15   21

In the second sequence, each number is <u>less</u> than the one before it. The sequence is always **decreasing**:

25   23   18   11   8

----

1. Write a **+** sign in the circle to show where the sequence <u>increases</u>. Write a **–** sign to show where it <u>decreases</u>. The first question is done for you:

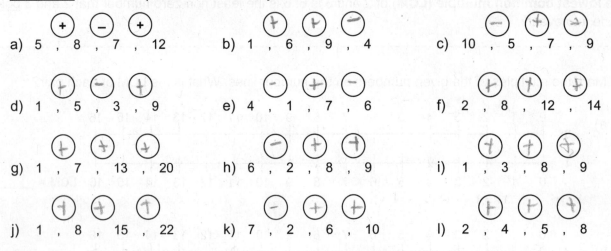

a) 5 , 8 , 7 , 12   b) 1 , 6 , 9 , 4   c) 10 , 5 , 7 , 9

d) 1 , 5 , 3 , 9   e) 4 , 1 , 7 , 6   f) 2 , 8 , 12 , 14

g) 1 , 7 , 13 , 20   h) 6 , 2 , 8 , 9   i) 1 , 3 , 8 , 9

j) 1 , 8 , 15 , 22   k) 7 , 2 , 6 , 10   l) 2 , 4 , 5 , 8

2. Write a **+** sign in the circle to show where the sequence <u>increases</u>. Write a **–** sign to show where it <u>decreases</u>. Then write...

    ... an **A** beside the sequence if it increases,

    ... a **B** beside the sequence if it decreases,

    ... a **C** beside the sequence if it increases *and* decreases.

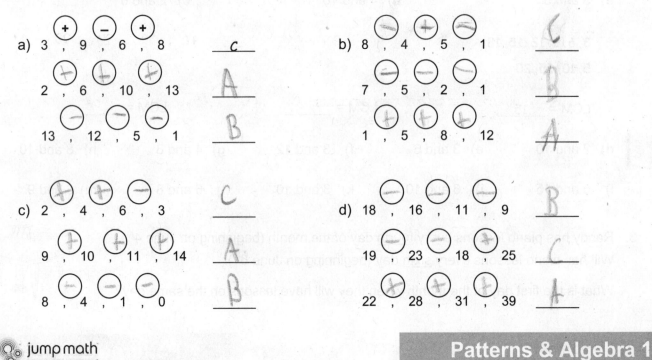

a) 3 , 9 , 6 , 8 _____ C

    2 , 6 , 10 , 13 _____ A

    13 , 12 , 5 , 1 _____ B

c) 2 , 4 , 6 , 3 _____ C

    9 , 10 , 11 , 14 _____ A

    8 , 4 , 1 , 0 _____ B

b) 8 , 4 , 5 , 1 _____ C

    7 , 5 , 2 , 1 _____ B

    1 , 5 , 8 , 12 _____ A

d) 18 , 16 , 11 , 9 _____ B

    19 , 23 , 18 , 25 _____ C

    22 , 28 , 31 , 39 _____ A

3. Find the <u>amount</u> by which the sequence increases or decreases and write it in the circle.
   (Write a number with a **+** sign if the sequence increases, and a **−** sign if it decreases.)

a) 2 , (+4) 6 , (−2) 4 , (+7) 11 , (−4) 7

b) 1 , (+5) 6 , (−3) 3 , (+6) 9 , (−5) 4

c) 1 , (+3) 4 , (+4) 8 , (+4) 12 , (+6) 18

d) 5 , (−2) 3 , (+6) 9 , (−8) 1 , (+9) 10

e) 3 , (+2) 5 , (+4) 9 , (−3) 6 , (+5) 11

f) 19 , (−6) 13 , (−3) 10 , (+6) 16 , (−5) 11

g) 17 , (−7) 10 , (+5) 15 , (+4) 19 , (−5) 14

h) 38 , (+3) 41 , (−7) 34 , (+8) 42 , (+6) 48

4. Match each sequence with the sentence that describes it. This sequence ...

a) **A** ... increases by 5 each time.
   B ... increases by different amounts.

   __A__ 9 , 12 , 14 , 17 , 21

   __A__ 7 , 12 , 17 , 22 , 27

b) **A** ... increases by 6 each time.
   B ... increases by different amounts.

   __A__ 10 , 16 , 22 , 28 , 34

   __A__ 5 , 8 , 13 , 15 , 21

c) **A** ... decreases by different amounts.
   B ... decreases by the same amount.

   __B__ 11 , 10 , 8 , 7 , 5

   __B__ 11 , 9 , 7 , 5 , 3

d) **A** ... decreases by 9 each time.
   B ... decreases by different amounts.

   __B__ 41 , 30 , 22 , 16 , 8

   __B__ 47 , 38 , 29 , 20 , 11

BONUS

e) **A** ... increases by 5 each time.
   B ... decreases by different amounts.
   C ... increases by different amounts.

   __C__ 16 , 21 , 27 , 31 , 33

   __B__ 18 , 13 , 9 , 8 , 5

   __A__ 17 , 22 , 27 , 32 , 37

f) **A** ... increases and decreases.
   B ... increases by the same amount.
   C ... decreases by different amounts.
   D ... decreases by the same amount.

   __A__ 20 , 23 , 19 , 17 , 13

   __C__ 15 , 12 , 11 , 9 , 7

   __D__ 20 , 18 , 16 , 14 , 12

   __B__ 10 , 13 , 16 , 19 , 22

5. Write a rule for each pattern (use the words <u>add</u> or <u>subtract</u>, and say what number the pattern starts with):

    a) 2 , 5 , 8 , 11   Start at 2 and add 3

    b) 3 , 9 , 15 , 21   Start at 3 add 6

    c) 18 , 15 , 12 , 9   Start at 18 Subtract 3

    d) 43 , 38 , 33 , 28   Start at 43 Subtract 5

6. Write a rule for each pattern.
    NOTE: One sequence doesn't have a rule – see if you can find this sequence.

    a) 8 , 13 , 18 , 23   Start at 8 add 5

    b) 26 , 19 , 12 , 5   Start at 26 subtract 7

    c) 29 , 21 , 17 , 14 , 9

    d) 71 , 75 , 79 , 83   Start at 71 add 4

7. Describe each pattern as <u>increasing</u>, <u>decreasing</u> or <u>repeating</u>:

    a) 1 , 5 , 9 , 13 , 17 , 21   increasing   b) 2 , 7 , 9 , 2 , 7 , 9   repeating

    c) 19 , 17 , 15 , 13 , 12   decreasing   d) 2 , 5 , 8 , 11 , 14 , 17   increasing

    e) 4 , 9 , 4 , 9 , 4 , 9   repeating   f) 31 , 26 , 20 , 17 , 15   decreasing

8. Write the first five numbers in the pattern:

    a) Start at 8 and add 4   b) Start at 37 and subtract 6   c) Start at 99 and add 7

9. Create an increasing number pattern. Write the rule for your pattern. Do the same for a decreasing number pattern.

10. Create a repeating pattern using: a) letters   b) shapes   c) numbers

11. Create a pattern and ask a friend to find the rule for your pattern.

PA5-18: 2-Dimensional Patterns

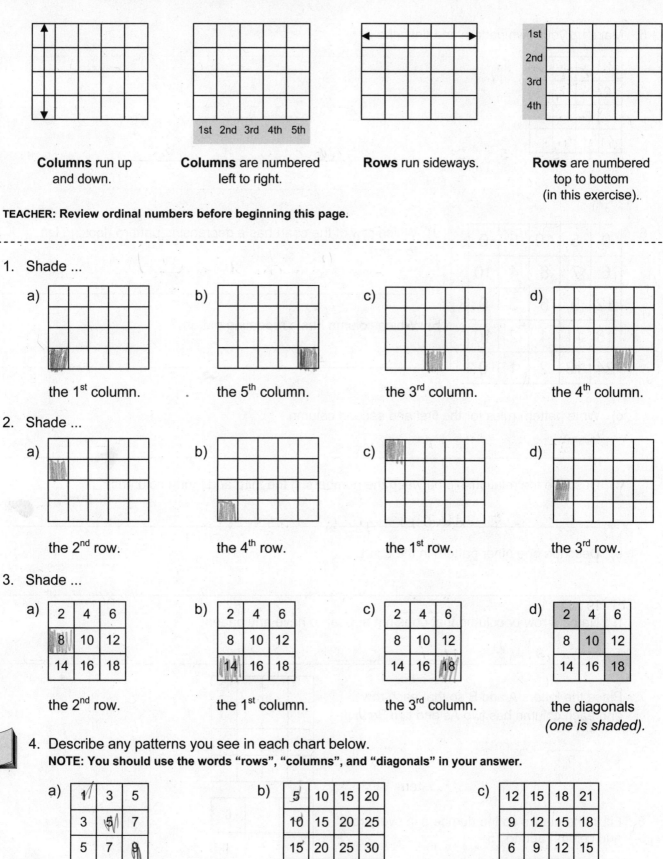

Columns run up and down.

Columns are numbered left to right.

Rows run sideways.

Rows are numbered top to bottom (in this exercise).

TEACHER: Review ordinal numbers before beginning this page.

1. Shade ...

   a) the 1st column.

   b) the 5th column.

   c) the 3rd column.

   d) the 4th column.

2. Shade ...

   a) the 2nd row.

   b) the 4th row.

   c) the 1st row.

   d) the 3rd row.

3. Shade ...

   a)
2	4	6
8	10	12
14	16	18

   the 2nd row.

   b)
2	4	6
8	10	12
14	16	18

   the 1st column.

   c)
2	4	6
8	10	12
14	16	18

   the 3rd column.

   d)
2	4	6
8	10	12
14	16	18

   the diagonals *(one is shaded)*.

4. Describe any patterns you see in each chart below.

   NOTE: You should use the words "rows", "columns", and "diagonals" in your answer.

   a)
1	3	5
3	5	7
5	7	9

   b)
5	10	15	20
10	15	20	25
15	20	25	30
20	25	30	35

   c)
12	15	18	21
9	12	15	18
6	9	12	15
3	6	9	12

5. Make up your own pattern and describe it.

3	6	9	12
15	18	21	24
27	30	33	36
39	42	45	48

colour The 3rd row

6.

0	5	10	5	0
6	7	8	4	10
12	9	6	3	0
18	11	4	2	10
24	13	2	1	0

a) Which row of the chart has a decreasing pattern (looking left to right)?

5th 3rd row

b) Which column has a repeating pattern?

5th

c) Write pattern rules for the first and second column.

1, add 6 2. add 2

d) Describe the relationship between the numbers in the third and fourth columns.

4th is half the 3rd

e) Describe one other pattern in the chart.

3rd column

f) Name a row or column that does not appear to have any pattern.

2nd row

7. Place the letters A and B so that each row and each column has two As and two Bs in it:

A	B	A	B
B	A	B	A
A	B	A	B
B	A	B	A

8. Fill in the blanks so the numbers in every row and column add to 15:

2	7	6
9	5	1
4	3	8

1. Here are some **number pyramids**:

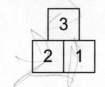

Can you find the rule by which the patterns in the pyramids were made? Describe it here:

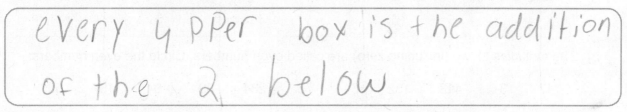

every upper box is the addition of the 2 below

2. Using the rule you described in Question 1 above, find the missing numbers:

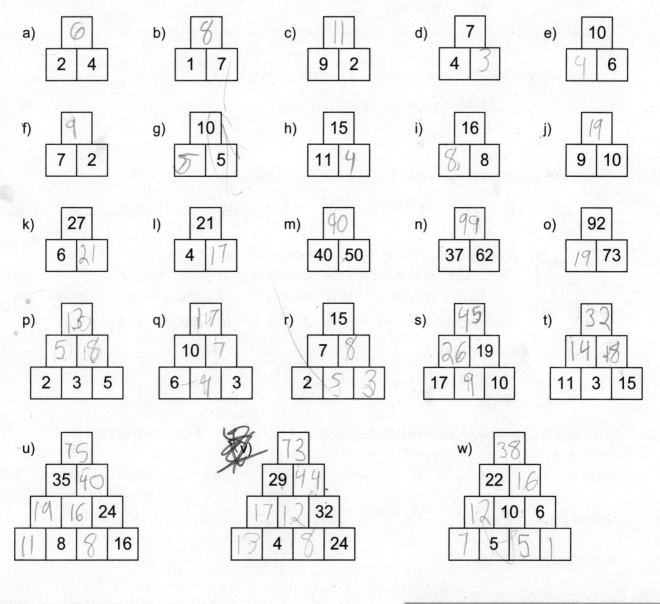

a)
6
2	4

b)
8
1	7

c)
11
9	2

d)
7
4	3

e)
10
4	6

f)
9
7	2

g)
10
5	5

h)
15
11	4

i)
16
8	8

j)
19
9	10

k)
27
6	21

l)
21
4	17

m)
90
40	50

n)
99
37	62

o)
92
19	73

p)
13
5	18
2	3	5

q)
17
10	7
6	4	3

r)
15
7	8
2	5	3

s)
45
26	19
17	9	10

t)
32
14	18
11	3	15

u)
75
35	40
19	16	24
11	8	8	16

v)
73
29	44
17	12	32
13	4	8	24

w)
38
22	16
12	10	6
7	5	5	1

1. a)

1	2	3	4	5	6	7	8	9	10
11	12	13	14	15	16	17	18	19	20

Look at the ones digit in the multiples of 2.

How can you tell whether a number is a multiple of two?

If it has any of these numbers 0,2,4,6,8,

b) The multiples of two (including zero) are called <u>even</u> numbers. Circle the even numbers:

17   3   (418)   (132)   (64)   (76)   234   89   (94)   167   (506)

2. a) Write out the first 12 multiples of 5 greater than zero:

<u>5</u> , <u>10</u> , 15 , 20 , 25 , 30 , 35 , 40 , 45 , 50 , 55 , 60

b) How can you tell whether a number is a multiple of five?

because you just add five over again

c) Without counting up, circle the numbers that are multiples of 5:

83   17   (45)   37   (150)   64   (190)   (65)   71   (235)   618   (1645)

3.

1	2	3
11	12	13
21	22	23

Example

Shade all the multiples of 3 on a hundreds chart.

You should find that the shaded squares lie in diagonal lines.

Now add the ones digit and the tens digit of each number along any diagonal line.

Describe what you notice below. (Try this for each shaded diagonal.)

4. A number is a multiple of 3 if the sum of its digits is a multiple of 3. Fill in the chart below:

Number	28	37	42	61	63	87	93	123
Sum of digits	2 + 8 = 10	3+7=10	4+2=6	6+1=7	6+3=9	8+7=15	9+3=12	12+3=15
Multiple of 3?	No	NO	Yes	NO	Yes	Yes	Yes	Yes

PA5-21: Patterns in the Eight Times Table

1. On a hundreds chart, shade every eighth number (i.e. shade the numbers you would say when counting by eights: 8, 16, 24, ...).

   The numbers you shaded are the <u>multiples</u> of eight (up to 100).

2. Complete the following:

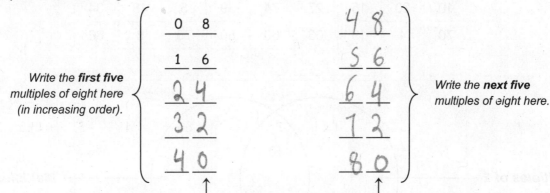

   Write the **first five** multiples of eight here (in increasing order).

0	8
1	6
2	4
3	2
4	0

   Write the **next five** multiples of eight here.

4	8
5	6
6	4
7	2
8	0

   Look down the columns marked by the arrows. What pattern do you see in the <u>ones</u> digits?

3. What pattern do you see in the number of tens?

TEACHER:
Review the answers to Questions 2 and 3 above before allowing your students to go further.

4. Use the pattern you found in Questions 2 and 3 to write out the multiples of 8 from 88 to 160:

   ___ ___   ___ ___ ___

   ___ ___   ___ ___ ___

   ___ ___ ___   ___ ___ ___

   ___ ___ ___   ___ ___ ___

   ___ ___ ___   ___ ___ ___

PA5-22: Times Tables (Advanced)

TEACHER:
Review Venn diagrams with your students before assigning the questions below.

1. a) Sort the numbers below into the Venn diagram.
   The first number has been done for you:

10	20	15	27	74	39	5	48	34
70	4	19	63	60	50	75	6	66

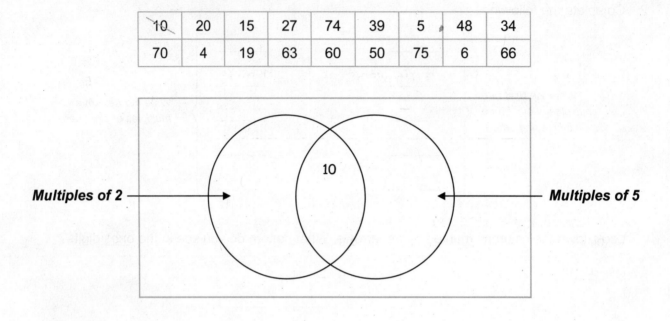

b) Think of two numbers from 50 to 100 that would go in the middle of the diagram: _____, _____

c) Think of two numbers from 50 to 100 that could not be placed in either circle: _____, _____

2. Sort the numbers below into the Venn diagram.
   REMEMBER: A number is a multiple of 3 if the sum of its digits is a multiple of 3.

24	30	47	21	26	60	80	13	11
48	35	56	72	10	75	16	40	6

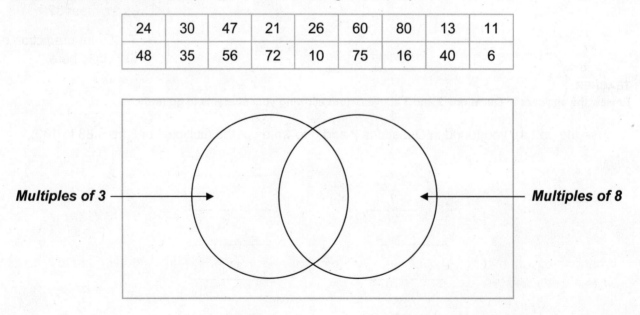

Patterns & Algebra 1

TEACHER:
For this exercise, your students will need a copy of the hundreds chart from the Teacher's Guide.

1. Underline the ones digits of the multiples of 4 listed below:

    <u>0</u>   <u>4</u>   <u>8</u>   1<u>2</u>   16   20   24

    28   32   36   40   44   48

    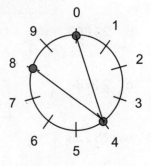

    Mark the digits that you underlined with a dot on the circle chart.
    Then join the dots in the order that you marked them (as shown).

    What pattern do you see? _____

    _____

    _____

2. On a hundreds chart, circle the first 10 multiples of 6. Underline the ones
    digits of the numbers you circled. Plot the ones digits on this circle chart
    and join the dots in the order that you marked them.

    What do you notice? _____

    _____

    _____

    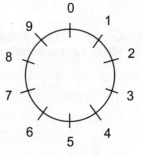

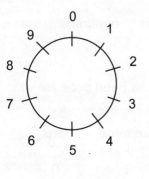

3. Repeat the exercise in
    Question 2 for the number 8.

    What do you notice?

4. Repeat the exercise
    again for multiples of 3.

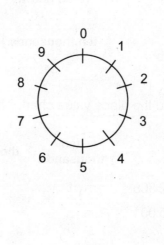

5. Which one-digit number
    (2, 5, 7 or 9) do you think
    will give the same pattern
    as the circle pattern for
    the number 3?

    Test your prediction on
    the circle here:

    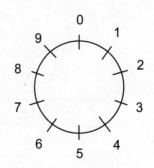

6. What one-digit number (2, 5, 7 or 9) do you think will give the same circle pattern as the number 8?
    Draw a circle and test your prediction.

NS5-1: Place Value

1. Write the place value of the underlined digit.

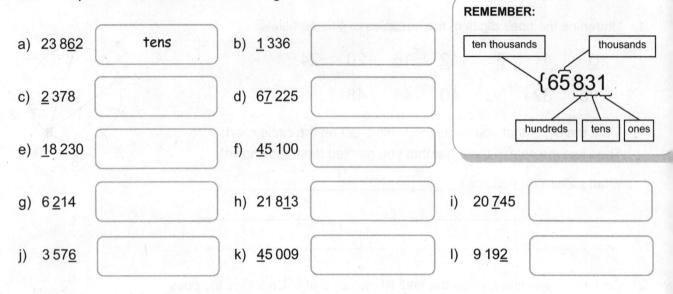

REMEMBER:

a) 23 8<u>6</u>2   tens   b) <u>1</u> 336

c) <u>2</u> 378   d) 6<u>7</u> 225

e) <u>1</u>8 230   f) <u>4</u>5 100

g) 6 <u>2</u>14   h) 21 8<u>1</u>3   i) 20 <u>7</u>45

j) 3 57<u>6</u>   k) <u>4</u>5 009   l) 9 19<u>2</u>

2. Give the place value of the number 5 in each of the numbers below:
    HINT: First underline the 5 in each question.

a) 15 640   b) 358   c) 45 636

d) 2 415   e) 51 188   f) 451

g) 1 512   h) 125   i) 35 380

3. You can also write numbers using a place value chart:

    Example:

    In a place value chart, the number
    52 953 is:

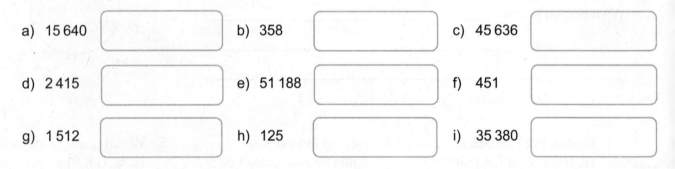

ten thousands	thousands	hundreds	tens	ones
5	2	9	5	3

Write the following numbers into the place value chart. The first one has been done for you:

	ten thousands	thousands	hundreds	tens	ones
a) 12 305	1	2	3	0	5
b) 45 001					
c) 3 699					
d) 19 053					
e) 546					
f) 20 127					

jump math
MULTIPLYING POTENTIAL

The number 23 967 is a **5-digit number**:

- The **digit** 2 stands for 20 000 – the **value** of the digit 2 is 20 000.

- The **digit** 3 stands for 3 000 – the **value** of the digit 3 is 3 000.

- The **digit** 9 stands for 900 – the **value** of the digit 9 is 900.

- The **digit** 6 stands for 60 – the **value** of the digit 6 is 60.

- The **digit** 7 stands for 7 – the **value** of the digit 7 is 7.

4. Write the **value** of each digit:

5	4	3	6	2

2	8	5	3	7

1	3	2	7	5

5. What does the digit 4 stand for in each number? The first one is done for you:

a) 847

40

b) 5 243

c) 16 423

d) 43 228

e) 4 207

f) 3 742

g) 43 092

h) 54 283

6. Fill in the blanks:

a) In the number 36 572, the <u>digit</u> 5 stands for _____ .

b) In the number 24 236, the <u>digit</u> 3 stands for _____ .

c) In the number 62 357, the <u>digit</u> 6 stands for _____ .

d) In the number 8 021, the <u>value</u> of the digit 8 is _____ .

e) In the number 26 539, the <u>value</u> of the digit 2 is _____ .

f) In the number 7 253, the digit _____ is in the <u>thousands place</u>.

g) In the number 57 320, the digit _____ is in the <u>ten thousands place</u>.

NS5-2: Writing Numbers

1. Write numerals for the number words.

   a) twenty-three _____   b) thirty-two _____   c) ninety-five _____

   d) two hundred seventy _____   e) four hundred seventy-nine _____

   f) nineteen thousand, two hundred seventeen _____

   g) forty-seven thousand, five hundred nine _____

Number Words for the Tens Place	
ten	sixty
twenty	seventy
thirty	eighty
forty	ninety
fifty	

2. Write the number words for the numerals.

   a) 245 _____   b) 451 _____

   c) 378 _____   d) 109 _____

3. Write the value of the underlined digits:

   a) <u>36</u> 123 ____thirty-six thousand____   b) <u>4</u> 752 _____

   c) <u>25</u> 751 _____   d) <u>19</u> 234 _____

4. Underline the digits that represent thousands or ten thousands:

   <u>24</u> 751   <u>6</u> 543   7 163   19 789   43 567   1 987   38 527   70 144

5. Writing numbers 1 000 to 99 999.

   Step 1: _Underline the thousands and the ten thousands digits. Write the value of those digits._

   a) <u>26</u> 124 ____twenty-six thousand____   b) <u>3</u> 124 ____three thousand____

   c) 37 456 _____   d) 19 254 _____

   Step 2: _Cover the underlined digits. Write the number words for the remaining digits._

   e) <u>17</u> 234 ___**seventeen thousand** two hundred thirty-four___

   f) <u>2</u> 697 ___**two thousand**_____

   g) <u>34</u> 121 ___**thirty-four thousand**_____

   Complete the number words.

   h) 4 621 ___four___ thousand, ___six___ hundred ___twenty-one___

   i) 25 768 ___twenty-five___ thousand, _____ hundred _____

   j) 37 954 _____

6. Write number words for the following numerals:

4 121 _____

53 672 _____

14 378 _____

99 999 _____

7. Write the numbers provided, in words, on the signs where they are missing.

a)

Mt. Everest
(Chomolungma) (8 848 m)

_____

_____

_____

_____ m high

Shanghai, China

Jakarta, Indonesia

Sydney, Australia

TORONTO

Buenos Aires, Argentina

b) The world's deepest living sea star
lives at the depth of (7 630 m)

_____

_____

_____ m

The distance from Toronto to…

c) Buenos Aires, Argentina: (8 894 km)

_____

_____

_____ km

d) Sydney, Australia: (15 562 km)

_____

_____

_____ km

e) Jakarta, Indonesia: (15 803 km)

_____

_____

_____ km

f) Shanghai, China: (11 445 km)

_____

_____

_____ km

1. Write each number in expanded word form (numerals and words).

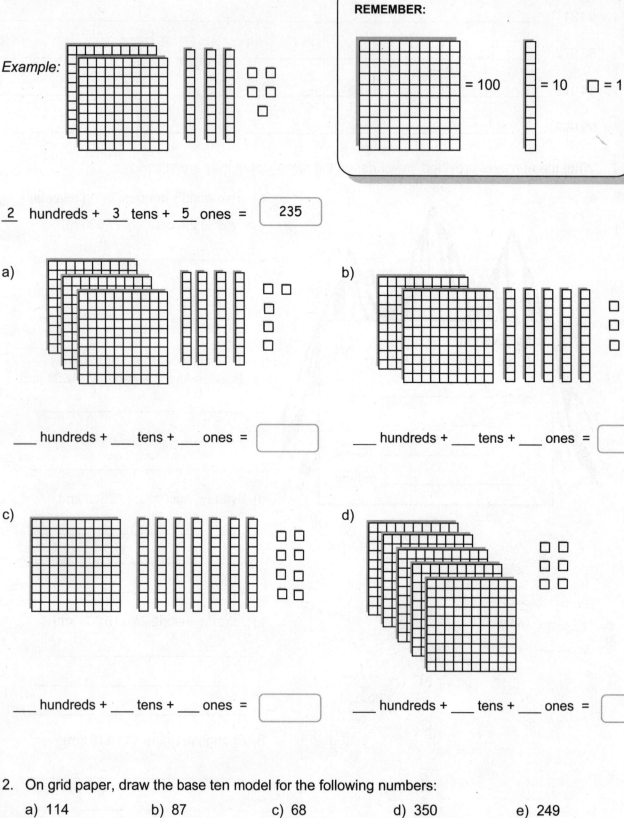

REMEMBER:

= 100   = 10   □ = 1

Example:

_2_ hundreds + _3_ tens + _5_ ones = [235]

a)

___ hundreds + ___ tens + ___ ones = [   ]

b)

___ hundreds + ___ tens + ___ ones = [   ]

c)

___ hundreds + ___ tens + ___ ones = [   ]

d)

___ hundreds + ___ tens + ___ ones = [   ]

2. On grid paper, draw the base ten model for the following numbers:

   a) 114   b) 87   c) 68   d) 350   e) 249

NS5-3: Representation with Base Ten Materials (continued)

3. Write each number in expanded word form (numerals and words) then as a numeral.

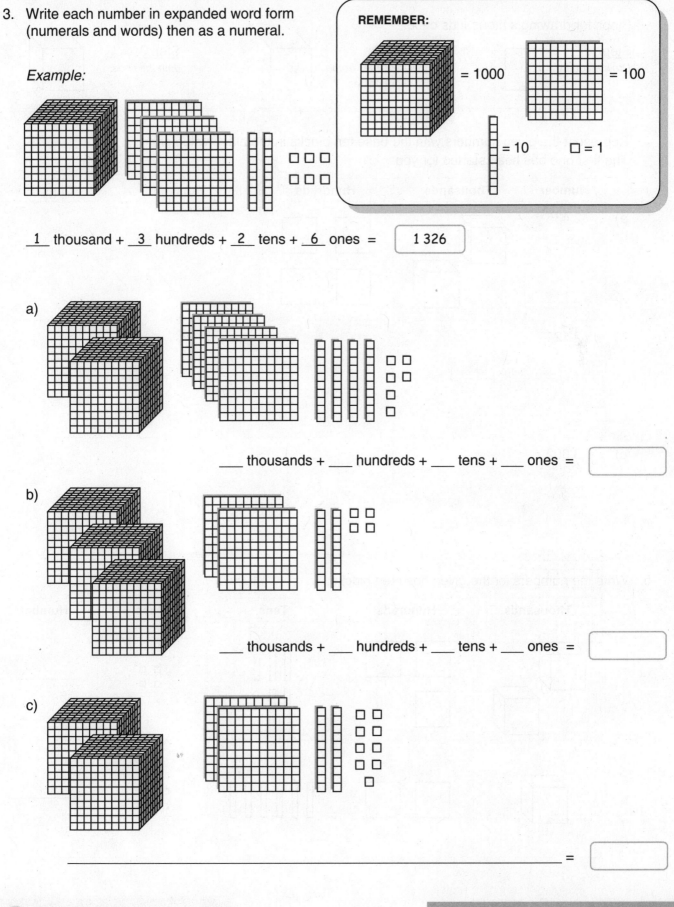

REMEMBER:

= 1000   = 100   = 10   □ = 1

Example:

__1__ thousand + __3__ hundreds + __2__ tens + __6__ ones = | 1 326 |

a)

___ thousands + ___ hundreds + ___ tens + ___ ones =

b)

___ thousands + ___ hundreds + ___ tens + ___ ones =

c)

_____ =

jump math
MULTIPLYING POTENTIAL

Steps for drawing a thousands cube:

Step 1:
Draw a square:

Step 2:
Draw lines from
its 3 vertices:

Step 3:
Join the lines:

4. Represent the given numbers with the base ten blocks in the place value chart.
The first one has been started for you:

	Number	Thousands	Hundreds	Tens	Ones
a)	2 435				
b)	2 124				
c)	3 302				

5. Write the numbers for the given base ten blocks:

	Thousands	Hundreds	Tens	Ones	Number
a)					_____
b)					_____

1. Expand the following numbers using <u>numerals</u> and <u>words</u>. The first one is done for you:

    a) 43 427   = _4_ ten thousands + _3_ thousands + _4_ hundreds + _2_ tens + _7_ ones

    b) 25 312   = ____ ten thousands + ____ thousands + ____ hundreds + ____ tens + ____ ones

    c) 28 547   = _____

        _____

2. Write the number in expanded form (using <u>numerals</u>). The first one is done for you:

    a) 2 613 = _____ 2 000 + 600 + 10 + 3 _____   b) 27 = _____

    c) 48 = _____   d) 1 232 = _____

    e) 36 273 = _____

    f) 19 384 = _____

    g) 49 805 = _____

3. Write the number for each sum:

    a) 4 000 + 900 + 50 + 3 = _____   b) 2 000 + 30 + 2 = _____

    c) 60 000 + 3 000 + 900 + 90 + 7 = _____

    d) 50 000 + 30 + 4 = _____

    BONUS

    e) 500 + 2 000 + 80 + 90 000 + 8 = _____

    f) 40 000 + 500 +1 000 = _____   g) 10 000 + 3 000 + 7 + 600 = _____

    h) 300 + 80 000 + 2 = _____   i) 90 + 400 + 70 000 + 6 = _____

    j) 90 000 + 5 = _____   k) 80 000 + 8 + 800 = _____

    l) 30 000 + 1 + 5 000 = _____   m) 3 000 + 20 000 = _____

4. Find the missing numbers:

   a) 4 000 + 800 + _____ + 7 = 4 827   b) 3 000 + 200 + _____ + 5 = 3 275

   c) 70 000 + 9 000 + _____ + 20 + 5 = 79 825   d) 60 000 + 5 000 + _____ + 60 + 3 = 65 263

   e) 10 000 + 7 000 + 200 + 10 + _____ = 17 212   f) 20 000 + 6 000 + 300 + _____ + 8 = 26 328

   BONUS

   g) _____ + 300 = 7 300   h) 6 000 + _____ = 6 080

   i) 30 000 + 9 000 + _____ + _____ = 39 260   j) 60 000 + _____ + _____ = 67 003

5. Write each number in expanded form. Then draw a base ten model.

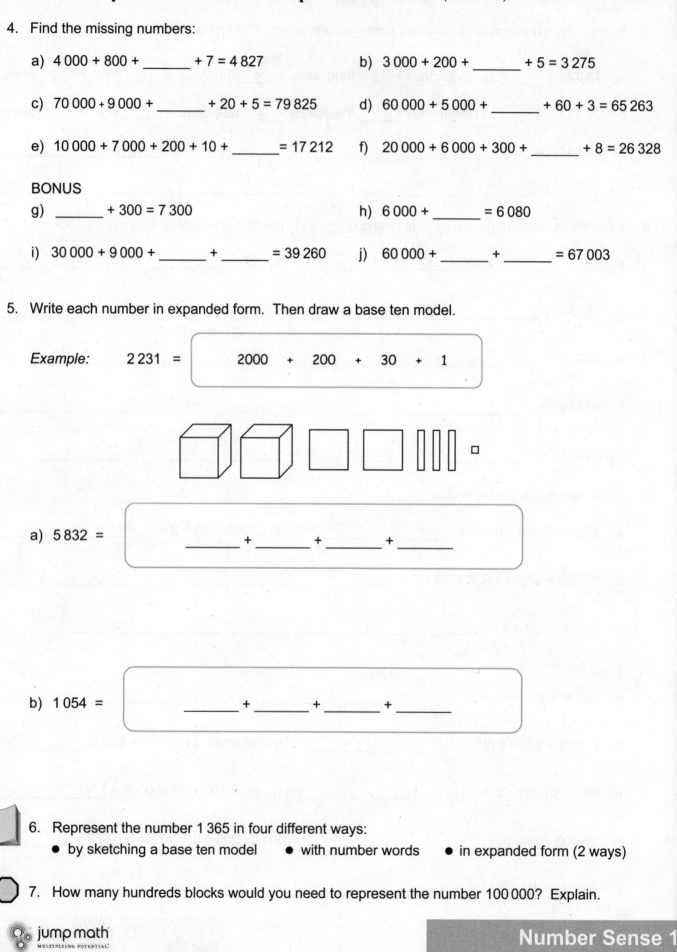

   Example: 2 231 =   2000 + 200 + 30 + 1

   a) 5 832 =   _____ + _____ + _____ + _____

   b) 1 054 =   _____ + _____ + _____ + _____

6. Represent the number 1 365 in four different ways:
   - by sketching a base ten model
   - with number words
   - in expanded form (2 ways)

7. How many hundreds blocks would you need to represent the number 100 000? Explain.

1. Write the **value** of each digit. Then complete the sentence:

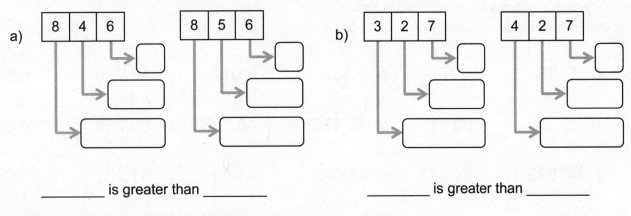

a)

b)

_____ is greater than _____   _____ is greater than _____

2. Circle the pair of digits that are different in each pair of numbers.
   Then write the greater number in the box:

a) 6 4 7 5
    6 4 6 5

    [6 475]

b) 73 605
    72 605

c) 14 852
    14 858

d) 3832
    4832

3. Read the numbers from left to right.
   Circle the first pair of digits you find that are different.
   Then write the greater number in the box:

a) 123
    134

b) 276
    374

c) 875
    869

d) 238
    221

e) 41 583
    41 597

f) 28 293
    28 542

g) 57 698
    60 347

h) 62 149
    62 148

4. Read the numbers from left to right.
   Underline the first pair of digits you find that are different.
   Then circle the greater number.

a) 32 547   32 562

b) 71 254   81 254

c) 37 123   37 321

d) 61 201   61 275

e) 63 235   63 233

f) 81 234   84 214

g) 32 153   31 278

h) 60 154   66 254

i) 96 567   96 528

5. The inequality sign **>** in **7 > 5** is read "seven is greater than five".
   The sign **<** in **8 < 10** is read "eight is less than ten".
   Write the correct inequality sign in each box.

   a) 3 129 ☐ 4 703   b) 5 332 ☐ 6 012   c) 16 726 ☐ 16 591

   d) 23 728 ☐ 23 729   e) 48 175 ☐ 48 123   f) 59 239 ☐ 60 009

   g) 64 872 ☐ 64 871   h) 48 025 ☐ 4 952   i) 91 232 ☐ 9 327

6. Circle the greater number in each pair:

   a) 32 or thirty-five   b) three hundred eighty-seven or 392   c) twenty-seven or 81

   d) one thousand one hundred six or 1 232   e) 50 273 or fifty thousand three hundred eighty-five

7. Mark each number on the number line. Then circle the greater number.

   A 23 800   **B** 23 400   **C** 23 600

   ├───┼───┼───┼───┼───┼───┼───┼───┼───┼───┤
   23 000   24 000

8. Fill in the boxes with any digit that will make the number statements true.

   a) ☐ 5 ☐ ☐ < 4 ☐ ☐ 1

   b) 3 ☐ ☐ ☐ 1 > ☐ 8 ☐ ☐ 9

9. Which number must be greater (no matter what digits are placed in the box)? Explain.

   ☐ 2 3 5 OR ☐ ☐ 1 2 3

10. How many numbers are greater than 59 990 and less than 60 000?

11. Buenos Aires, Argentina, is 9001 km away from Ottawa.
    Concepcion, Chile is 9106 km away.

    Which city is further from Ottawa?

    Explain how you know.

1. Write "10 more", "10 less", "100 more" or "100 less" in the blanks:

    a) 90 is _____ than 80

    b) 400 is _____ than 500

    c) 10 is _____ than 20

    d) 100 is _____ than 90

    e) 400 is _____ than 300

    f) 60 is _____ than 70

2. Write "100 more", "100 less", "1 000 more" or "1 000 less" in the blanks:

    a) 6 000 is _____ than 5 000

    b) 12 000 is _____ than 13 000

    c) 4 000 is _____ than 5 000

    d) 800 is _____ than 900

    e) 600 is _____ than 500

    f) 9 000 is _____ than 8 000

3. Write "1 000 more", "1 000 less", "10 000 more" or "10 000 less" in the blanks:

    a) 6 000 is _____ than 5 000

    b) 12 000 is _____ than 13 000

    c) 30 000 is _____ than 40 000

    d) 50 000 is _____ than 40 000

    e) 6 000 is _____ than 7 000

    f) 10 000 is _____ than 20 000

    g) 80 000 is _____ than 70 000

    h) 9 000 is _____ than 10 000

4. Circle the pair of digits that are different. Then fill in the blanks:

    a) 72 652
        72 752

        72 652 is ___100 less___
        than 72 752

    b) 91 385
        91 485

        91 385 is _____
        than 91 485

    c) 43 750
        33 750

        43 750 is _____
        than 33 750

    d) 62 250
        63 250

        62 250 is _____
        than 63 250

    e) 38 405
        38 415

        38 405 is _____
        than 38 415

    f) 85 871
        85 872

        85 871 is _____
        than 85 872

5. Fill in the blanks:

a) _____ is 10 more than 325

b) _____ is 10 less than 1 562

c) _____ is 100 more than 592

d) _____ is 100 less than 4 135

e) _____ is 100 more than 6 821

f) _____ is 100 less than 3 295

g) _____ is 1 000 less than 8 305

h) _____ is 1 000 more than 4 253

i) _____ is 10 000 less than 73 528

j) _____ is 1 000 less than 62 381

6. Fill in the blanks:

a) 234 + 10 = _____

b) 2 382 + 10 = _____

c) 19 035 + 10 = _____

d) 21 270 + 100 = _____

e) 3 283 + 100 = _____

f) 7 325 + 1 000 = _____

g) 357 − 10 = _____

h) 683 − 10 = _____

i) 837 − 100 = _____

j) 2 487 − 100 = _____

k) 1 901 − 100 = _____

l) 4 316 − 1 000 = _____

m) 3 301 − 10 = _____

n) 12 507 − 10 000 = _____

o) 39 397 + 10 = _____

7. Fill in the blanks:

a) 385 + _____ = 395

b) 608 + _____ = 708

c) 1 483 + _____ = 1 493

d) 2 617 + _____ = 2 717

e) 43 210 + _____ = 44 210

f) 26 287 + _____ = 26 387

g) 1 287 − _____ = 1 187

h) 325 − _____ = 315

i) 14 392 − _____ = 14 292

j) 87 001 − _____ = 86 001

k) 86 043 − _____ = 85 943

l) 61 263 − _____ = 51 263

8. Continue the number patterns:

a) 8 508, 8 518, 8 528, _____, _____

b) 35 730, 36 730, 37 730, _____, _____

c) 41 482, 41 492, _____, 41 512, _____

d) 28 363, _____, _____, 28 393, 28 403

9. Circle the pair of digits that are different. Then fill in the blanks:

a) 45241
45231

____45 231____ is ____10____

less than ____45 241____

b) 82350
92350

_____ is _____

more than _____

c) 68254
69254

_____ is _____

less than _____

NS5-7: Comparing Numbers (Advanced)

1. Write the number represented by the base ten materials in each box. Then circle the greater number in each pair.

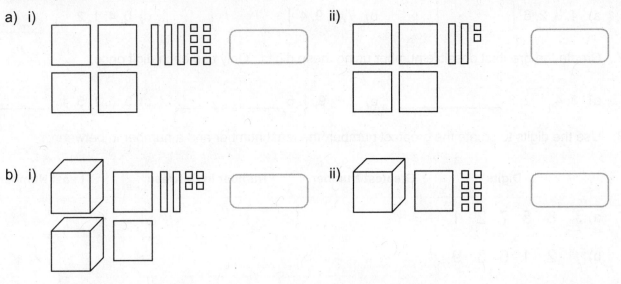

2. List all the two-digit numbers you can make using the digits provided. Then circle the greatest number:

   a) 7, 8 and 9

   b) 3, 4 and 0

3. What is the greatest number less than 1000 whose digits are all the same? _____

4. What is the greatest possible number you can create with:

   a) three digits _____   b) four digits _____   c) five digits _____

5. Identify the greater number by writing > or <.

   a) 37 432 ☐ 37 512

   b) 87 386 ☐ 87 384

   c) 17 329 ☐ 8 338

   d) 63 923 ☐ 62 857

6. Create the largest possible <u>four-digit</u> number using the digits given:

a) 4, 3, 2, 6 [   ]   b) 7, 8, 9, 4 [   ]   c) 0, 4, 1, 2 [   ]

7. Create the greatest possible number using these digits. Only use each digit once:

a) 3, 4, 1, 2, 8 _____   b) 2, 8, 9, 1, 5 _____   c) 3, 6, 1, 5, 4 _____

8. Use the digits to create the greatest number, the least number and a number in between:

	Digits	Greatest Number	Number in Between	Least Number
a)	8 5 7 2 1			
b)	2 1 5 3 9			
c)	3 0 1 5 3			

9. Arrange the numbers in order, starting with the <u>least</u> number:

a) 3 257, 3 352, 3 183   b) 17 251, 17 385, 17 256

_____ , _____ , _____   _____ , _____ , _____

c) 87 500, 87 498, 87 499   d) 36 725, 3 281, 93 859

_____ , _____ , _____   _____ , _____ , _____

e) 60 052, 60 001, 60 021   f) 273, 5 891, 17

_____ , _____ , _____   _____ , _____ , _____

10. Using the digits 0, 1, 2, 3, 4 create a number greater than 32 000 and less than 34 000.

_____

11. Using the digits 3, 5, 6, 7, 8 create an even number greater than 85 000 and less than 87 000.

_____

12. What digit can be substituted for [   ] to make each statement true?

a) 32 [   ] 56 is between 32 675 and 32 854   b) 68 [   ] 32 is between 68 379 and 68 464

jump math
MULTIPLYING POTENTIAL.

Number Sense 1

NS5-8: Regrouping

Gwendolyne has 2 hundreds blocks, 16 tens blocks, and 9 ones blocks.
She regroups 10 tens blocks as 1 hundreds block:

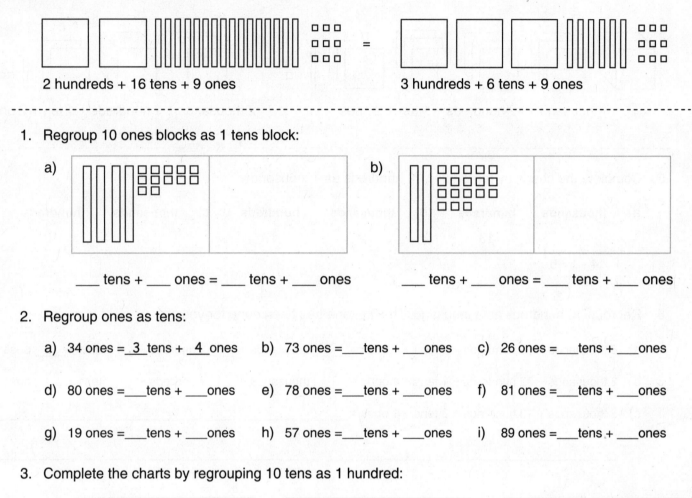

2 hundreds + 16 tens + 9 ones   3 hundreds + 6 tens + 9 ones

----

1. Regroup 10 ones blocks as 1 tens block:

   a)

   ___ tens + ___ ones = ___ tens + ___ ones

   b)

   ___ tens + ___ ones = ___ tens + ___ ones

2. Regroup ones as tens:

   a) 34 ones = _3_ tens + _4_ ones   b) 73 ones =___tens + ___ones   c) 26 ones =___tens + ___ones

   d) 80 ones =___tens + ___ones   e) 78 ones =___tens + ___ones   f) 81 ones =___tens + ___ones

   g) 19 ones =___tens + ___ones   h) 57 ones =___tens + ___ones   i) 89 ones =___tens + ___ones

3. Complete the charts by regrouping 10 tens as 1 hundred:

   a)

hundreds	tens
6	23
6 + 2 = 8	3

   b)

hundreds	tens
5	32

   c)

hundreds	tens
4	11

   d)

hundreds	tens
8	19

   e)

hundreds	tens
1	84

   f)

hundreds	tens
7	20

4. Regroup tens as hundreds or ones as tens.

   a) 5 hundreds + 4 tens + 24 ones = ___5 hundreds + 6 tens + 4 ones_____

   b) 7 hundreds + 0 tens + 47 ones = _____

   c) 3 hundreds + 57 tens + 8 ones = _____

jump math
MULTIPLYING POTENTIAL

Ara has 1 thousands block, 12 hundreds blocks, 1 tens block and 2 ones blocks.
She regroups 10 hundreds blocks as a thousands block:

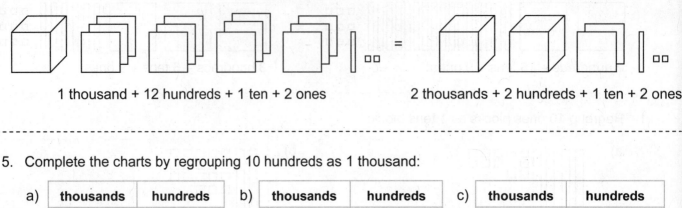

1 thousand + 12 hundreds + 1 ten + 2 ones   2 thousands + 2 hundreds + 1 ten + 2 ones

---

5. Complete the charts by regrouping 10 hundreds as 1 thousand:

a)

thousands	hundreds
4	13
4 + 1 = 5	3

b)

thousands	hundreds
2	17

c)

thousands	hundreds
8	10

6. Regroup 10 hundreds as a thousand. The first one has been done for you:

a) 6 thousands + 13 hundreds + 4 tens + 8 ones = __7__ thousands + __3__ hundreds + __4__ tens + __8__ ones

b) 2 thousands + 32 hundreds + 1 tens + 4 ones = ____ thousands + ____ hundreds + ____ tens + ____ ones

c) 5 thousands + 10 hundreds + 3 tens + 1 ones = _____

_____

7. Regroup thousands as ten thousands, hundreds as thousands, tens as hundreds, or ones as tens.

a) 2 thousands + 25 hundreds + 4 tens + 2 ones = ____ thousands + ____ hundreds + ____ tens + ____ ones

b) 3 thousands + 7 hundreds + 24 tens + 5 ones = _____

_____

c) 4 ten thousands + 25 thousands + 6 hundreds + 1 tens + 45 ones = _____

_____

8. Karim wants to build a model of four thousand three hundred forty-six.

He has 3 thousands blocks, 13 hundreds blocks and 50 ones blocks.

Can he build the model? Explain.

NS5-9: Adding with Regrouping

1. Add the numbers below by drawing a picture and by adding the digits.

a) **14 + 37**   b) **35 + 27**

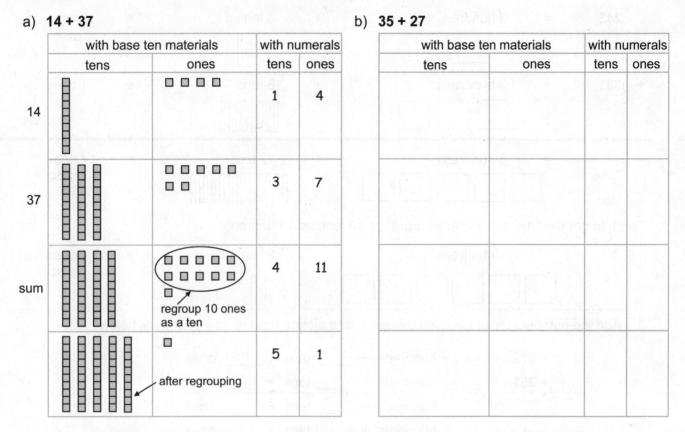

2. Add the ones digits. Show how you would regroup 10 ones as 1 ten.

a)
```
    ┌ ─ ┐   ← tens go here
    ┊ 1 ┊         ┌ ─ ┐                      ┌ ─ ┐                 ┌ ─ ┐               ┌ ─ ┐
    └ ─ ┘         └ ─ ┘                      └ ─ ┘                 └ ─ ┘               └ ─ ┘
      1  4    b)    3  6     c)    6  4   d)    3  5    e)    2  6
    + 1  9       + 4  9         + 2  8       + 4  5       + 1  9
   ─────────    ─────────      ─────────    ─────────    ─────────
    ┌ ─ ┐       ┌ ─ ┐          ┌ ─ ┐        ┌ ─ ┐        ┌ ─ ┐
    ┊ 3 ┊       ┊   ┊          ┊   ┊        ┊   ┊        ┊   ┊
    └ ─ ┘       └ ─ ┘          └ ─ ┘        └ ─ ┘        └ ─ ┘
      ↑
   ones go here
```

3. Add the numbers by regrouping.

a)
```
    1
     2  5    b)    1  9     c)    6  4   d)    7  7    e)    3  6
   + 1  6       + 3  2         + 2  9       + 1  8       + 3  6
   ─────────    ─────────      ─────────    ─────────    ─────────
     4  1
```

f)
```
     8  5    g)    2  9     h)    4  3   i)    2  1    j)    7  8
   +    6       + 3  2         + 1  8       + 5  9       + 2  8
   ─────────    ─────────      ─────────    ─────────    ─────────
```

 jump math
MULTIPLYING POTENTIAL

Allen adds 243 + 381 using base ten materials:

243	=	2 hundred	+	4 tens	+	3 ones ▫▫▫

+ 381	=	3 hundreds	+	8 tens	+	1 ones ▫

	=	5 hundreds	+	12 tens	+	4 ones ▫▫▫▫

Then, to get the final answer, Allen regroups 10 tens as 1 hundred:

	=	6 hundreds	+	2 tens	+	4 ones ▫▫▫▫

1. Add the numbers using base ten materials or a picture (and record your work below):

$$572 = \underline{\quad} \text{ hundreds} + \underline{\quad} \text{ tens} + \underline{\quad} \text{ ones}$$
$$+\,251 = \underline{\quad} \text{ hundreds} + \underline{\quad} \text{ tens} + \underline{\quad} \text{ ones}$$
$$= \underline{\quad} \text{ hundreds} + \underline{\quad} \text{ tens} + \underline{\quad} \text{ ones}$$
after regrouping $= \underline{\quad} \text{ hundreds} + \underline{\quad} \text{ tens} + \underline{\quad} \text{ ones}$

2. Add. You will need to regroup. The first one is started for you:

a) ₁
   2 5 8
  + 3 7 1
      2 9

b)
   3 6 1
  + 4 9 6

c)
   8 2 3
  +   9 6

d)
   9 5 0
  + 5 9 9

e)
   6 4 3
  + 2 6 4

3. Add, regrouping where necessary:

a)
   2 8 2
  + 3 7 1

b)
   1 5 6
  + 5 5 7

c)
   6 4 2
  + 1 8 9

d)
   3 9 0
  + 2 5 9

e)
   8 5 6
  + 1 0 6

f)
   2 8 9
  + 4 4 4

4. Add by lining the numbers up correctly in the grid. The first one has been started for you:

a) 643 + 182   b) 547 + 236   c) 405 + 368   d) 256 + 92

a) grid:
	6	4	3
+	1	8	2

NS5-11: Adding 4- and 5-Digit Numbers

Louisa adds 2 862 + 2 313 using base ten materials:

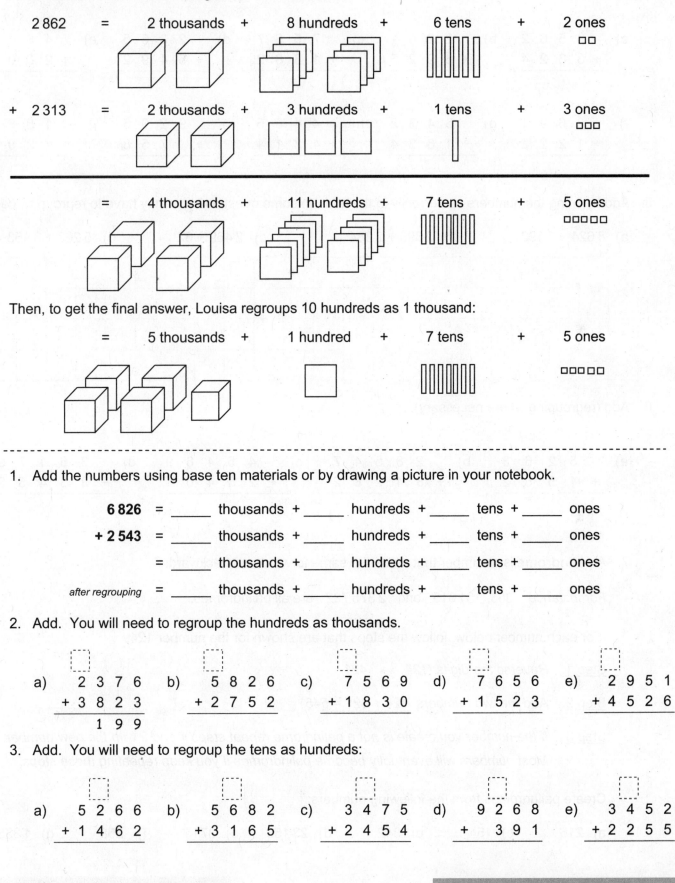

2 862   =   2 thousands   +   8 hundreds   +   6 tens   +   2 ones

+ 2 313   =   2 thousands   +   3 hundreds   +   1 tens   +   3 ones

=   4 thousands   +   11 hundreds   +   7 tens   +   5 ones

Then, to get the final answer, Louisa regroups 10 hundreds as 1 thousand:

=   5 thousands   +   1 hundred   +   7 tens   +   5 ones

1. Add the numbers using base ten materials or by drawing a picture in your notebook.

6 826   = _____ thousands + _____ hundreds + _____ tens + _____ ones

+ 2 543   = _____ thousands + _____ hundreds + _____ tens + _____ ones

= _____ thousands + _____ hundreds + _____ tens + _____ ones

after regrouping = _____ thousands + _____ hundreds + _____ tens + _____ ones

2. Add. You will need to regroup the hundreds as thousands.

a)   2 3 7 6
   + 3 8 2 3
   _____
       1 9 9

b)   5 8 2 6
   + 2 7 5 2

c)   7 5 6 9
   + 1 8 3 0

d)   7 6 5 6
   + 1 5 2 3

e)   2 9 5 1
   + 4 5 2 6

3. Add. You will need to regroup the tens as hundreds:

a)   5 2 6 6
   + 1 4 6 2

b)   5 6 8 2
   + 3 1 6 5

c)   3 4 7 5
   + 2 4 5 4

d)   9 2 6 8
   +   3 9 1

e)   3 4 5 2
   + 2 2 5 5

4. Add (regrouping when necessary):

a) 3 5 6 2
  + 3 6 2 4

b) 2 2 6 1
  + 6 9 2 5

c) 7 5 6 7
  + 1 3 8 2

d) 2 3 6 5
  + 5 4 9 2

e) 4 8 4 7
  + 2 0 0 5

f) 8 6 9 1
  + 1 2 2 2

g) 5 4 3 2
  + 1 8 3 4

h) 4 4 8 5
  + 4 8 1 4

i) 9 2 0 5
  +   7 5 8

j) 1 5 6 7
  + 7 2 9 1

5. Add by lining the numbers up correctly in the grid. In some questions you may have to regroup twice:

a) 8 624 + 1 192   b) 2 895 + 2 384   c) 2 469 + 62   d) 5 263 + 3 953

6. Add (regrouping where necessary):

a) 5 2 6 3
  + 1 5 5 2

b) 2 8 5 4 7
  + 3 4 2 8 2

c) 4 5 4 8 9
  + 2 6 4 0 1

d) 3 6 1 7 9
  + 3 3 4 5 2

7. A **palindrome** is a number that reads the same forward and backwards.

   For instance: 363, 51 815 and 2 375 732 are all palindromes.

   For each number below, follow the steps that are shown for the number 124:

   Step 1: *Reverse the digits: 124 → 421*

   Step 2: *Add the two numbers: 124 + 421 = 545*

   Step 3: *If the number you create is not a palindrome repeat steps 1 and 2 with the new number. Most numbers will eventually become palindromes if you keep repeating these steps.*

   Create palindromes from the following numbers:

   a) 216   b) 154   c) 342   d) 23 153   e) 371   f) 258   g) 1 385

NS5-12: Subtraction

Ken subtracts 34 – 16 using base ten blocks:

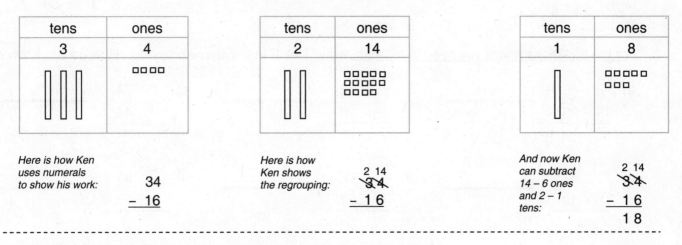

Step 1:
Ken represents 34 with base ten materials …

tens	ones
3	4

Here is how Ken uses numerals to show his work:

34
– 16

Step 2:
6 (the ones digit of 16) is greater than 4 (the ones digit of 34) so Ken exchanges a tens block for 10 ones …

tens	ones
2	14

Here is how Ken shows the regrouping:

2 14
3̷4̷
– 16

Step 3:
Ken subtracts 16 (he takes away 1 tens block and 6 ones) …

tens	ones
1	8

And now Ken can subtract 14 – 6 ones and 2 – 1 tens:

2 14
3̷4̷
– 16
18

----

1. Show how Ken can subtract by regrouping a tens block as 10 ones.

a) **66 – 37**

tens	ones
6	6

tens	ones
5	16

	6	6
–	3	7

	5	16
	6̷	6̷
–	3	7

b) **75 – 46**

tens	ones
7	5

tens	ones

	7	5
–	4	6

	7	5
–	4	6

c) **34 – 18**

tens	ones
3	4

tens	ones

	3	4
–	1	8

	3	4
–	1	8

d) **77 – 29**

tens	ones
7	7

tens	ones

	7	7
–	2	9

	7	7
–	2	9

Number Sense 1

2. Subtract by regrouping.

a)
```
      4 16
     5̶ 6̶
  -  1  8
  ─────────
     3  8
```

b)
```
     7  8
  -  3  9
  ─────────
```

c)
```
     5  3
  -  2  9
  ─────────
```

d)
```
     8  2
  -  4  3
  ─────────
```

e)
```
     6  6
  -  4  8
  ─────────
```

3. <u>For the questions where you need to regroup</u>, write "Help!" in the space provided. How do you know?

a)
```
    46
  - 28
```
Help!
6 is less than 8

b)
```
    52
  - 26
```
_____

c)
```
    73
  - 41
```
_____

d)
```
    32
  - 19
```
_____

e)
```
    56
  - 22
```
_____

f)
```
    95
  - 58
```
_____

g)
```
    66
  - 13
```
_____

h)
```
    24
  -  9
```
_____

i)
```
    84
  - 26
```
_____

j)
```
    79
  - 27
```
_____

k)
```
    52
  - 43
```
_____

l)
```
    41
  - 17
```
_____

4. To subtract 456 −283, Laura regroups 1 hundreds block as 10 tens blocks:

hundreds	tens	ones
4	5	6

hundreds	tens	ones
3	15	6

hundreds	tens	ones
1	7	3

Subtract by regrouping <u>hundreds</u> as tens. The first one has been started for you:

a)
```
    5 15
   6̶ 5̶ 2
 - 3 8 1
 ────────
```

b)
```
   6 7 9
 - 1 9 4
 ────────
```

c)
```
   8 1 6
 - 2 9 6
 ────────
```

d)
```
   9 5 8
 - 7 6 5
 ────────
```

5. Subtract by regrouping the <u>tens</u>. The first one has been started for you:

a)
```
      4  13
   6  5̶  3̶
-  5  2  6
_____
```

b)
```
   5  7  2
-  4  3  9
_____
```

c)
```
   9  6  4
-  6  3  8
_____
```

d)
```
   8  9  0
-  4  1  6
_____
```

6. For the questions below, you will have to regroup <u>twice</u>.

Example:

Step 1:
```
   3  12
7  4̶  2̶
- 2 7 4
```

Step 2:
```
   3  12
7  4̶  2̶
- 2 7 4
_____
       8
```

Step 3:
```
      13
6  3̶  12
7̶  4̶  2̶
- 2 7 4
_____
       8
```

Step 4:
```
      13
6  3̶  12
7̶  4̶  2̶
- 2 7 4
_____
    6  8
```

Step 5:
```
      13
6  3̶  12
7̶  4̶  2̶
- 2 7 4
_____
 4  6  8
```

a)
```
   7  5  2
-  3  6  3
_____
```

b)
```
   8  2  3
-  1  7  5
_____
```

c)
```
   3  0  4
-     2  7
_____
```

d)
```
   9  8  3
-  5  8  4
_____
```

7. To subtract 4 135 − 2 314, Laura exchanges a thousands block for 10 hundreds blocks:

thousands	hundreds	tens	ones
4	1	3	5

thousands	hundreds	tens	ones
3	11	3	5

thousands	hundreds	tens	ones
1	8	2	1

Subtract by regrouping thousands as hundreds. The first one has been done for you:

a)
```
   5  15
6̶  5̶  2  6
- 2  7  1  4
_____
   3  8  1  2
```

b)
```
   4  2  8  5
-  1  8  5  3
_____
```

c)
```
   9  6  4  3
-  5  7  2  2
_____
```

d)
```
   6  5  7  9
-  3  8  5  7
_____
```

8. In some of the questions below, you will need to regroup twice:

a)

	2	5	8	7
−	1	2	5	9

b)

	8	5	3	7
−	6	7	2	5

c)

	9	6	2	8
−	5	4	3	4

d)

	3	5	6	0
−	1	9	6	0

e)

	5	6	2	7	3
−	4	2	0	1	6

f)

	8	2	5	2	9
−	3	7	2	5	1

g)

	9	0	5	2	3
−	1	8	2	1	9

9. In the questions below, you will have to regroup three times.

> **Step 1:**
>
> ```
>        2  16
>    8 4 3̶ 6̶
>  − 2 5 6 8
>  ───────────
> ```
>
> **Step 2:**
>
> ```
>        2  16
>    8 4 3̶ 6̶
>  − 2 5 6 8
>  ───────────
>          8
> ```
>
> **Step 3:**
>
> ```
>      12
>    3 2̶ 16
>    8 4 3̶ 6̶
>  − 2 5 6 8
>  ───────────
>        6 8
> ```
>
> **Step 4:**
>
> ```
>  7 13 12
>    3̶ 2̶ 16
>    8̶ 4 3̶ 6̶
>  − 2 5 6 8
>  ───────────
>        8 6 8
> ```
>
> **Step 5:**
>
> ```
>  7 13 12
>    3̶ 2̶ 16
>    8̶ 4 3̶ 6̶
>  − 2 5 6 8
>  ───────────
>      5 8 6 8
> ```

a)

	7	6	5	2
−	1	8	9	5

b)

	8	3	2	4
−	3	8	6	5

c)

	4	5	7	1
−	1	8	8	4

d)

	9	0	6	8
−	1	5	7	9

10. In the questions below you will have to regroup two or three times:

> **Step 1:**
>
> ```
>    0  10
>    1̶ 0̶ 0 0
>  −    5 3 2
>  ───────────
> ```
>
> **Step 2:**
>
> ```
>        9
>    0  1̶0 10
>    1̶ 0̶ 0̶ 0
>  −    5 3 2
>  ───────────
> ```
>
> **Step 3:**
>
> ```
>      9  9
>    0 1̶0 1̶0 10
>    1̶ 0̶ 0̶ 0̶
>  −    5 3 2
>  ───────────
> ```
>
> **Step 4:**
>
> ```
>      9  9
>    0 1̶0 1̶0 10
>    1̶ 0̶ 0̶ 0̶
>  −    5 3 2
>  ───────────
>        4 6 8
> ```

a)

	1	0	0	0
−		3	5	8

b)

	1	0	0
−		4	8

c)

	1	0	0	0
−		7	6	2

d)

	1	0	0	0
−		2	5	9

Number Sense 1

NS5-13: Parts and Totals

1. The bars in each picture represent a quantity of red and green apples. Fill in the blanks:

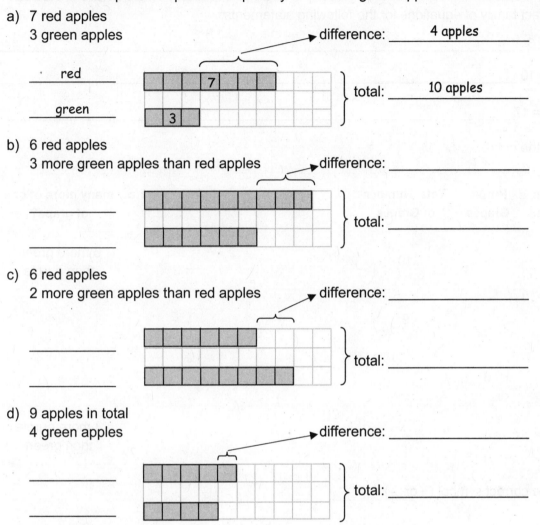

a) 7 red apples
    3 green apples

    difference: ___4 apples___

    red

    green

    total: ___10 apples___

b) 6 red apples
    3 more green apples than red apples

    difference: _____

    total: _____

c) 6 red apples
    2 more green apples than red apples

    difference: _____

    total: _____

d) 9 apples in total
    4 green apples

    difference: _____

    total: _____

2. Write the missing numbers.

Red Apples	Green Apples	Total Number of Apples	How many more of one colour of apple?
3	5	8	2 more green apples than red
4		9	
	1	8	
8			3 more red apples than green

3. Draw a picture (as in 1) and make a chart for each question.

    a) 5 red apples
        4 more green apples
        than red apples

    b) 13 apples in total
        6 green apples

    BONUS
    c) 9 apples in total
        1 more red apple
        than green apples

Number Sense 1

1. The fact family for the addition statement **3 + 4 = 7** is: **4 + 3 = 7**; **7 − 4 = 3** and **7 − 3 = 4**.

    Write the fact family of equations for the following statements:

    a) 2 + 4 = 6 _____

    b) 7 + 3 = 10 _____

    c) 12 + 5 = 17 _____

2. Complete the chart.

	Green Grapes	Purple Grapes	Total Number of Grapes	Fact Family		How many more of one type of grape?
a)	8	2	10	8 + 2 = 10 10 − 8 = 2	2 + 8 = 10 10 − 2 = 8	6 more green than purple
b)	5		9			
c)	3	6				
d)		4				3 more purple than green

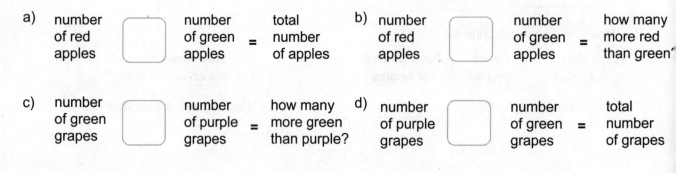

3. Use the correct symbol (+ or −).

    a) number of red apples [ ] number of green apples = total number of apples

    b) number of red apples [ ] number of green apples = how many more red than green?

    c) number of green grapes [ ] number of purple grapes = how many more green than purple?

    d) number of purple grapes [ ] number of green grapes = total number of grapes

4. Draw a picture on grid paper (as in question 1 on the previous page) for each question:

    a) Alan has 12 red stickers and 5 blue stickers.
        How many stickers does he have?

    b) Claire has 6 pets. Two are cats.
        The rest are dogs. How many dogs does she have?

    c) Peter walked 8 km. Layi walked 5 km.
        How much further did Peter walk?

Answer the following questions in your notebook.

1. Alex has $57 and Borana has $12.
   How much money do they have altogether?

2. Camile cycled 2 375 km one year and 5 753 the next. How many km did she cycle altogether?

3. The maximum depth of Lake Ontario is 244 m.
   The maximum depth of Lake Superior is 406 m.

   How much deeper is Lake Superior than Lake Ontario?

4. Mount Kilimanjaro in Tanzania is 5 895 m high and Mount Fuji in Japan is 3 776 m high.

   How much higher is Mount Kilimanjaro than Mount Fuji?

5. In space, the Apollo 10 command module travelled 39 666 km per hour.

   How far did it travel in 2 hours?

6. Two nearby towns have populations of 12 475 and 14 832 people.

   What is the total population of both towns?

7. Canada was founded in 1867.
   How many years ago was Canada founded?

8. In the number 432 ...

   The 100s digit is 1 more than the 10s digit
   The 10s digit is 1 more than the 1s digit

   Make up your own number with this property:

   _____ _____ _____

   Now write the number backwards:

   _____ _____ _____

   Write your two numbers in the grid and subtract (put the greater number on top).

   Try this again with several other numbers.
   You will always get 198!

   BONUS
   Can you explain why this works?

9. Sahar had 20 stickers.
   She put 5 in a book and gave 4 to her friend Nina.
   How many were leftover?

10. John has 26 marbles.
    David has 15 fewer marbles than John.
    Claude has 10 more marbles than John.

    How many marbles do David and Claude have altogether?

NS5-16: Larger Numbers

1. Write the place value of the underlined digit.

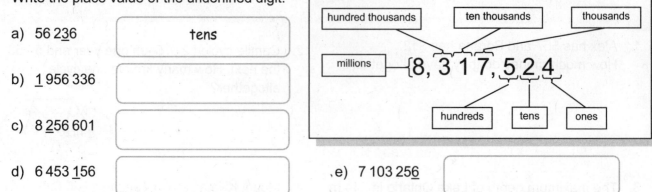

REMEMBER:

hundred thousands | ten thousands | thousands

millions — {8, 3 1 7, 5 2 4}

hundreds | tens | ones

a) 56 2<u>3</u>6   tens

b) <u>1</u> 956 336

c) 8 2<u>5</u>6 601

d) 6 453 <u>1</u>56

e) 7 103 25<u>6</u>

2. Write a numeral for the following number words:

a) five million six hundred forty-seven thousand one hundred ten _____

b) seven million eight hundred twenty-three thousand nine hundred twenty-five _____

3. Write the number words for the following numerals:

a) 2 325 853 _____

_____

b) 9 307 211 _____

_____

4. Write the numbers in expanded form (using numerals):

a) 4 238 215   4 000 000 + 200 000 + 30 000 + 8 000 + 200 + 10 + 5 _____

b) 5 218 967 _____

5. Circle the greater number:

a) 3 205 138   OR   3 215 139   b) 4 238 537   OR   423 854

6. Add or subtract.

a)

	2	8	1	5	3	7	2
+	1	1	9	2	1	3	5

b)

	6	9	1	3	5	2	1
−	1	3	8	5	5	2	3

c)

	2	8	5	9	3	2	1
−		1	3	8	1	5	9

jump math
MULTIPLYING POTENTIAL

Answer the following questions in your notebook.

1. The chart gives the area of some of the largest lakes in North America.

   a) How much more area does Lake Michigan cover than Lake Erie?

   b) Write the areas of the lakes in order from least to greatest.

   c) How much more area does the largest lake cover than the smallest lake?

   d) The largest lake in the world is the Caspian Sea in Asia. Its area is 370 990 km^2.

      How much greater than the area of Lake Superior is the area of the Caspian Sea?

Lake	Area (in km^2)
Erie	25 690
Great Slave	28 570
Michigan	58 020
Great Bear	31 340
Superior	82 100

2. A clothing store had 500 shirts. In one week, they sold:

   • 20 red shirts   • 50 blue shirts   • 100 green shirts

   How many shirts were left?

3. Use the digits 1, 2, 3, 4, 5, 6, 7 and 8 once each to fill in the boxes.

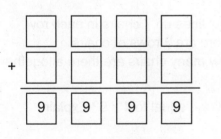

4. Use each of the digits 4, 5, 6, 7, 8 once to create …

   a) The greatest odd number possible.

   b) A number between 56 700 and 57 000.

   c) An odd number whose tens digit and hundreds digit add to 12.

   d) An odd number whose thousands digit is twice its hundreds digit.

5. Design your own problem using the numbers in the chart in Question 1.
   Write it in your notebook and then exchange it with a partner.

6. What is the greatest number you can add to 74 253 without having to regroup?

When you multiply a pair of numbers, the result is called the **product** of the numbers.

In the **array** shown, there are 3 **rows** of dots.
There are 5 dots **in each row**.

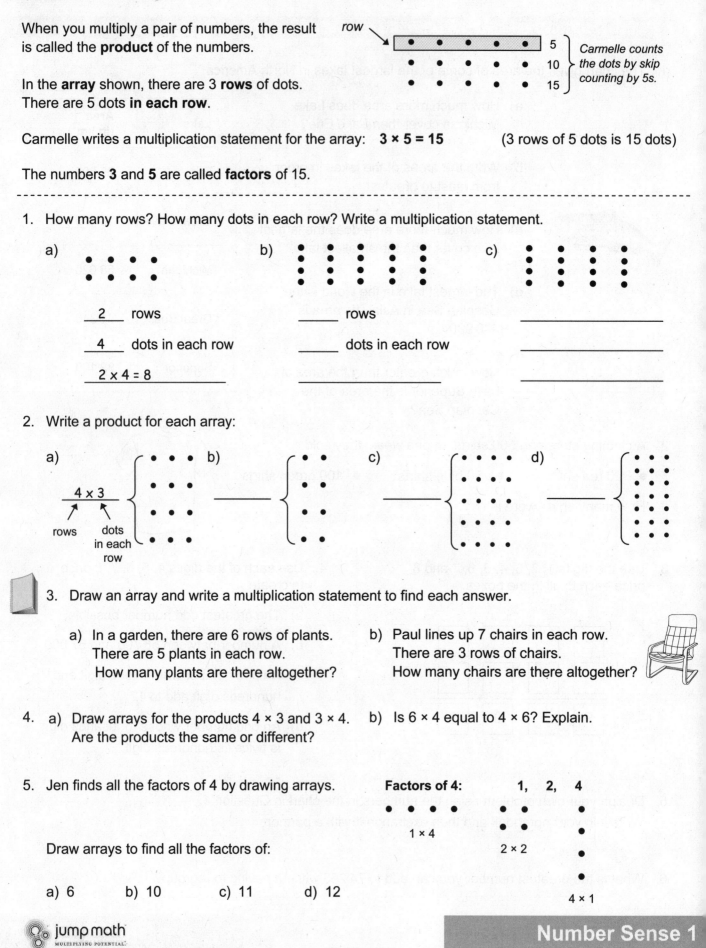

row

5
10 } Carmelle counts the dots by skip counting by 5s.
15

Carmelle writes a multiplication statement for the array: **3 × 5 = 15**   (3 rows of 5 dots is 15 dots)

The numbers **3** and **5** are called **factors** of 15.

----

1. How many rows? How many dots in each row? Write a multiplication statement.

    a)

    __2__ rows

    __4__ dots in each row

    __2 × 4 = 8__

    b)

    _____ rows

    _____ dots in each row

    _____

    c)

    _____

    _____

    _____

2. Write a product for each array:

    a)

    __4 × 3__

    ↗   ↖
    rows   dots
           in each
           row

    b)

    c)

    d)

3. Draw an array and write a multiplication statement to find each answer.

    a) In a garden, there are 6 rows of plants.
       There are 5 plants in each row.
       How many plants are there altogether?

    b) Paul lines up 7 chairs in each row.
       There are 3 rows of chairs.
       How many chairs are there altogether?

4. a) Draw arrays for the products 4 × 3 and 3 × 4.
       Are the products the same or different?

    b) Is 6 × 4 equal to 4 × 6? Explain.

5. Jen finds all the factors of 4 by drawing arrays.

    Factors of 4:   **1,   2,   4**

    1 × 4

    2 × 2

    4 × 1

    Draw arrays to find all the factors of:

    a) 6   b) 10   c) 11   d) 12

Amy finds the product of **3** and **5** by skip counting on a number line. She counts off three 5s. From the picture, Amy can see that the **product** of 3 and 5 is 15.

$3 \times 5 =$ ⌒5⌒ + ⌒5⌒ + ⌒5⌒ $= 15$

0 1 2 3 4 5 6 7 8 9 10 11 12 13 14 15

---

1. Draw arrows to find the products by skip counting.

   a) **4 x 2 =**

   0 1 2 3 4 5 6 7 8 9 10 11 12 13 14 15

   b) **3 x 4 =**

   0 1 2 3 4 5 6 7 8 9 10 11 12 13 14 15

2. Use the number line to skip count by 4s, 6s and 7s. Fill in the boxes below as you count:

0 1 2 3 4 5 6 7 8 9 **10** 11 12 13 14 15 16 17 18 19 **20** 21 22 23 24 25 26 27 28 29 **30** 31 32 33 34 35 36 37 38 39 **40** 41 42

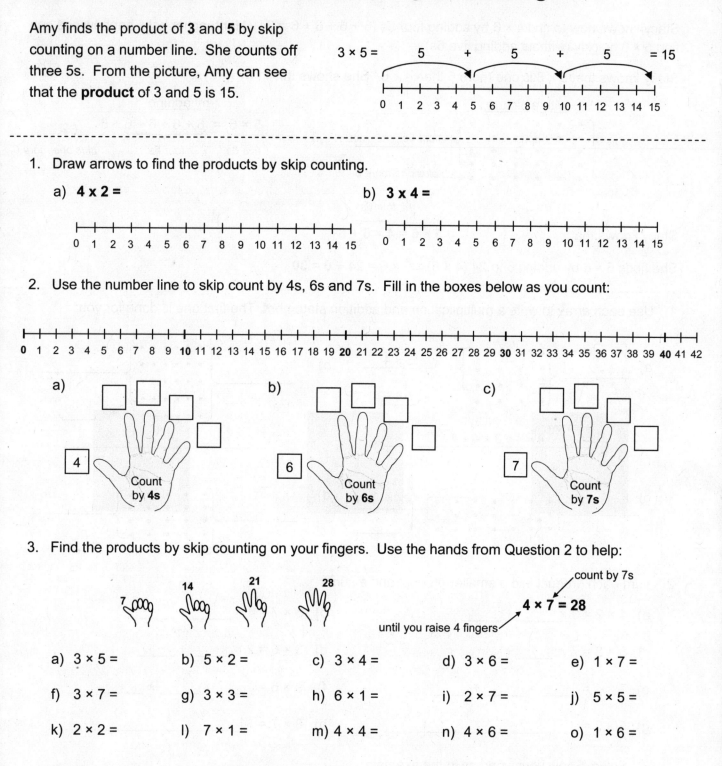

   a) ☐ ☐ ☐ ☐ [4] Count by **4s**

   b) ☐ ☐ ☐ ☐ [6] Count by **6s**

   c) ☐ ☐ ☐ ☐ [7] Count by **7s**

3. Find the products by skip counting on your fingers. Use the hands from Question 2 to help:

   7 ~~ 14 ~~ 21 ~~ 28 ~~   count by 7s
   4 × 7 = 28
   until you raise 4 fingers

   a) $3 \times 5 =$ b) $5 \times 2 =$ c) $3 \times 4 =$ d) $3 \times 6 =$ e) $1 \times 7 =$

   f) $3 \times 7 =$ g) $3 \times 3 =$ h) $6 \times 1 =$ i) $2 \times 7 =$ j) $5 \times 5 =$

   k) $2 \times 2 =$ l) $7 \times 1 =$ m) $4 \times 4 =$ n) $4 \times 6 =$ o) $1 \times 6 =$

4. Find the number of items in each picture. Write a multiplication statement for each picture:

   a) 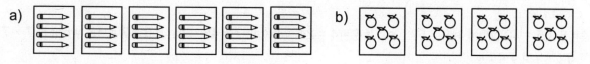   b)

   _____   _____

NS5-20: Multiplying by Adding On

Stacy knows how to find 4 × 6 by adding four 6s (6 + 6 + 6 + 6 = 24). Her teacher asks her how she can find 5 × 6 <u>quickly</u> (without adding five 6s):

Stacy knows that 5 × 6 is one more 6 than 4 × 6. She shows this in two ways:

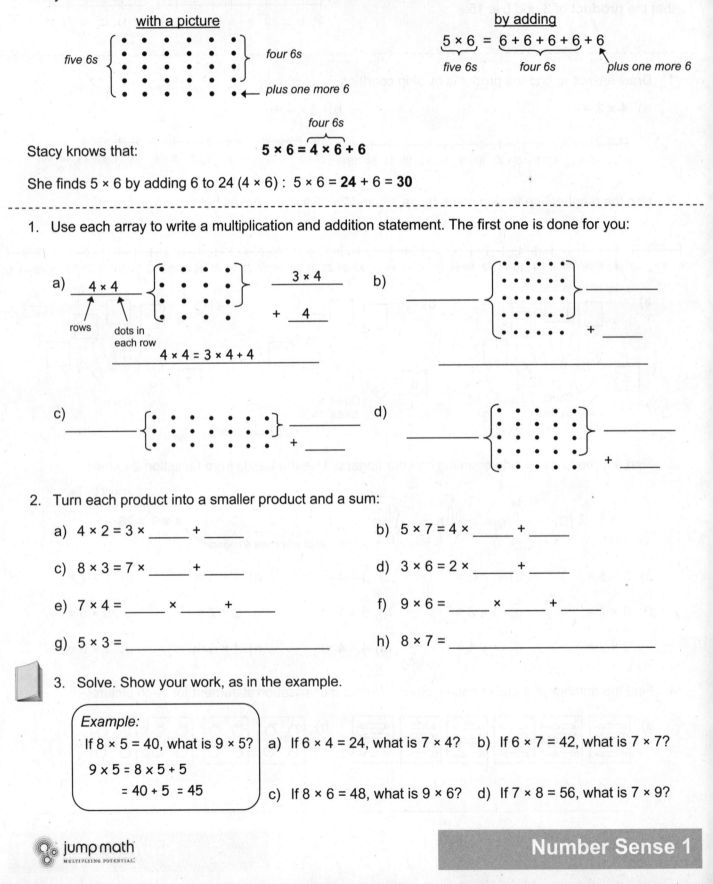

Stacy knows that: **5 × 6 = 4 × 6 + 6**

She finds 5 × 6 by adding 6 to 24 (4 × 6) : 5 × 6 = **24** + 6 = **30**

---

1. Use each array to write a multiplication and addition statement. The first one is done for you:

a) __4 × 4__ { : : : : } __3 × 4__
   rows / dots in each row
   + __4__
   __4 × 4 = 3 × 4 + 4__

b) _____ { } _____
   + _____

c) _____ { : : : : : : } _____
   + _____

d) _____ { } _____
   + _____

2. Turn each product into a smaller product and a sum:

a) 4 × 2 = 3 × _____ + _____

b) 5 × 7 = 4 × _____ + _____

c) 8 × 3 = 7 × _____ + _____

d) 3 × 6 = 2 × _____ + _____

e) 7 × 4 = _____ × _____ + _____

f) 9 × 6 = _____ × _____ + _____

g) 5 × 3 = _____

h) 8 × 7 = _____

3. Solve. Show your work, as in the example.

Example:
If 8 × 5 = 40, what is 9 × 5?
9 × 5 = 8 × 5 + 5
      = 40 + 5 = 45

a) If 6 × 4 = 24, what is 7 × 4?   b) If 6 × 7 = 42, what is 7 × 7?

c) If 8 × 6 = 48, what is 9 × 6?   d) If 7 × 8 = 56, what is 7 × 9?

To multiply **4 × 20**, Allen makes 4 groups containing 2 <u>tens</u> blocks (20 = 2 tens):

To multiply **4 × 200**, Allen makes 4 groups containing 2 <u>hundreds</u> blocks (200 = 2 hundreds):

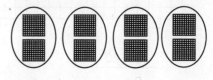

$$4 \times 20 = 4 \times 2 \text{ tens} = 8 \text{ tens} = 80$$

$$4 \times 200 = 4 \times 2 \text{ hundreds} = 8 \text{ hundreds} = 800$$

Allen notices a pattern: **4 × 2 = 8**   **4 × 20 = 80**   **4 × 200 = 800**

----

1. Draw a model for each multiplication statement, then calculate the answer. The first one is started:

    a) 4 × 30   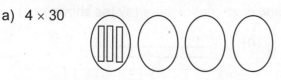   b) 2 × 20

    4 × 30 = 4 × ____ tens = ____ tens = ____   2 × 20 = 2 × ____ tens = ____ tens = ____

2. Regroup to find the answer. The first one is done for you:

    a) 3 × 70 = 3 × ____7____ tens = ____21____ tens = ____210____

    b) 4 × 50 = 4 × _____ tens = _____ tens = _____

    c) 3 × 40 = 3 × _____ tens = _____ tens = _____

    d) 6 × 30 = 6 × _____ tens = _____ tens = _____

3. Complete the pattern by multiplying:

    a) 2 × 3 = _____   b) 5 × 1 = _____   c) 5 × 4 = _____   d) 4 × 2 = _____

        2 × 30 = _____   5 × 10 = _____   5 × 40 = _____   4 × 20 = _____

        2 × 300 = _____   5 × 100 = _____   5 × 400 = _____   4 × 200 = _____

4. Multiply:

    a) 5 × 30 = _____   b) 30 × 4 = _____   c) 4 × 40 = _____   d) 50 × 3 = _____

    e) 3 × 500 = _____   f) 500 × 6 = _____   g) 3 × 80 = _____   h) 500 × 5 = _____

    i) 2 × 900 = _____   j) 70 × 6 = _____   k) 8 × 40 = _____   l) 900 × 3 = _____

5. Draw a base ten model (using cubes to represent thousands) to show: 6 × 1 000 = 6000.

6. Knowing that 4 × 2 = 8, how can you use this fact to multiply 4 × 2 000? Explain.

NS5-22: Advanced Arrays

1. Write a multiplication statement for each array.

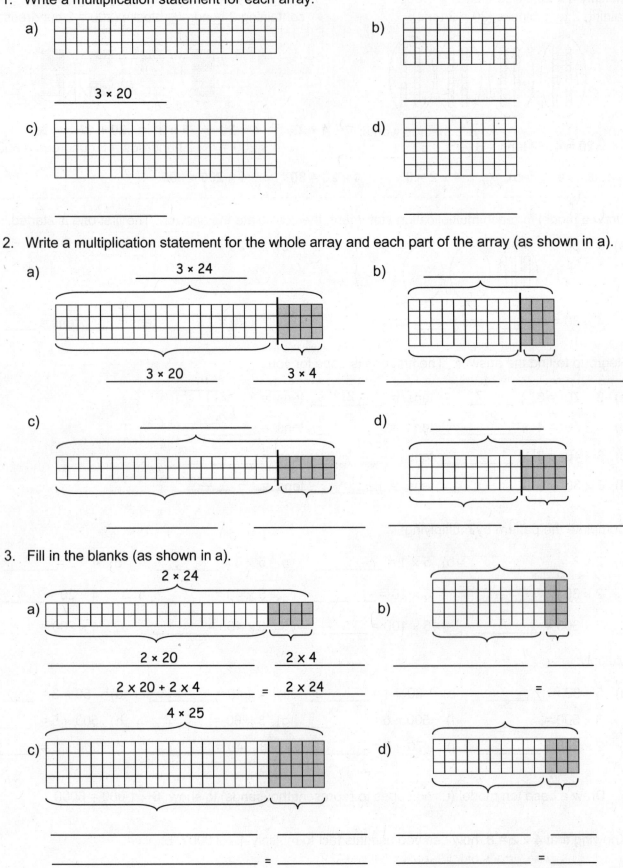

a)

3×20

b)

c)

d)

2. Write a multiplication statement for the whole array and each part of the array (as shown in a).

a) 3×24

3×20 3×4

b)

c)

d)

3. Fill in the blanks (as shown in a).

a) 2×24

2×20 2×4

$2 \times 20 + 2 \times 4$ = 2×24

c) 4×25

=

b)

=

d)

=

Number Sense 1

To multiply 4 × 23, Anya rewrites 23 as a sum:

23 = 20 + 3

She multiplies 20 by 4:	**4 × 20 = 80**
Then she multiplies 4 × 3:	**4 × 3 = 12**
Finally she adds the result:	**80 + 12 = 92**

The picture shows why Anya's method works: **4 × 23 = 4 × 20 + 4 × 3 = 80 + 12 = 92**

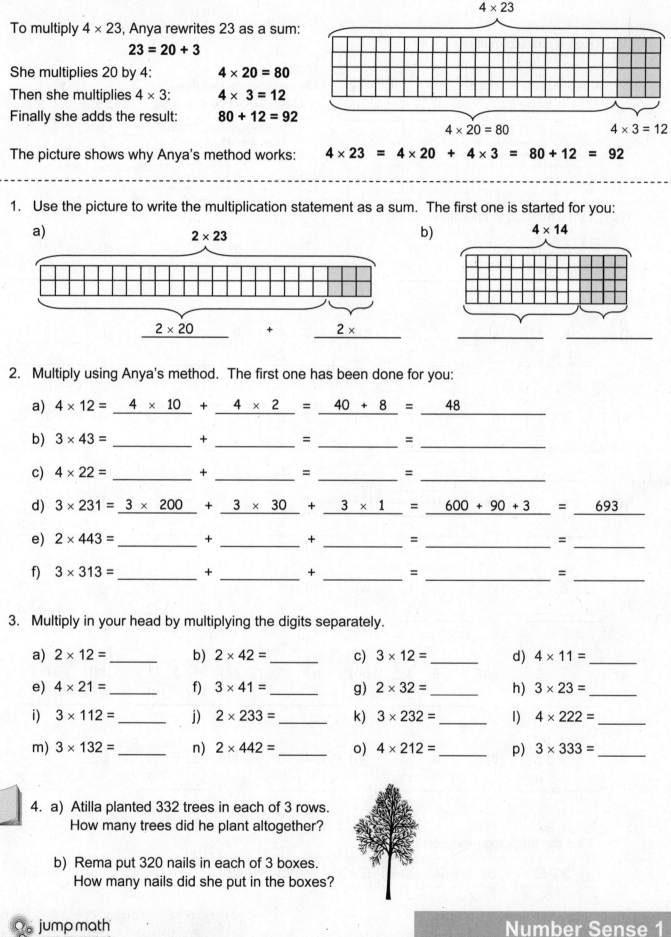

4 × 23

4 × 20 = 80   4 × 3 = 12

----

1. Use the picture to write the multiplication statement as a sum. The first one is started for you:

a)   **2 × 23**

2 × 20 _____ + 2 × _____

b)   **4 × 14**

_____ _____

2. Multiply using Anya's method. The first one has been done for you:

a) 4 × 12 = __4 × 10__ + __4 × 2__ = __40 + 8__ = __48__

b) 3 × 43 = _____ + _____ = _____ = _____

c) 4 × 22 = _____ + _____ = _____ = _____

d) 3 × 231 = __3 × 200__ + __3 × 30__ + __3 × 1__ = __600 + 90 + 3__ = __693__

e) 2 × 443 = _____ + _____ + _____ = _____ = _____

f) 3 × 313 = _____ + _____ + _____ = _____ = _____

3. Multiply in your head by multiplying the digits separately.

a) 2 × 12 = _____   b) 2 × 42 = _____   c) 3 × 12 = _____   d) 4 × 11 = _____

e) 4 × 21 = _____   f) 3 × 41 = _____   g) 2 × 32 = _____   h) 3 × 23 = _____

i) 3 × 112 = _____   j) 2 × 233 = _____   k) 3 × 232 = _____   l) 4 × 222 = _____

m) 3 × 132 = _____   n) 2 × 442 = _____   o) 4 × 212 = _____   p) 3 × 333 = _____

4. a) Atilla planted 332 trees in each of 3 rows.
        How many trees did he plant altogether?

    b) Rema put 320 nails in each of 3 boxes.
        How many nails did she put in the boxes?

Clara uses a chart to multiply 3 × 42:

Step 1:
She multiplies the ones digit
of 42 by 3 (3 × 2 = 6).

	4	2
×		3
		6

Step 2:
She multiplies the tens digit
of 42 by 3 (3 × 4 tens = 12 tens).

She regroups 10 tens
as 1 hundred.

	4	2
×		3
1	2	6

hundreds *tens*

1. Use Clara's method to find the products:

a)
	5	1
×		4

b)
	6	3
×		2

c)
	7	1
×		4

d)
	2	1
×		6

e)
	9	1
×		3

f)
	8	1
×		2

g)
	7	2
×		3

h)
	9	4
×		2

i)
	4	2
×		4

j)
	9	2
×		2

k)
	8	1
×		5

l)
	7	3
×		2

m)
	2	2
×		3

n)
	7	3
×		3

o)
	7	4
×		2

p)
	8	3
×		3

q)
	6	4
×		2

r)
	3	2
×		4

s)
	4	1
×		9

t)
	9	1
×		5

u)
	6	3
×		3

v)
	8	1
×		9

w)
	7	1
×		5

x)
	7	2
×		2

y)
	8	1
×		8

z)
	7	2
×		4

aa)
	9	3
×		3

bb)
	7	1
×		9

cc)
	5	1
×		6

dd)
	6	1
×		8

ee)
	9	2
×		4

ff)
	6	5
×		1

gg)
	5	3
×		3

hh)
	8	1
×		7

ii)
	9	1
×		8

2. Find the following products.

a) 2 × 62   b) 2 × 64   c) 5 × 31   d) 4 × 62   e) 6 × 41   f) 7 × 21

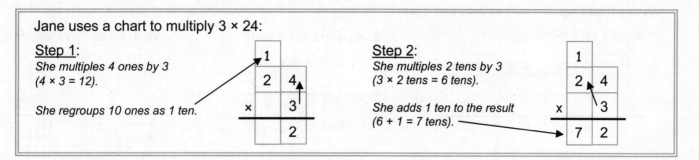

Jane uses a chart to multiply 3 × 24:

Step 1:
She multiples 4 ones by 3
(4 × 3 = 12).

She regroups 10 ones as 1 ten.

Step 2:
She multiples 2 tens by 3
(3 × 2 tens = 6 tens).

She adds 1 ten to the result
(6 + 1 = 7 tens).

1. Using Jane's method, complete the first step of the multiplication. The first one has been done:

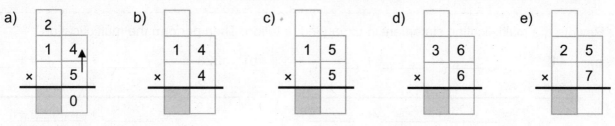

a) b) c) d) e)

2. Using Jane's method, complete the second step of the multiplication:

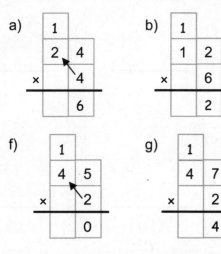

a) b) c) d) e)

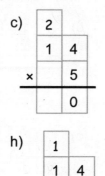

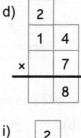

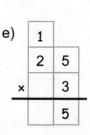

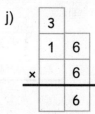

f) g) h) i) j)

3. Using Jane's method, complete the first and second step of the multiplication:

a) b) c) d)

| 3 | 5 |
| × | 2 |

| 2 | 6 |
| × | 6 |

| 4 | 5 |
| × | 4 |

| 5 | 5 |
| × | 3 |

TEACHER:
Be sure to give
your students
extra practice
at this skill.

e) f) g) h) i)

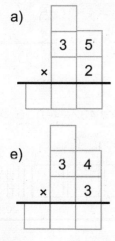

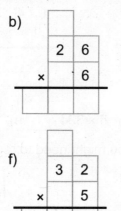

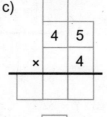

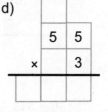

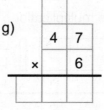

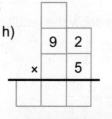

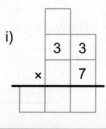

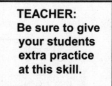

Murray multiplies 2 × 321 in 3 different ways:

1. With a chart:

hundreds	tens	ones
3	2	1
×		2
6	4	2

2. In expanded form:

$$
\begin{array}{r}
300 + 20 + 1 \\
\times\ 2 \\
\hline
=\ 600 + 40 + 2 \\
=\ 642
\end{array}
$$

3. With base ten materials:

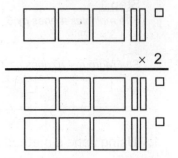

---

1. Rewrite the multiplication statement in expanded notation. Then perform the multiplication.

   a) 412   _____ + _____ + _____

       × 3   _____ × 3

             = _____ + _____ + _____

             = _____

   b) 323   _____ + _____ + _____

       × 2   _____ × 2

             = _____ + _____ + _____

             = _____

2. Multiply:

   a)
	3	4
×		2

   b)
3	1	2
×		3

   c)
2	1	2
×		4

   d)
3	2	3
×		3

   e)
2	1	3
×		3

3. Multiply by regrouping ones as tens:

   a)
1	1	4
×		4

   b)
2	2	6
×		3

   c)
2	2	4
×		4

   d)
2	1	6
×		3

   e)
1	1	4
×		6

4. Multiply by regrouping tens as hundreds. In the last question, you will also regroup ones as tens:

   a)
2	5	2
×		3

   b)
1	6	1
×		5

   c)
2	5	3
×		3

   d)
1	4	2
×		4

   e)
2	7	4
×		3

5. Multiply:

   a) 4 × 142   b) 6 × 311   c) 7 × 223   d) 8 × 324   e) 9 × 1 432   f) 6 × 2 537

6. Draw a picture to show the result of the multiplication. You might need to regroup.

   a) _____ × 2

   b) _____ × 3

   c) _____ × 4

Erin wants to multiply 20 × 32. She knows how to find 10 × 32. She rewrites 20 x 32 as <u>double</u> 10 × 32:

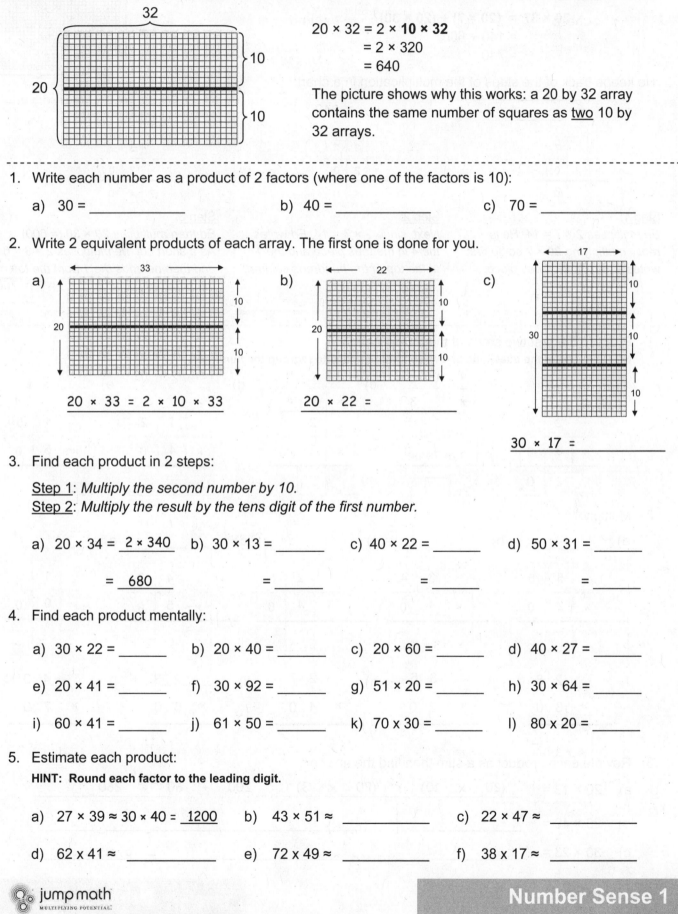

$20 × 32 = 2 × \mathbf{10 × 32}$
$= 2 × 320$
$= 640$

The picture shows why this works: a 20 by 32 array contains the same number of squares as <u>two</u> 10 by 32 arrays.

---

1. Write each number as a product of 2 factors (where one of the factors is 10):

   a) 30 = _____

   b) 40 = _____

   c) 70 = _____

2. Write 2 equivalent products of each array. The first one is done for you.

   a)

   20 × 33 = 2 × 10 × 33

   b)

   20 × 22 = _____

   c)

   30 × 17 = _____

3. Find each product in 2 steps:

   <u>Step 1</u>: *Multiply the second number by 10.*
   <u>Step 2</u>: *Multiply the result by the tens digit of the first number.*

   a) 20 × 34 = <u>2 × 340</u>

       = <u>680</u>

   b) 30 × 13 = _____

       = _____

   c) 40 × 22 = _____

       = _____

   d) 50 × 31 = _____

       = _____

4. Find each product mentally:

   a) 30 × 22 = _____

   b) 20 × 40 = _____

   c) 20 × 60 = _____

   d) 40 × 27 = _____

   e) 20 × 41 = _____

   f) 30 × 92 = _____

   g) 51 × 20 = _____

   h) 30 × 64 = _____

   i) 60 × 41 = _____

   j) 61 × 50 = _____

   k) 70 x 30 = _____

   l) 80 x 20 = _____

5. Estimate each product:

   HINT: Round each factor to the leading digit.

   a) 27 × 39 ≈ 30 × 40 = <u>1200</u>

   b) 43 × 51 ≈ _____

   c) 22 × 47 ≈ _____

   d) 62 x 41 ≈ _____

   e) 72 × 49 ≈ _____

   f) 38 x 17 ≈ _____

Ed multiplies **20 × 37** by splitting the product into a sum of two smaller products:

20 × 37 = (20 × 7) + (20 × 30)
= 140 + 600
= 740

He keeps track of the steps of the multiplication in a chart:

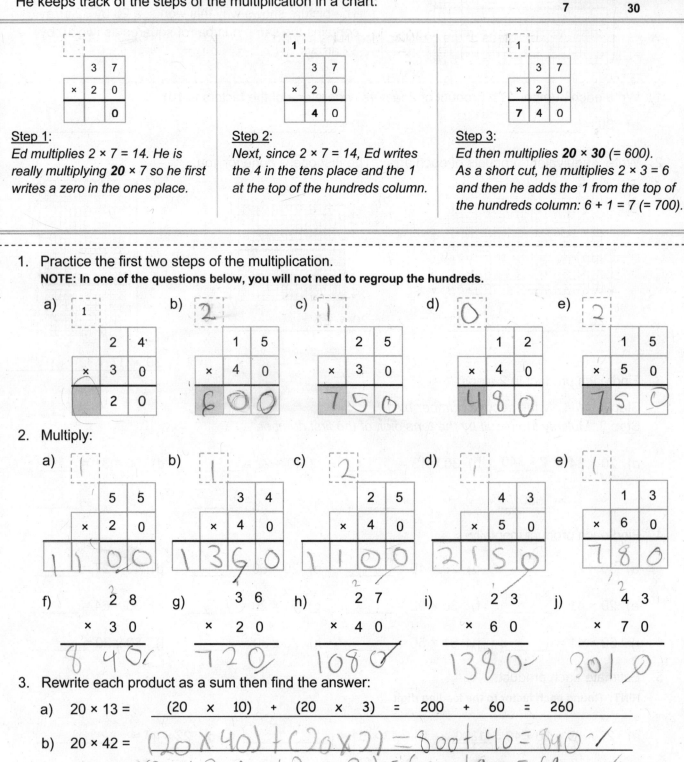

Step 1:
Ed multiplies 2 × 7 = 14. He is really multiplying **20 × 7** so he first writes a zero in the ones place.

Step 2:
Next, since 2 × 7 = 14, Ed writes the 4 in the tens place and the 1 at the top of the hundreds column.

Step 3:
Ed then multiplies **20 × 30** (= 600). As a short cut, he multiplies 2 × 3 = 6 and then he adds the 1 from the top of the hundreds column: 6 + 1 = 7 (= 700).

1. Practice the first two steps of the multiplication.
   NOTE: In one of the questions below, you will not need to regroup the hundreds.

a)
```
    2 4
  × 3 0
    2 0
```
(1)

b)
```
    1 5
  × 4 0
  6 0 0
```
(2)

c)
```
    2 5
  × 3 0
  7 5 0
```
(1)

d)
```
    1 2
  × 4 0
  4 8 0
```
(0)

e)
```
    1 5
  × 5 0
  7 5 0
```
(2)

2. Multiply:

a)
```
    5 5
  × 2 0
  1 1 0 0
```
(1)

b)
```
    3 4
  × 4 0
  1 3 6 0
```
(1)

c)
```
    2 5
  × 4 0
  1 1 0 0
```
(2)

d)
```
    4 3
  × 5 0
  2 1 5 0
```
(1)

e)
```
    1 3
  × 6 0
  7 8 0
```
(1)

f)
```
    2 8
  × 3 0
  8 4 0
```

g)
```
    3 6
  × 2 0
  7 2 0
```

h)
```
    2 7
  × 4 0
  1 0 8 0
```

i)
```
    2 3
  × 6 0
  1 3 8 0
```

j)
```
    4 3
  × 7 0
  3 0 1 0
```

3. Rewrite each product as a sum then find the answer:

a) 20 × 13 = (20 × 10) + (20 × 3) = 200 + 60 = 260

b) 20 × 42 = (20 × 40) + (20 × 2) = 800 + 40 = 840

c) 30 × 23 = (30 × 20) + (30 × 3) = 600 + 90 = 690

Grace multiplies 26 × 28 by splitting the product into a sum
of two smaller products:

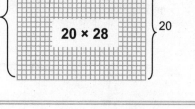

26 × 28 = 6 × 28 + 20 × 28

       = 168 + 560

       = 728

She keeps track of the steps of the multiplication using a chart.

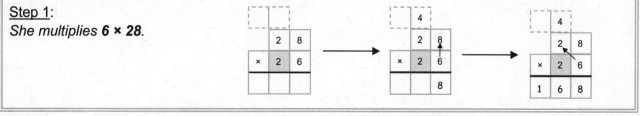

Step 1:
*She multiplies **6 × 28**.*

1. Practice the first step of the multiplication:

a)   b)   c)   d)   e)

f)   g)   h)   i)   j)

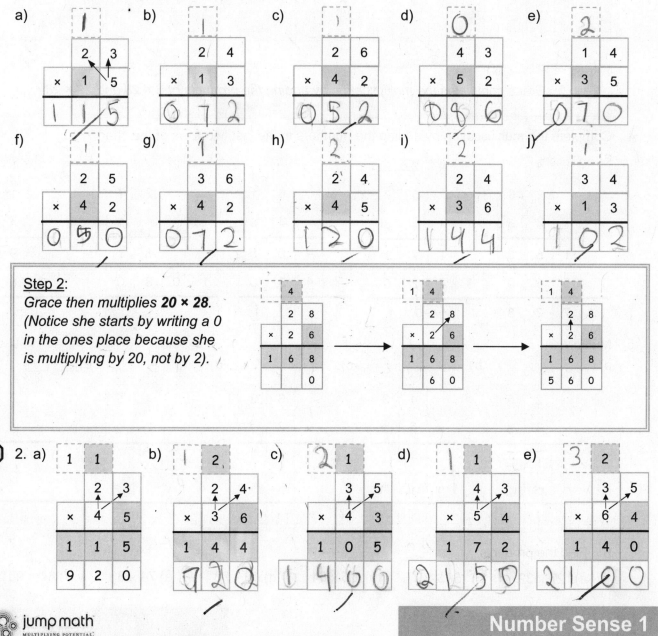

Step 2:
*Grace then multiplies **20 × 28**.
(Notice she starts by writing a 0
in the ones place because she
is multiplying by 20, not by 2).*

2. a)   b)   c)   d)   e)

3. Practice the first 2 steps of the multiplication.

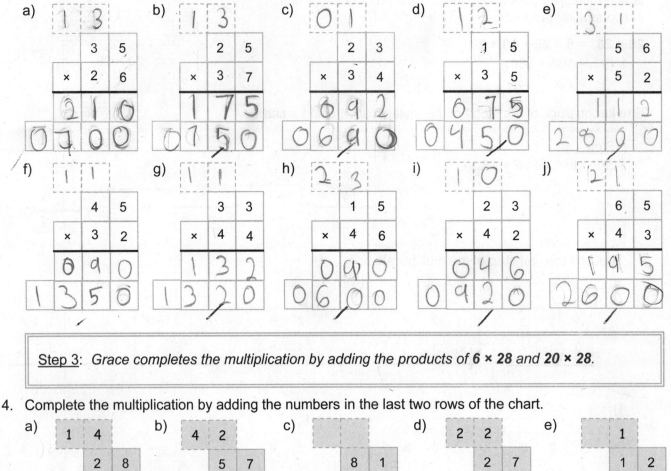

Step 3: *Grace completes the multiplication by adding the products of **6 × 28** and **20 × 28**.*

4. Complete the multiplication by adding the numbers in the last two rows of the chart.

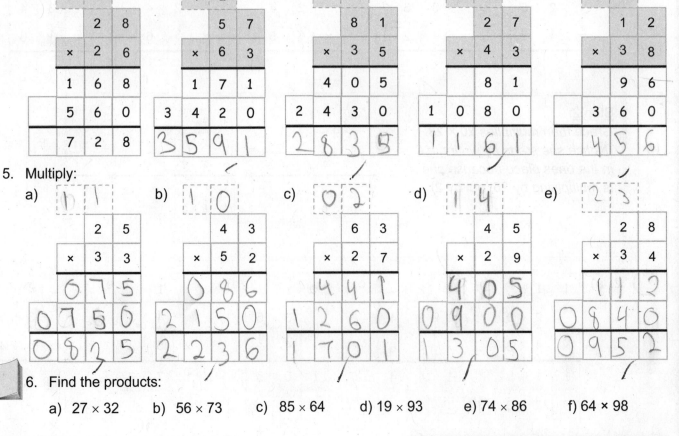

5. Multiply:

6. Find the products:

   a) 27 × 32   b) 56 × 73   c) 85 × 64   d) 19 × 93   e) 74 × 86   f) 64 × 98

1. Double each number mentally by doubling the ones digit and the tens digit separately.

23	44	12	31	43	54	83	92	71
Double 46	88	24	62	86	108	166	184	142

2. Double the ones and tens separately and add the result: $2 \times 36 = 2 \times 30 + 2 \times 6 = 60 + 12 = 72$.

25	45	16	28	18	17	35	55	39
Double 50	80	32	56	36	34	79	110	78

3. a) One flower costs 34¢. How much do two flowers cost? _____ 68¢

    b) One lizard costs 48¢. How much do two lizards cost? _____ 96¢

4. From the arrays you can see:
    3×2 is the same as 2×3.

    Is 4×5 the same as 5×4? Explain.

    3×2
    (3 rows of 2)

    2×3
    (2 rows of 3)

5. Rearrange the products so you can find the answer mentally.

    Example: $2 \times 8 \times 35$
    $= 2 \times 35 \times 8$
    $= 70 \times 8$
    $= 560$

    Example: $4 \times 18 \times 25$
    $= 4 \times 25 \times 18$
    $= 100 \times 18$
    $= 1800$

    a) $2 \times 4 \times 25$

    b) $2 \times 3 \times 45$

    c) $2 \times 6 \times 35$

    d) $2 \times 27 \times 50$

    e) $4 \times 75 \times 250$

    f) $2 \times 97 \times 500$

    g) $372 \times 4 \times 25$

    h) $2 \times 2 \times 15 \times 250$

    i) $25 \times 2 \times 50 \times 4$

6. Double the number in the box and halve the number in the circle.

    Example: $\boxed{8} \times \bigcirc{4} \rightarrow \boxed{16} \times \bigcirc{2}$

    $\boxed{6} \times \bigcirc{4} \rightarrow \boxed{12} \times \bigcirc{2}$

    $\boxed{10} \times \bigcirc{2} \rightarrow \boxed{20} \times \bigcirc{1}$

    $\boxed{7} \times \bigcirc{12} \rightarrow \boxed{14} \times \bigcirc{6}$

    Does the product change or stay the same? Explain

7. Use halving and doubling to find each product mentally.

    Example: 32×5
    $= 16 \times 10$
    $= 160$

    a) 42×5

    b) 64×5

    c) 86×5

jump math
MULTIPLYING POTENTIAL

1. Fill in the blanks.

a)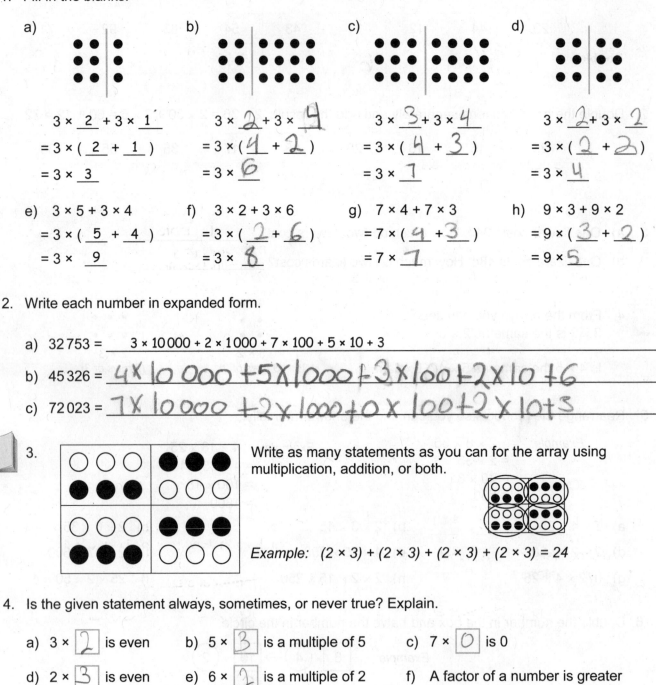

$3 \times \underline{2} + 3 \times \underline{1}$

$= 3 \times (\underline{2} + \underline{1})$

$= 3 \times \underline{3}$

b) $3 \times \underline{2} + 3 \times \underline{4}$

$= 3 \times (\underline{4} + \underline{2})$

$= 3 \times \underline{6}$

c) $3 \times \underline{3} + 3 \times \underline{4}$

$= 3 \times (\underline{4} + \underline{3})$

$= 3 \times \underline{7}$

d) $3 \times \underline{2} + 3 \times \underline{2}$

$= 3 \times (\underline{2} + \underline{2})$

$= 3 \times \underline{4}$

e) $3 \times 5 + 3 \times 4$

$= 3 \times (\underline{5} + \underline{4})$

$= 3 \times \underline{9}$

f) $3 \times 2 + 3 \times 6$

$= 3 \times (\underline{2} + \underline{6})$

$= 3 \times \underline{8}$

g) $7 \times 4 + 7 \times 3$

$= 7 \times (\underline{4} + \underline{3})$

$= 7 \times \underline{7}$

h) $9 \times 3 + 9 \times 2$

$= 9 \times (\underline{3} + \underline{2})$

$= 9 \times \underline{5}$

2. Write each number in expanded form.

a) $32\,753 = \underline{3 \times 10\,000 + 2 \times 1000 + 7 \times 100 + 5 \times 10 + 3}$

b) $45\,326 = \underline{4 \times 10\,000 + 5 \times 1000 + 3 \times 100 + 2 \times 10 + 6}$

c) $72\,023 = \underline{7 \times 10\,000 + 2 \times 1000 + 0 \times 100 + 2 \times 10 + 3}$

3. Write as many statements as you can for the array using multiplication, addition, or both.

Example: $(2 \times 3) + (2 \times 3) + (2 \times 3) + (2 \times 3) = 24$

4. Is the given statement always, sometimes, or never true? Explain.

a) $3 \times \boxed{2}$ is even

b) $5 \times \boxed{3}$ is a multiple of 5

c) $7 \times \boxed{0}$ is 0

d) $2 \times \boxed{3}$ is even

e) $6 \times \boxed{2}$ is a multiple of 2

f) A factor of a number is greater than the number

5. Explain why the product of two 2-digit numbers must be at least 100.

6. Using the digits 1, 2, 3, and 4, create …

a) the greatest product

$\boxed{4} \times \boxed{3}\,\boxed{2}\,\boxed{1}$

b) the least product

$\boxed{1} \times \boxed{2}\,\boxed{3}\,\boxed{4}$

Number Sense 1

Answer the questions below in your notebook.

1. A bee has 6 legs. How many legs do 325 bees have?

2. How many hours are there in the month of January?

3. A 12-sided field has sides 87 metres long. What is the perimeter of the field?

4. Sapin's heart beats 98 times a minute. How many times would it beat in an hour?

5. A harp has 47 strings. How many strings do 12 harps have?

6. Find the first four products. (Show your work on a separate piece of paper.) Use the pattern in the products to find the products in e) and f) without multiplying:

   a)
	3	7
×		9

   b)
	3	7
×	1	2

   c)
	3	7
×	1	5

   d)
	3	7
×	1	8

   e)
	3	7
x	2	1

   f)
	3	7
x	2	4

7. A hummingbird flaps its wings 15 times a second.

   How many times does it flap its wings in a minute?

8.

Planets	Width (in km)
Mercury	4 850
Mars	6 790
Pluto	3 400

The circumference of a planet is the distance around the planet.

The circumference is always about 3 times the width of the planet.

Use the numbers in the charts to find the approximate circumferences of the planets.

9. Tickets to a play cost $14.

   How much will it cost for a class of 26 students to attend the play?

   How much change will they receive from a $500 payment?

10. Recall that **factors** of a number are whole numbers that multiply to give the number. Two **factors** of 15 are 3 and 5. 15 is called the **product** of 3 and 5.

   Say whether each statement below is true or false. Explain your answer.

   a) The factors of a number are never greater than the number.

   b) The least factor of a number is always 1.

   c) A number is always a factor of itself.

   d) The sum of a pair of factors of a number is <u>always</u> less than the number (i.e. 3 and 2 are factors of 6 and 3 + 2 < 6).

Rita has 12 sandwiches. A tray holds 4 sandwiches:

There are 3 trays:

What has been shared or divided into <u>sets</u> or <u>groups</u>? *(Sandwiches)*

How many sets are there? *(There are 3 sets of sandwiches.)*

How many of the things being divided are in each set? *(There are 4 sandwiches in each set.)*

---

1. a)

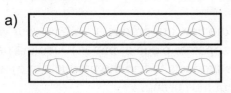

What has been shared or divided into sets?

there a hats in each set

How many sets? _2_

How many in each set? _5_

b)

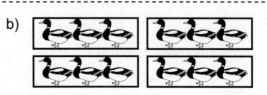

What has been shared or divided into sets?

ducks

How many sets? _4_

How many in each set? _3_

2. Using circles for <u>sets</u> and dots for <u>things</u>, draw a picture to show…

a) 5 sets
    4 things in each set

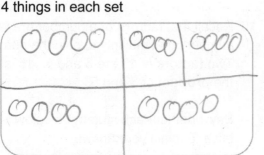

b) 6 groups
    3 things in each group

c) 7 sets
    3 things in each set

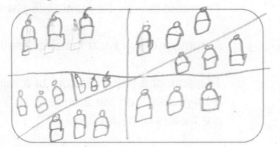

d) 3 sets
    4 things in each set

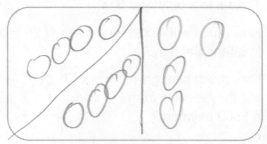

 jump math
MULTIPLYING POTENTIAL

Number Sense 1

3.

	What has been shared or divided into sets?	How many sets?	How many in each set?

a) 24 toys
      4 toys for each girl/boy
      6 girls/boys
	24 toys	6	4

b) 8 children
      32 crackers
      4 crackers for each child
	32 crackers	8	4

c) 18 flowers
      3 bouquets
      6 flowers in each bouquet
	18 flowers	3	6

d) 9 trees
      45 oranges
      5 oranges in each tree
	45 oranges	9	5

e) 8 apples in each pack
      80 apples
      10 packs
	80 apples	8	10

f) 6 taxis
      24 passengers
      4 passengers in each taxi
	24 passengers	6	4

g) 35 cows
      7 cows in each herd
      5 herds
	35 cows	7	5

h) 7 litters
      42 puppies
      6 puppies in each litter
	42 puppies	6	7

4. Draw a picture for Questions 3 a), b) and c) using <u>circles</u> for sets and <u>dots</u> for the things being divided.

Tory has 18 cookies. There are two ways she can share or <u>divide</u> her cookies equally:

I • She can decide how many <u>sets</u> (or <u>groups</u>) of cookies she wants to make:

For example:
Tory wants to make 3 sets of cookies. She draws 3 circles:

She then puts one cookie at a time into the circles until she has placed 18 cookies.

II • She can decide how many cookies she wants to put <u>in each set</u>:

For example:
Tory wants to put 6 cookies in each set. She counts out 6 cookies:

She counts out sets of 6 cookies until she has placed 18 cookies in sets.

----

1. Share **12** dots equally. How many dots are in each set? **HINT: Place one dot at a time.**

    a) 4 sets:

    There are _____ dots in each set.

    b) 3 sets:

    There are _____ dots in each set.

2. Share the triangles equally among the sets. **HINT: Count the triangles first. Divide by the number of circles.**

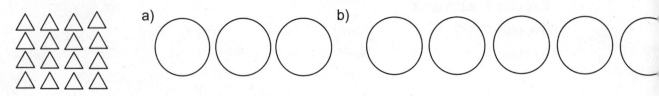

    a)   b)

3. Share the squares equally among the sets:

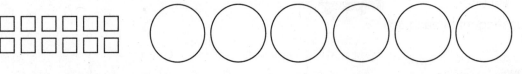

4. Group the lines so that there are 4 lines in each set. Say how many sets there are:

    a) | | | | | | | | b) | | | | | | | | | | | | | | | | c) | | | | | | | | | | | |

    There are _____ sets.   There are _____ sets   There are _____ sets.

5. Group **16** flowers so that …

    a) there are 8 flowers in each set.   b) there are 4 flowers in each set.

NS5-34: Two Ways of Sharing (continued)

6. In each question fill in what you know. Write a question mark for what you don't know:

	What has been shared or divided into sets?	How many sets?	How many in each set?
a) Kathy has 30 stickers. She put 6 stickers in each box.	30 stickers	?	6
b) 24 children are in 6 vans.	24 children	6	?
c) Andy has 14 apples. He gives them to 7 friends.			
d) Manju has 24 comic books. She puts 3 in each bin.			
e) 35 children sit at 7 tables.			
f) 24 people are in 2 boats.			
g) 12 books are shared among 4 children.			
h) 10 flowers are in 2 rows.			
i) 8 hamsters are in 4 cages.			

7. Draw a picture using dots and circles to solve each question.

a) 10 dots; 5 sets

_____ dots in each set

b) 12 dots; 4 dots in each set

_____ sets

c) 15 dots; 5 dots in each set

_____ sets

d) 8 dots; 4 sets

_____ dots in each set

e) 3 friends share 12 tickets.

How many tickets does each friend get? _____

f) 10 students go canoeing in 5 boats.

How many kids are in each boat? _____

g) Pria has 14 stickers.
She gives 7 to each friend.

How many friends receive stickers? _____

h) Each basket holds 5 plums.
There are 15 plums altogether.

How many baskets are there? _____

i) 16 flowers are planted in 2 pots.

How many flowers are in each pot? _____

j) Keith has 15 stamps.
He puts 3 on each page.

How many pages does he use? _____

Every **division** statement implies an **addition** statement.

For example, the statement "20 divided into sets of size 4 gives 5 sets" can be represented as:

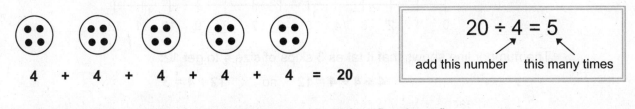

4 + 4 + 4 + 4 + 4 = 20

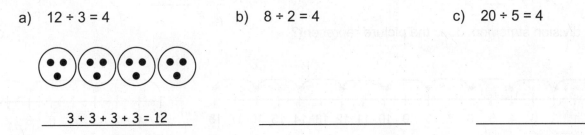

add this number   this many times

Hence the division statement 20 ÷ 4 = 5 can be read as "add four five times."
The number 4 is called the **divisor** and the number 5 is called the **quotient** of the division statement.

----

1. Draw a picture and write an <u>addition</u> statement for each <u>division</u> statement.

   a) 12 ÷ 3 = 4

   b) 8 ÷ 2 = 4

   c) 20 ÷ 5 = 4

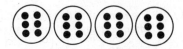

   _____3 + 3 + 3 + 3 = 12_____   _____   _____

2. Draw a picture and write a <u>division</u> statement for each <u>addition</u> statement.

   a) 6 + 6 + 6 + 6 = 24

   b) 4 + 4 + 4 + 4 + 4 + 4 = 24

   _____   _____

   c) 7 + 7 + 7 = 21

   d) 3 + 3 + 3 + 3 + 3 = 15

   _____   _____

   e) 4 + 4 + 4 + 4 = 16

   f) 8 + 8 + 8 = 24

   _____   _____

Number Sense 1

You can solve the division problem **12 ÷ 4 = ?** by skip counting on the number line:

```
0  1  2  3  4  5  6  7  8  9  10  11  12
```

The number line shows that it takes 3 skips of size 4 to get 12:

4 + 4 + 4 = 12   so ...   **12 ÷ 4 = 3**

3.   Draw arrows to show how you can divide by skip counting:

a)
```
0  1  2  3  4  5  6  7  8
```
8 ÷ 4 = _____

b)
```
0  1  2  3  4  5  6  7  8  9  10  11  12  13  14  15  16
```
16 ÷ 2 = _____

4.   What division statement does the picture represent?

a)
```
0  1  2  3  4  5  6  7  8  9  10  11  12  13  14  15  16  17  18
```
_____

b)
```
0  1  2  3  4  5  6  7  8  9
```
_____

5.   You can also find the answer to a division question by skip counting on your fingers.

For instance, to find **40 ÷ 8**, count by 8s until you reach 40.

The number of fingers you have up when you say "40" is the answer:

8   16   24   32   40

So 40 ÷ 8 = 5

Find the answers by skip counting on your fingers:

a) 18 ÷ 6 = _____   b) 12 ÷ 6 = _____   c) 32 ÷ 8 = _____   d) 21 ÷ 7 = _____   e) 45 ÷ 5 = _____

f) 25 ÷ 5 = _____   g) 36 ÷ 4 = _____   h) 35 ÷ 5 = _____   i) 27 ÷ 3 = _____   j) 16 ÷ 2 = _____

k) 36 ÷ 9 = _____   l) 35 ÷ 7 = _____   m) 12 ÷ 3 = _____   n) 18 ÷ 3 = _____   o) 24 ÷ 6 = _____

6.   8 friends split the cafeteria bill of $32.
How much does each friend have to pay?

_____

7.   35 candles are in 5 rows.
How many candles are in each row?

_____

NS5-36: Division and Multiplication

Every division statement implies a multiplication statement. The statement:

"14 divided into sets of size 2 gives 7 sets" (or **14 ÷ 2 = 7**)

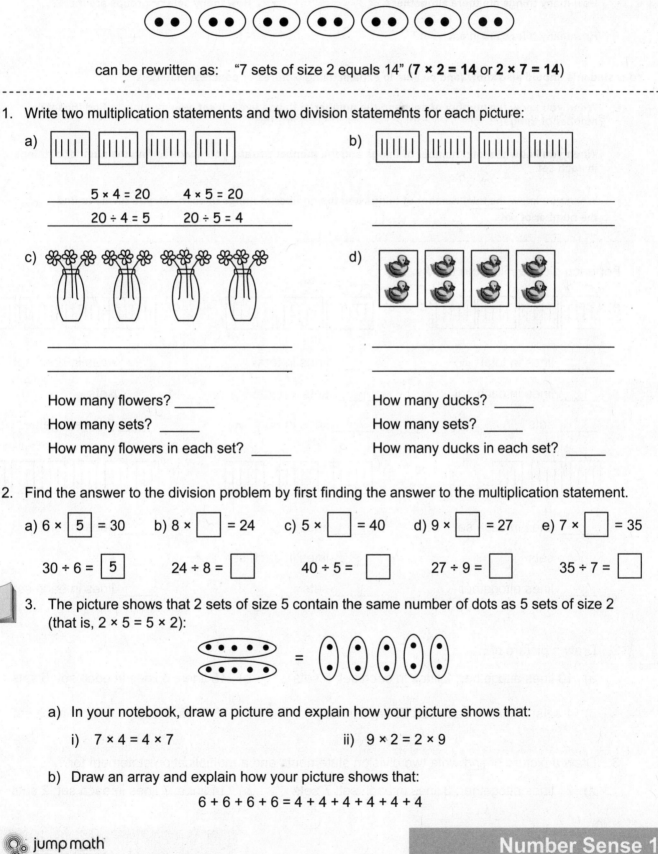

can be rewritten as: "7 sets of size 2 equals 14" (**7 × 2 = 14** or **2 × 7 = 14**)

- -

1. Write two multiplication statements and two division statements for each picture:

   a)

   $$5 × 4 = 20 \qquad 4 × 5 = 20$$
   $$20 ÷ 4 = 5 \qquad 20 ÷ 5 = 4$$

   b)

   _____

   _____

   c)

   _____

   _____

   How many flowers? _____

   How many sets? _____

   How many flowers in each set? _____

   d)

   _____

   _____

   How many ducks? _____

   How many sets? _____

   How many ducks in each set? _____

2. Find the answer to the division problem by first finding the answer to the multiplication statement.

   a) 6 × ⟦5⟧ = 30   b) 8 × ☐ = 24   c) 5 × ☐ = 40   d) 9 × ☐ = 27   e) 7 × ☐ = 35

   30 ÷ 6 = ⟦5⟧   24 ÷ 8 = ☐   40 ÷ 5 = ☐   27 ÷ 9 = ☐   35 ÷ 7 = ☐

3. The picture shows that 2 sets of size 5 contain the same number of dots as 5 sets of size 2 (that is, 2 × 5 = 5 × 2):

   a) In your notebook, draw a picture and explain how your picture shows that:

   i) 7 × 4 = 4 × 7   ii) 9 × 2 = 2 × 9

   b) Draw an array and explain how your picture shows that:

   6 + 6 + 6 + 6 = 4 + 4 + 4 + 4 + 4 + 4

TEACHER:

To solve word problems involving multiplication or division, students should ask:

- **How many things are there altogether?**
- **How many sets or groups are there?**
- **How many things are in each set?**

Your students should also know (and be able to explain using pictures or concrete materials):

- When you know the number of sets and the number of things in each set, you multiply to find the total number of things.

- When you know the total number of things and the number of sets, you divide to find the number of things in each set.

- When you know the total number of things and the number of things in each set, you divide to find the number of sets.

---

1. For each picture, fill in the blanks:

a)
_____ lines in total

_____ lines in each set

_____ sets

b)
_____ lines in total

_____ sets

_____ lines in each set

c)
_____ lines in each set

_____ sets

_____ lines altogether

d)
_____ lines in each set

_____ sets

_____ lines altogether

e)
_____ lines

_____ lines in each set

_____ sets

f)
_____ lines in total

_____ sets

_____ lines in each set

2. Draw a picture of...

a) 10 lines altogether; 2 lines in each set; 5 sets

b) 15 lines; 3 lines in each set; 5 sets

c) 4 sets; 7 lines in each set; 28 lines in total

d) 18 lines; 3 sets; 6 lines in each set

3. Draw a picture of <u>and</u> write two division statements and a multiplication statement for...

a) 21 lines altogether; 3 lines in each set; 7 sets

b) 14 lines; 7 lines in each set; 2 sets

4. In each question below some information is missing (indicated by a question mark).

    Write a multiplication or division statement to find the missing information.

	Total number of things	Number of sets	Number of things in each set	Multiplication or division statement
a)	?	6	3	6 × 3 = 18
b)	20	4	?	20 ÷ 4 = 5
c)	15	?	5	
d)	10	2	?	
e)	?	4	6	
f)	21	7	?	

5. For each question, write a multiplication or a division statement to solve the problem:

a) 15 things in total
    5 things in each set

    _____

    How many sets?

    _____

b) 6 sets
    4 things in each set

    _____

    How many things in total?

    _____

c) 25 things in total
    5 sets

    _____

    How many things in each set?

    _____

d) 9 groups
    4 things in each group

    _____

    How many things in total?

    _____

e) 9 things in each set
    18 things in total

    _____

    How many sets?

    _____

f) 3 groups
    18 things altogether

    _____

    How many in each group?

    _____

g) 16 things in each set
    3 sets

    _____

    How many things in total?

    _____

h) 8 things in each set
    24 things in total

    _____

    How many sets?

    _____

i) 20 things in total
    5 sets

    _____

    How many things in each set?

    _____

jump math
MULTIPLYING POTENTIAL

Number Sense 1

6. Fill in the chart. Use a question mark to show what you don't know.
    Then write a multiplication or division statement in the right hand column.

	Total Number of things	Number of sets	Number in each set	Multiplication or division statement
a) 8 chairs at each table 3 tables	?	3	8	3 × 8 = 24 How many chairs? _____ 24
b) 9 marbles in each jar 5 jars				How many marbles? _____
c) 35 flowers 7 pots				How many flowers in each pot? _____
d) 32 people 4 boats				How many people in each boat? _____
e) 24 flowers 6 plants				How many flowers on each plant? _____
f) 36 candles 6 candles in each packet				How many packets? _____

7. The fact family for the multiplication statement **3 × 5 = 15** is: **5 × 3 = 15**; **15 ÷ 3 = 5** and **15 ÷ 5 = 3**.
    Write the fact family of equations for the following statements:

a) 4 × 2 = 8   b) 6 × 3 = 18   c) 7 × 8 = 56   d) 9 × 4 = 36

    _____   _____   _____   _____

    _____   _____   _____   _____

    _____   _____   _____   _____

Guy wants to share 9 apples with 3 friends.
He sets out 4 plates, one for himself and one for each of his friends.
He puts one apple at a time on a plate:

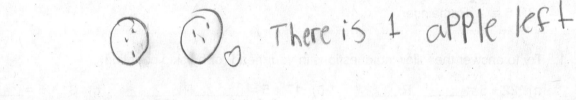

← *There is one apple left over.*

9 apples cannot be shared equally into 4 sets. Each person gets 2 apples, but one is left over.

$$9 \div 4 = 2 \text{ Remainder } 1 \quad \text{OR} \quad 9 \div 4 = 2 \text{ R } 1$$

----

1. Can you share 7 apples equally onto 2 plates? Show your work using dots and circles:

 There is 1 apple left

2. Share the dots as equally as possible among the circles.

   a) 8 dots in 3 circles

   b) 13 dots in 4 circles

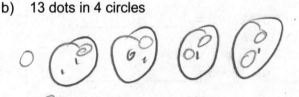

   __2__ dots in each circle; __2__ dots remaining   __3__ dots in each circle; __1__ dot remaining

 3. Share the dots as equally as possible. Draw a picture and write a division statement.

   Example: 9 dots in 2 circles

   $9 \div 2 = 4 \text{ R}1$

   a) 14 dots in 4 circles
   b) 18 dots in 6 circles
   c) 17 dots in 4 circles
   d) 22 dots in 3 circles

4. Five children want to share 22 sea shells.
   How many shells will each child receive?
   How many will be left over?

5. Find two different ways to share 29 pens into equal groups so that one is left over.

6. Four friends have more than 7 stickers and less than 13 stickers.
   They share the stickers evenly. How many stickers do they have?
   (Is there more than one answer?)

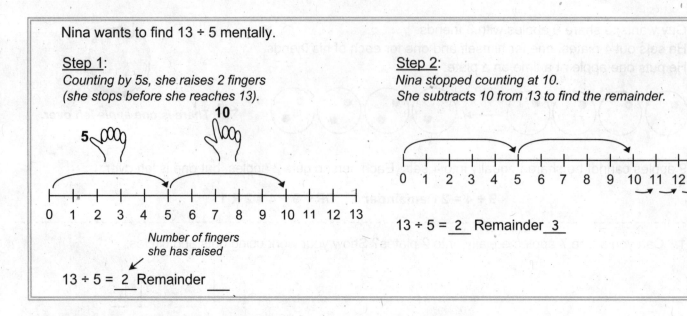

Nina wants to find 13 ÷ 5 mentally.

Step 1:
*Counting by 5s, she raises 2 fingers
(she stops before she reaches 13).*

Step 2:
*Nina stopped counting at 10.
She subtracts 10 from 13 to find the remainder.*

13 ÷ 5 = 2 Remainder 3

*Number of fingers
she has raised*

13 ÷ 5 = 2 Remainder ___

1. Try to answer the following questions in your head (or by skip counting):

 a) 22 ÷ 5 = _4_ R _2_   b) 17 ÷ 5 = _3_ R _2_   c) 31 ÷ 5 = _6_ R _1_

 d) 27 ÷ 5 = _5_ R _2_   e) 13 ÷ 5 = _2_ R _3_   f) 7 ÷ 5 = _1_ R _2_

 g) 13 ÷ 3 = _4_ R _1_   h) 17 ÷ 3 = _5_ R _2_   i) 23 ÷ 3 = _7_ R _2_

 j) 23 ÷ 7 = _3_ R _2_   k) 19 ÷ 6 = _4_ R _1_   l) 25 ÷ 8 = _3_ R _1_

 m) 37 ÷ 9 = _4_ R _1_   n) 43 ÷ 7 = _6_ R _3_   o) 29 ÷ 8 = _3_ R _5_

 p) 13 ÷ 6 = _2_ R _1_   q) 47 ÷ 9 = _5_ R _2_   r) 64 ÷ 7 = _9_ R _1_

 s) 53 ÷ 9 = _5_ R _8_   t) 46 ÷ 6 = _7_ R _4_   u) 23 ÷ 4 = _5_ R _3_

2. Richard wants to divide 18 peaches between 5 friends.

 How many peaches will each friend get? _3_

 How many will be left over? _3_

3. Paul puts 16 pencils in three boxes.

 How many pencils will go in each box? _5_

 How many will be left over? _1_

Manuel is preparing snacks for 4 classes.
He needs to divide 97 oranges into 4 groups.
He will use long division and a model to solve the problem:

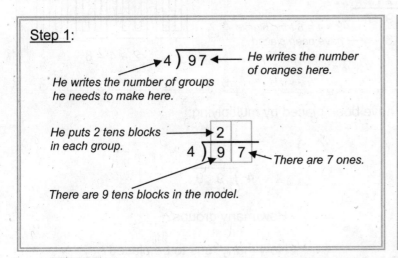

Step 1:

$4 \overline{) 97}$ ← He writes the number of oranges here.

He writes the number of groups he needs to make here.

He puts 2 tens blocks in each group.

There are 7 ones.

There are 9 tens blocks in the model.

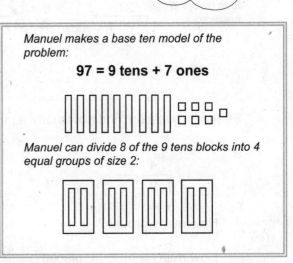

Manuel makes a base ten model of the problem:

97 = 9 tens + 7 ones

Manuel can divide 8 of the 9 tens blocks into 4 equal groups of size 2:

1. Manuel has written a division statement to solve a problem.
   How many groups does he want to make?
   How many tens and how many ones would he need to model the problem?

   a) $3 \overline{) 76}$

   groups __3__
   tens blocks __7__
   ones __6__

   b) $4 \overline{) 95}$

   groups __4__
   tens blocks __9__
   ones __5__

   c) $4 \overline{) 92}$

   groups __4__
   tens blocks __9__
   ones __2__

   d) $5 \overline{) 86}$

   groups __5__
   tens blocks __8__
   ones __6__

2. How many tens blocks can be put in each group?

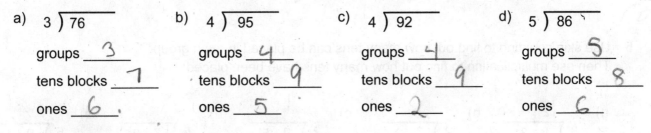

   a) $3 \overline{) 4\ 5}$ — 1

   b) $5 \overline{) 9\ 3}$ — 1

   c) $4 \overline{) 6\ 2}$ — 1

   d) $3 \overline{) 8\ 9}$ — 2

   e) $4 \overline{) 8\ 2}$ — 2

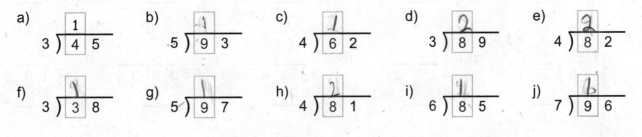

   f) $3 \overline{) 3\ 8}$ — 1

   g) $5 \overline{) 9\ 7}$ — 1

   h) $4 \overline{) 8\ 1}$ — 2

   i) $6 \overline{) 8\ 5}$ — 1

   j) $7 \overline{) 9\ 6}$ — 1

3. For each division statement, how many groups have been made?
   How many tens are in each group?

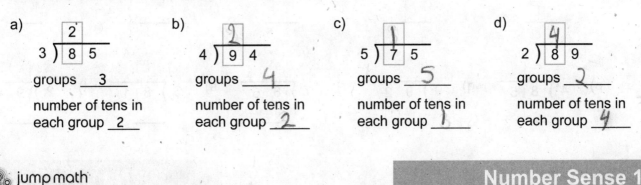

   a) $3 \overline{) 8\ 5}$ — 2

   groups __3__

   number of tens in each group __2__

   b) $4 \overline{) 9\ 4}$ — 2

   groups __4__

   number of tens in each group __2__

   c) $5 \overline{) 7\ 5}$ — 1

   groups __5__

   number of tens in each group __1__

   d) $2 \overline{) 8\ 9}$ — 4

   groups __2__

   number of tens in each group __4__

Step 2:

There are 2 tens blocks in each group.

$4\overline{)9\ 7}$ with 2

There are 4 groups.

$4\overline{)9\ 7}$ ← 8   2 × 4 = 8 tens blocks have been placed.

In the model:

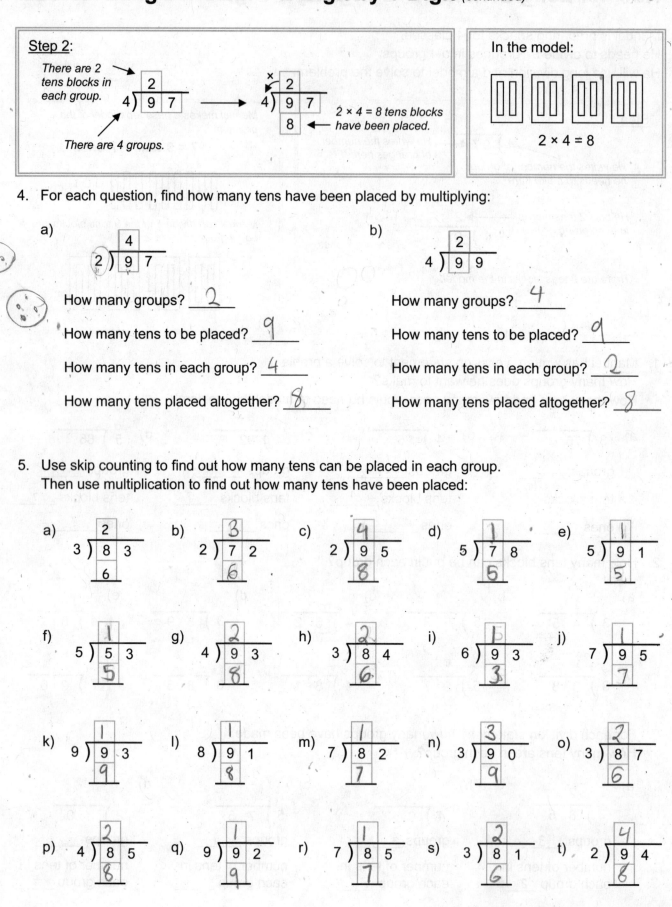

2 × 4 = 8

4. For each question, find how many tens have been placed by multiplying:

a)
$2\overline{)9\ 7}$ with 4

How many groups? **2**

How many tens to be placed? **9**

How many tens in each group? **4**

How many tens placed altogether? **8**

b)
$4\overline{)9\ 9}$ with 2

How many groups? **4**

How many tens to be placed? **9**

How many tens in each group? **2**

How many tens placed altogether? **8**

5. Use skip counting to find out how many tens can be placed in each group.
    Then use multiplication to find out how many tens have been placed:

a) $3\overline{)8\ 3}$ 2 / 6

b) $2\overline{)7\ 2}$ 3 / 6

c) $2\overline{)9\ 5}$ 4 / 8

d) $5\overline{)7\ 8}$ 1 / 5

e) $5\overline{)9\ 1}$ 1 / 5

f) $5\overline{)5\ 3}$ 1 / 5

g) $4\overline{)9\ 3}$ 2 / 8

h) $3\overline{)8\ 4}$ 2 / 6

i) $6\overline{)9\ 3}$ 5 / 3

j) $7\overline{)9\ 5}$ 1 / 7

k) $9\overline{)9\ 3}$ 1 / 9

l) $8\overline{)9\ 1}$ 1 / 8

m) $7\overline{)8\ 2}$ 1 / 7

n) $3\overline{)9\ 0}$ 3 / 9

o) $3\overline{)8\ 7}$ 2 / 6

p) $4\overline{)8\ 5}$ 2 / 8

q) $9\overline{)9\ 2}$ 1 / 9

r) $7\overline{)8\ 5}$ 1 / 7

s) $3\overline{)8\ 1}$ 2 / 6

t) $2\overline{)9\ 4}$ 4 / 8

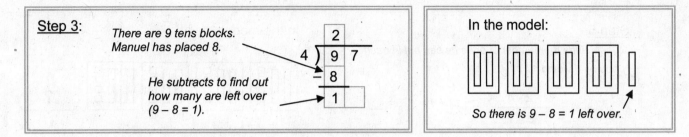

Step 3:

There are 9 tens blocks. Manuel has placed 8.

He subtracts to find out how many are left over (9 – 8 = 1).

In the model:

So there is 9 – 8 = 1 left over.

6. For each question, carry out the first 3 steps of the long division:

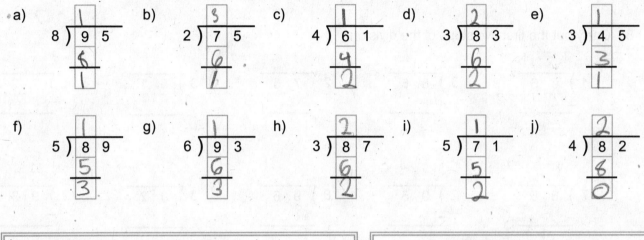

a) 8)95   b) 2)75   c) 4)61   d) 3)83   e) 3)45

f) 5)89   g) 6)93   h) 3)87   i) 5)71   j) 4)82

Step 4:

There is one tens block left over and 7 ones. So there are 17 ones left over. Manuel writes the 7 beside the 1 to show this.

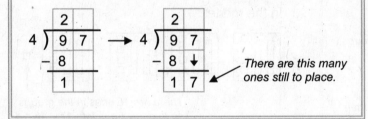

There are this many ones still to place.

In the model:

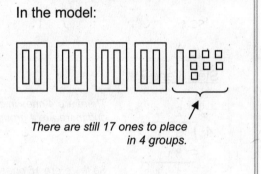

There are still 17 ones to place in 4 groups.

7. Carry out the first four steps of the division:

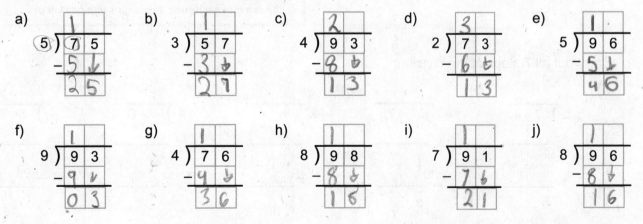

a) 5)75   b) 3)57   c) 4)93   d) 2)73   e) 5)96

f) 9)93   g) 4)76   h) 8)98   i) 7)91   j) 8)96

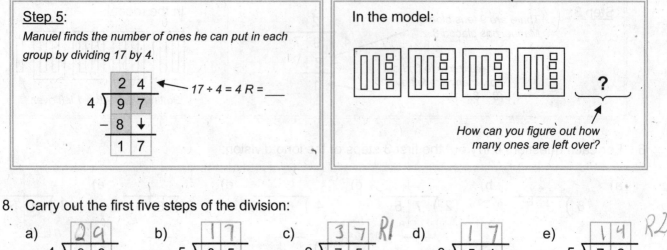

Step 5:

Manuel finds the number of ones he can put in each group by dividing 17 by 4.

$$17 \div 4 = 4 \, R = \underline{\quad}$$

In the model:

?

How can you figure out how many ones are left over?

8. Carry out the first five steps of the division:

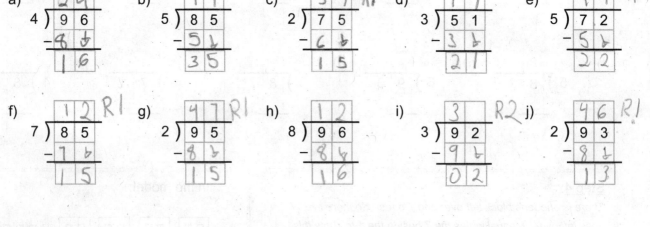

a) 4) 9 6

b) 5) 8 5

c) 2) 7 5   R1

d) 3) 5 1

e) 5) 7 2   R2

f) 7) 8 5   R1

g) 2) 9 5   R1

h) 8) 9 6

i) 3) 9 2   R2

j) 2) 9 3   R1

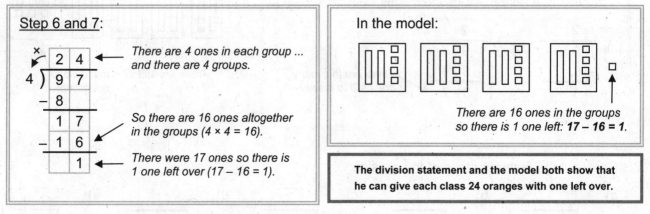

Step 6 and 7:

There are 4 ones in each group ... and there are 4 groups.

So there are 16 ones altogether in the groups (4 × 4 = 16).

There were 17 ones so there is 1 one left over (17 − 16 = 1).

In the model:

*There are 16 ones in the groups so there is 1 one left: **17 − 16 = 1**.*

The division statement and the model both show that he can give each class 24 oranges with one left over.

9. Carry out all 7 steps of the division:

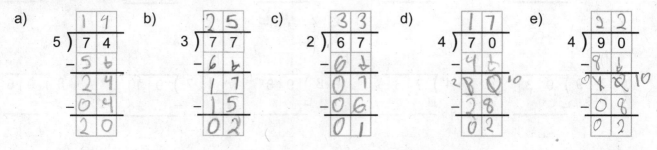

a) 5) 7 4

b) 3) 7 7

c) 2) 6 7

d) 4) 7 0

e) 4) 9 0

Number Sense 1

f)
```
      1 6
  5 ) 8 1
    - 5 ↴
      3 1
    - 3 0
      0 1
```

g)
```
      2 1
  4 ) 8 4
    - 8 ↴
      0 4
    - 0 4
      0 0
```

h)
```
      1 9
  5 ) 9 6
    - 5 ↴
      4 6
    - 4 5
      0 1
```

i)
```
      1 4
  6 ) 8 9
    - 6 ↴
      2 9
    - 2 4
      0 5
```

j)
```
      1 0
  9 ) 9 7
    - 9 ↴
      0 7
```

k)
```
      2 3
  4 ) 9 3
    - 8 ↴
      1 3
    - 1 2
      0 1
```

l)
```
      1 2
  8 ) 9 7
    - 8 ↴
      1 7
    - 1 6
      0 1
```

m)
```
      1 4
  6 ) 8 6
    - 6 ↴
      2 6
    - 2 4
      0 2
```

n)
```
      1 3
  7 ) 9 5
    - 7 ↴
      2 5
    - 2 1
      0 4
```

o)
```
      4 0
  2 ) 8 0
    - 8 ↴
      0 0
```

10. Avi put 98 flowers in bouquets of 8. How many flowers are left over?

```
      1 2
  8 ) 9 8
    - 8 ↴
      1 8
    - 1 6
      0 2
```

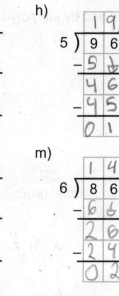

11. How many weeks are in 93 days?

```
      1 3
  7 ) 9 3
    - 7 ↴
      2 3
    - 2 1
      0 2
```

12. Michelle jogs for 3 km everyday. How many days will she take to run 45 km?

```
      1 5
  3 ) 4 5
    - 3 ↴
      1 5
    - 1 5
      0 0
```

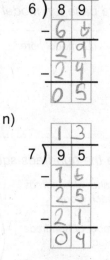

13. A six sided pool has perimeter 72 m. How long is each side?

```
      1 2
  6 ) 7 2
    - 6 ↴
      1 2
    - 1 2
      0 0
```

14. Guerdy packs 85 books into boxes of 6, and Tyree packs 67 books into boxes of 4. Who uses more boxes?

```
      1 4
  6 ) 8 5
    - 6 ↴
      2 5
    - 2 4
      0 1
```

```
      1 6
  4 ) 6 7
    - 4 ↴
      2 7
    - 2 4
      0 3
```

1. Find 335 ÷ 2 by drawing a base ten model and by long division:

   Step 1:   *Draw a base ten model of 335.*

   > Draw your model here.

   Step 2:   *Divide the hundreds squares into 2 equal groups.*

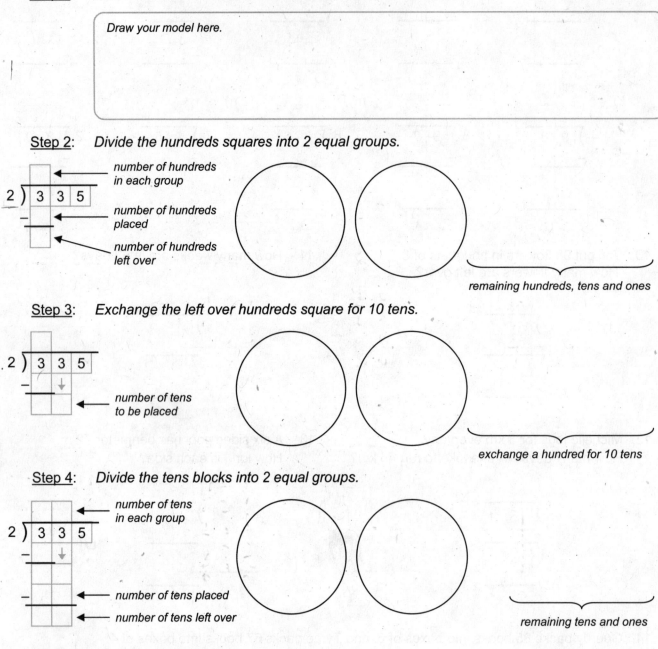

   number of hundreds
   in each group

   $2 \overline{\smash{)}\,3\,3\,5}$

   number of hundreds
   placed

   number of hundreds
   left over

   remaining hundreds, tens and ones

   Step 3:   *Exchange the left over hundreds square for 10 tens.*

   $2 \overline{\smash{)}\,3\,3\,5}$

   number of tens
   to be placed

   exchange a hundred for 10 tens

   Step 4:   *Divide the tens blocks into 2 equal groups.*

   number of tens
   in each group

   $2 \overline{\smash{)}\,3\,3\,5}$

   number of tens placed

   number of tens left over

   remaining tens and ones

   Step 5:   *Exchange the left over tens blocks for 10 ones.*

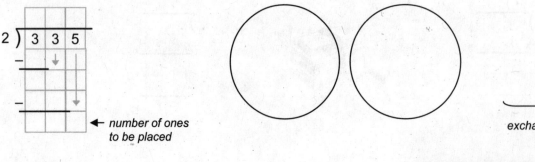

   $2 \overline{\smash{)}\,3\,3\,5}$

   number of ones
   to be placed

   exchange a ten for 10 ones

Steps 6 and 7:   Divide the ones into 2 equal groups.

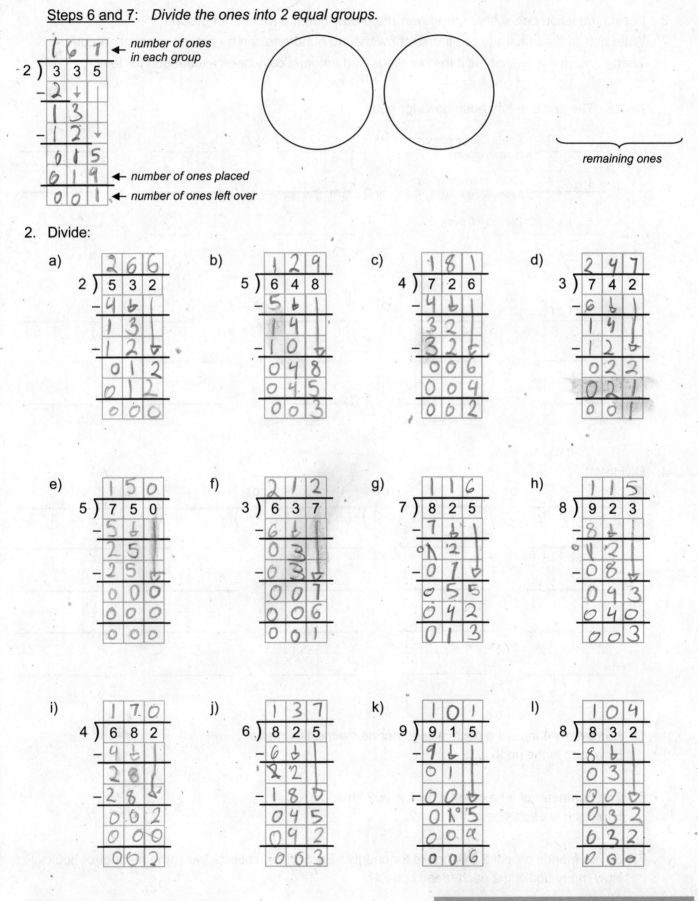

← number of ones in each group

← number of ones placed

← number of ones left over

remaining ones

2. Divide:

a) 2) 532

b) 5) 648

c) 4) 726

d) 3) 742

e) 5) 750

f) 3) 637

g) 7) 825

h) 8) 923

i) 4) 682

j) 6) 825

k) 9) 915

l) 8) 832

Number Sense 1

3. In each question below, there are fewer hundreds than the number of groups.

   Write a '0' in the hundreds position to show that no hundreds can be placed in equal groups.

   Then perform the division as if the hundreds had automatically been exchanged for tens.

   Divide. The first one has been done for you:

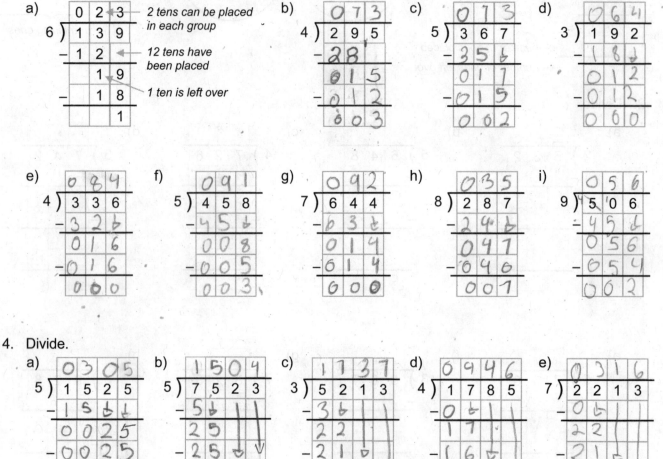

a) 2 tens can be placed in each group; 12 tens have been placed; 1 ten is left over

b) c) d)

e) f) g) h) i)

4. Divide.

a) b) c) d) e)

5. Ken swims 4 laps of a pool. Altogether he swims 144 metres.
   How long is the pool?

6. The perimeter of a hexagonal park is 852 km.
   How long is each side of the park?

7. Seven friends collect 2 744 books for charity. Each friend collects the same number of books.
   How many books did each friend collect?

Answer the following questions in your notebook.

1. A class paid $20 for a cake and $4 per child for a slice of pizza.

   They paid $140.

   How many children are in the class?

2. Make as many 3-digit numbers as you can using the digits 5, 1, and 0. (Use each digit once).

   Which of your numbers are divisible by…

   a) 2   b) 5

   c) 10   d) 3

3. A number has…

   • remainder 2 when divided by 3
   • remainder 4 when divided by 5

   What is the number?

4. Raj wants to divide 24 apricots, 64 raisins, and 56 peanuts evenly into packets (with no food left over).

   What is the greatest number of packets he can make? Explain.

In questions below, you will have to interpret what the remainder means.

   Example: Cindy wants to put 64 cookies onto trays. Each tray holds 5 cookies.

   How many trays will she need?

   64 ÷ 5 = 12 remainder 4

   She will need 13 trays (because she needs a tray for the four leftover cookies).

5. A car can hold 5 passengers.

   How many cars will 29 passengers need?

6. Manu colours 4 pictures in her picture book every day.

   How many days will she take to colour 50 pictures?

7. Jay shares 76 plums as evenly as possible among 9 friends.

   How many plums does each friend get?

8. Siru wants to place her stamps in an album.

   Each page holds 9 stamps.

   How many pages will she need for 95 stamps?

Answer the following questions in your notebook.

1. A bus carries 36 students.

   How many students can 25 buses carry?

2. A racer snake lays at least 3 eggs and no more than 40 eggs.

   What is the least number of eggs 6 snakes would lay?

   What is the greatest number?

3. If 2 pencils cost 17¢, how much will 8 pencils cost? Show your work.

4. How much do 7 books cost at $19 per book?

5. A tiger beetle is the fastest land insect. It can scuttle 9 km in an hour.

   How many metres could it crawl in half an hour?

6. Create a division problem to go with the expression below.

   $$72 \div 8$$

7. What is the least number of whole apples that can be shared equally among 2, 3, or 4 people?

8. a) Alice is between 20 and 40 years old. Last year, her age was a multiple of 4. This year, her age is a multiple of 5. How old is Alice?

   b) George is between 30 and 50 years old. Last year, his age was a multiple of 6. This year it is a multiple of 7. How old is George?

9. Nandita ran 24 laps of her school track. The track is 75 metres long.

   a) How far has she run?

   b) How much further must she run if she wants to run 2000 metres?

   c) About how many extra laps must she run?

10. If 3 CDs cost $23, how would you calculate the cost of 12 CDs?

11. What digit could be in the box? Explain.

    $\boxed{}569 \div 6$ is about 400.

12. Three letter carriers delivered a different number of letters in 1 week:

    - Carl: 2 624 letters
    - Sally: 1 759 letters
    - Selma: 3 284 letters

    Did any one letter carrier deliver more than half of all the letters?

NS5-44: Rounding on a Number Line

1. Draw an arrow to the 0 or 10 to show whether the circled number is closer to **0 or 10**:

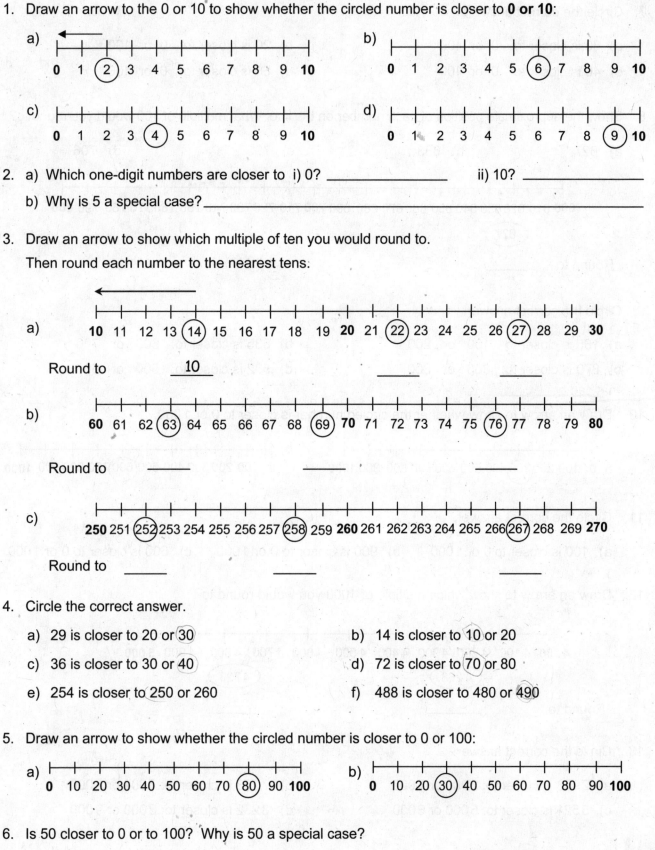

a)

$$0 \quad 1 \quad ② \quad 3 \quad 4 \quad 5 \quad 6 \quad 7 \quad 8 \quad 9 \quad \mathbf{10}$$

b)

$$0 \quad 1 \quad 2 \quad 3 \quad 4 \quad 5 \quad ⑥ \quad 7 \quad 8 \quad 9 \quad \mathbf{10}$$

c)

$$0 \quad 1 \quad 2 \quad 3 \quad ④ \quad 5 \quad 6 \quad 7 \quad 8 \quad 9 \quad \mathbf{10}$$

d)

$$0 \quad 1 \quad 2 \quad 3 \quad 4 \quad 5 \quad 6 \quad 7 \quad 8 \quad ⑨ \quad \mathbf{10}$$

2. a) Which one-digit numbers are closer to i) 0? _____ ii) 10? _____

   b) Why is 5 a special case?_____

3. Draw an arrow to show which multiple of ten you would round to.

   Then round each number to the nearest tens.

   a)

   $$\mathbf{10} \quad 11 \quad 12 \quad 13 \quad ⑭ \quad 15 \quad 16 \quad 17 \quad 18 \quad 19 \quad \mathbf{20} \quad 21 \quad ㉒ \quad 23 \quad 24 \quad 25 \quad 26 \quad ㉗ \quad 28 \quad 29 \quad \mathbf{30}$$

   Round to _____10_____   _____   _____

   b)

   $$\mathbf{60} \quad 61 \quad ㉓ \quad 64 \quad 65 \quad 66 \quad 67 \quad 68 \quad ㉙ \quad \mathbf{70} \quad 71 \quad 72 \quad 73 \quad 74 \quad 75 \quad ㉖ \quad 77 \quad 78 \quad 79 \quad \mathbf{80}$$

   Round to _____   _____   _____

   c)

   $$\mathbf{250} \; 251 \; ㉒ \; 253 \; 254 \; 255 \; 256 \; 257 \; ㉘ \; 259 \; \mathbf{260} \; 261 \; 262 \; 263 \; 264 \; 265 \; 266 \; ㉗ \; 268 \; 269 \; \mathbf{270}$$

   Round to _____   _____   _____

4. Circle the correct answer.

   a) 29 is closer to 20 or ⟨30⟩   b) 14 is closer to ⟨10⟩ or 20

   c) 36 is closer to 30 or ⟨40⟩   d) 72 is closer to ⟨70⟩ or 80

   e) 254 is closer to ⟨250⟩ or 260   f) 488 is closer to 480 or ⟨490⟩

5. Draw an arrow to show whether the circled number is closer to 0 or 100:

   a)
   $$\mathbf{0} \quad 10 \quad 20 \quad 30 \quad 40 \quad 50 \quad 60 \quad 70 \quad ⑧⓪ \quad 90 \quad \mathbf{100}$$

   b)
   $$\mathbf{0} \quad 10 \quad 20 \quad ③⓪ \quad 40 \quad 50 \quad 60 \quad 70 \quad 80 \quad 90 \quad \mathbf{100}$$

6. Is 50 closer to 0 or to 100? Why is 50 a special case?

   _____

NS5-44: Rounding on a Number Line (continued)

7. Circle the correct answer:

    a) 80 is closer to: 0 or 100

    b) 20 is closer to: 0 or 100

    c) 40 is closer to: 0 or 100

    d) 60 is closer to: 0 or 100

8. Show the approximate position of each number on the line. What multiple of 100 would you round to?

    a) 627   b) 683   c) 795   d) 706

    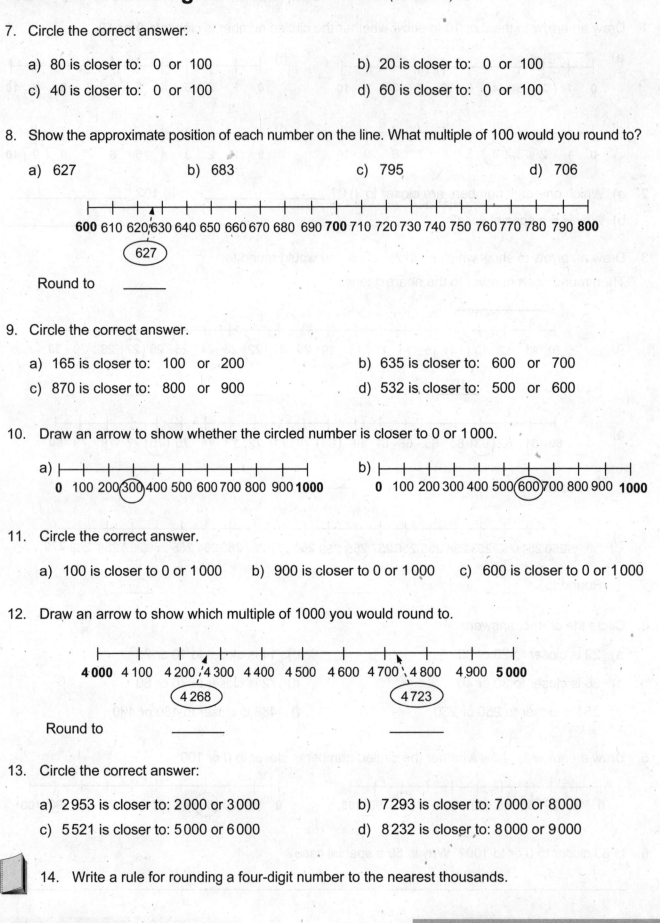

    Round to _____

9. Circle the correct answer.

    a) 165 is closer to: 100 or 200

    b) 635 is closer to: 600 or 700

    c) 870 is closer to: 800 or 900

    d) 532 is closer to: 500 or 600

10. Draw an arrow to show whether the circled number is closer to 0 or 1 000.

11. Circle the correct answer.

    a) 100 is closer to 0 or 1 000   b) 900 is closer to 0 or 1 000   c) 600 is closer to 0 or 1 000

12. Draw an arrow to show which multiple of 1 000 you would round to.

    Round to _____   _____

13. Circle the correct answer:

    a) 2 953 is closer to: 2 000 or 3 000

    b) 7 293 is closer to: 7 000 or 8 000

    c) 5 521 is closer to: 5 000 or 6 000

    d) 8 232 is closer to: 8 000 or 9 000

14. Write a rule for rounding a four-digit number to the nearest thousands.

1. Round to the nearest **tens** place:

a) 22 ☐

b) 26 ☐

c) 73 ☐

d) 58 ☐

e) 94 ☐

f) 83 ☐

g) 15 ☐

h) 49 ☐

i) 27 ☐

j) 37 ☐

k) 91 ☐

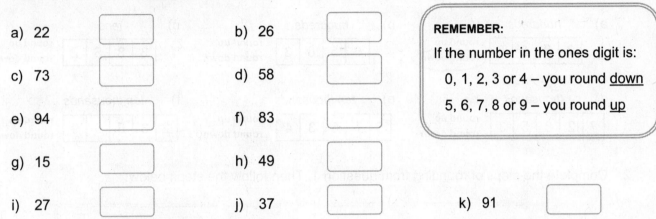

REMEMBER:

If the number in the ones digit is:

0, 1, 2, 3 or 4 – you round <u>down</u>

5, 6, 7, 8 or 9 – you round <u>up</u>

2. Round to the nearest **tens** place. Underline the tens digit first. Then put your pencil on the digit to the right (the ones digit). This digit tells you whether to round up or down:

a) 14<u>5</u> [150]

b) 183 ☐

c) 361 ☐

d) 342 ☐

e) 554 ☐

f) 667 ☐

g) 656 ☐

h) 847 ☐

i) 938 ☐

3. Round the following numbers to the nearest **hundreds** place. Underline the hundreds digit first. Then put your pencil on the digit to the right (the tens digit):

a) <u>7</u>30 [700]

b) 490 ☐

c) 540 ☐

d) 270 ☐

e) 167 ☐

f) 317 ☐

g) 160 ☐

h) 873 ☐

i) 791 ☐

j) 6 <u>2</u>37 [6 200]

k) 1 286 ☐

l) 8 218 ☐

m) 4 905 ☐

n) 6 321 ☐

o) 9 583 ☐

4. Round the following numbers to the nearest thousands place. Underline the thousands digit first. Then put your pencil on the digit to the right (the hundreds digit).

a) <u>7</u> 872 [8 000]

b) 8 952 ☐

c) 5 231 ☐

d) 3 092 ☐

e) 3 871 ☐

f) 1680 ☐

jump math
MULTIPLYING POTENTIAL.

Number Sense 1

1. Underline the digit you wish to round to. Then say whether you would round up or down.

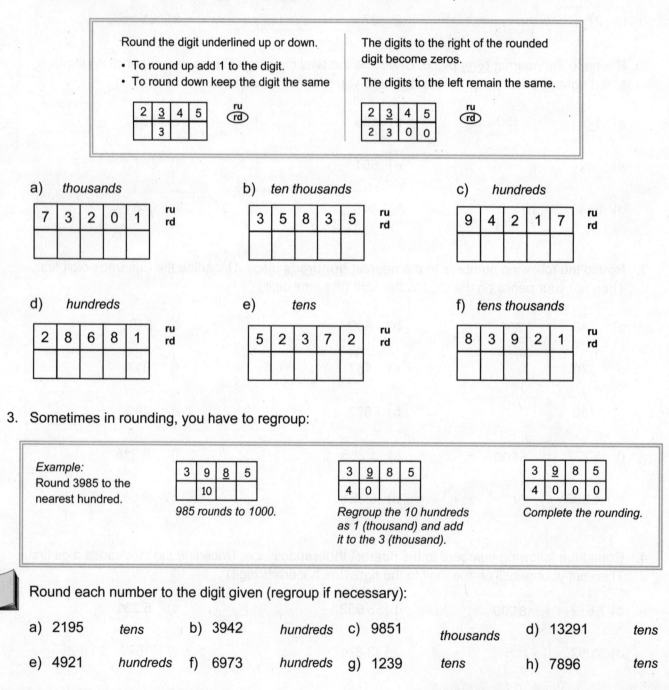

2. Complete the steps of rounding from question 1. Then follow the steps below:

3. Sometimes in rounding, you have to regroup:

Round each number to the digit given (regroup if necessary):

a) 2195   *tens*   b) 3942   *hundreds*   c) 9851   *thousands*   d) 13291   *tens*

e) 4921   *hundreds*   f) 6973   *hundreds*   g) 1239   *tens*   h) 7896   *tens*

NS5-47: Estimating Sums and Differences

1. Estimate by rounding to the nearest tens.

> $\approx$ ← Mathematicians use this symbol to mean **"approximately equal to"**.

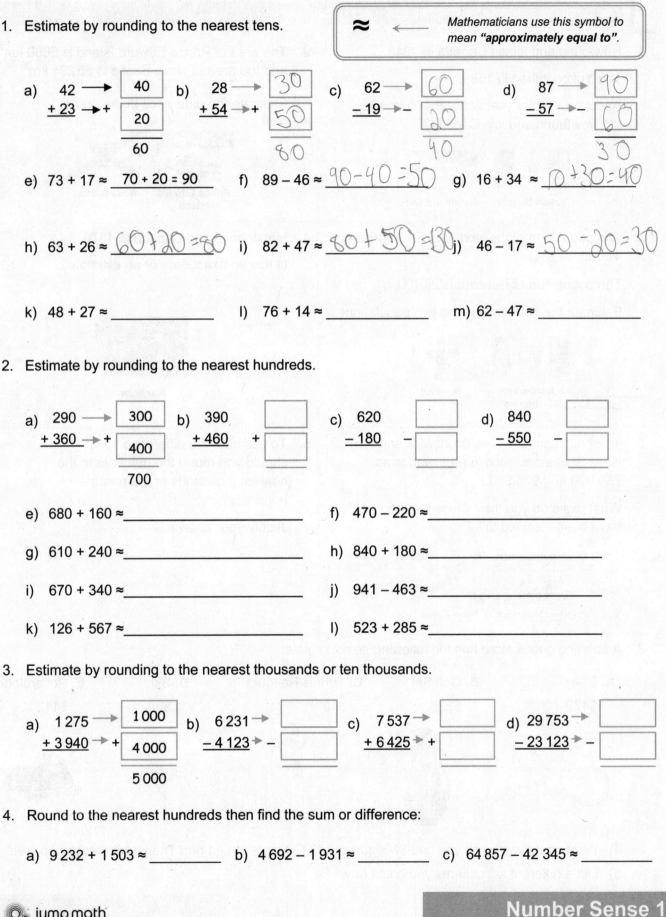

a) $42 \rightarrow \boxed{40}$
   $+ 23 \rightarrow + \boxed{20}$
   $\overline{60}$

b) $28 \rightarrow \boxed{30}$
   $+ 54 \rightarrow + \boxed{50}$
   $\overline{80}$

c) $62 \rightarrow \boxed{60}$
   $- 19 \rightarrow - \boxed{20}$
   $\overline{40}$

d) $87 \rightarrow \boxed{90}$
   $- 57 \rightarrow - \boxed{60}$
   $\overline{30}$

e) $73 + 17 \approx$ __70 + 20 = 90__

f) $89 - 46 \approx$ 90 - 40 = 50

g) $16 + 34 \approx$ 10 + 30 = 40

h) $63 + 26 \approx$ 60 + 20 = 80

i) $82 + 47 \approx$ 80 + 50 = 130

j) $46 - 17 \approx$ 50 - 20 = 30

k) $48 + 27 \approx$ _____

l) $76 + 14 \approx$ _____

m) $62 - 47 \approx$ _____

2. Estimate by rounding to the nearest hundreds.

a) $290 \rightarrow \boxed{300}$
   $+ 360 \rightarrow + \boxed{400}$
   $\overline{700}$

b) $390 \rightarrow \boxed{}$
   $+ 460 \rightarrow + \boxed{}$

c) $620 \rightarrow \boxed{}$
   $- 180 \rightarrow - \boxed{}$

d) $840 \rightarrow \boxed{}$
   $- 550 \rightarrow - \boxed{}$

e) $680 + 160 \approx$ _____

f) $470 - 220 \approx$ _____

g) $610 + 240 \approx$ _____

h) $840 + 180 \approx$ _____

i) $670 + 340 \approx$ _____

j) $941 - 463 \approx$ _____

k) $126 + 567 \approx$ _____

l) $523 + 285 \approx$ _____

3. Estimate by rounding to the nearest thousands or ten thousands.

a) $1\,275 \rightarrow \boxed{1\,000}$
   $+ 3\,940 \rightarrow + \boxed{4\,000}$
   $\overline{5\,000}$

b) $6\,231 \rightarrow \boxed{}$
   $- 4\,123 \rightarrow - \boxed{}$

c) $7\,537 \rightarrow \boxed{}$
   $+ 6\,425 \rightarrow + \boxed{}$

d) $29\,753 \rightarrow \boxed{}$
   $- 23\,123 \rightarrow - \boxed{}$

4. Round to the nearest hundreds then find the sum or difference:

a) $9\,232 + 1\,503 \approx$ _____

b) $4\,692 - 1\,931 \approx$ _____

c) $64\,857 - 42\,345 \approx$ _____

Answer the following questions in your notebook.

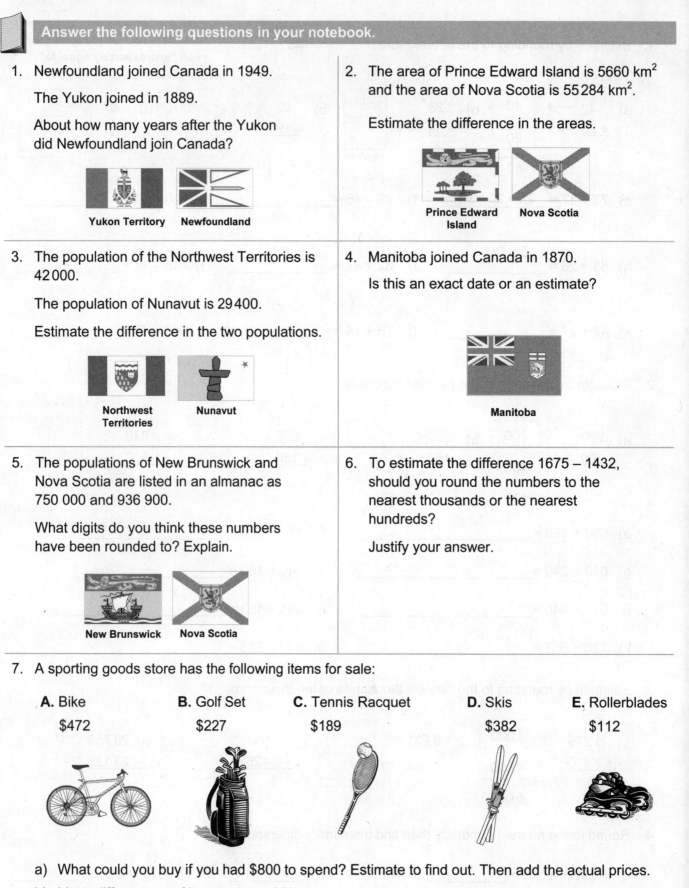

1. Newfoundland joined Canada in 1949.

   The Yukon joined in 1889.

   About how many years after the Yukon did Newfoundland join Canada?

   Yukon Territory   Newfoundland

2. The area of Prince Edward Island is 5660 km² and the area of Nova Scotia is 55 284 km².

   Estimate the difference in the areas.

   Prince Edward Island   Nova Scotia

3. The population of the Northwest Territories is 42 000.

   The population of Nunavut is 29 400.

   Estimate the difference in the two populations.

   Northwest Territories   Nunavut

4. Manitoba joined Canada in 1870.

   Is this an exact date or an estimate?

   Manitoba

5. The populations of New Brunswick and Nova Scotia are listed in an almanac as 750 000 and 936 900.

   What digits do you think these numbers have been rounded to? Explain.

   New Brunswick   Nova Scotia

6. To estimate the difference 1675 – 1432, should you round the numbers to the nearest thousands or the nearest hundreds?

   Justify your answer.

7. A sporting goods store has the following items for sale:

   A. Bike   **B.** Golf Set   **C.** Tennis Racquet   **D.** Skis   **E.** Rollerblades
   $472 $227 $189 $382 $112

   a) What could you buy if you had $800 to spend? Estimate to find out. Then add the actual prices.

   b) List a different set of items you could buy.

NS5-49: Multiplying by 10, 100, 1000 and 10000

1. a) Skip count by 10 <u>twelve</u> times. What number did you reach? _____

    b) Find the product: 10 × 12 = _____

    c) Skip count by 100 twelve times. What number did you reach? _____

    d) Find the product: 100 × 12 = _____

2. How many zeroes do you add to a number when you multiply the number by…

    a) 10: You add _____ zero.   b) 100: You add _____ zeroes.   c) 1000: You add _____ zeroes.

3. Continue the pattern.

    a)   10 × 8 = _____   b)   10 x 25 = _____   c)   10 x 62 = _____

         100 × 8 = _____   100 × 25 = _____   100 × 62 = _____

        1000 × 8 = _____   1000 × 25 = _____   1000 × 62 = _____

      10000 × 8 = _____   10000 × 25 = _____   10000 × 62 = _____

4. Find the products.

    a)   17 × 10 = _____   b)   10 × 50 = _____   c)   10 × 97 = _____

    d)   69 × 100 = _____   e)   20 × 100 = _____   f)   19 × 100 = _____

    g)   100 × 89 = _____   h)   37 × 100 = _____   i) 46 × 10000 = _____

5. Round each number to the leading digit.
    Then find the product of the rounded numbers:

    leading digit

    a) 11 × 79   b) 12 × 22   c) 13 × 79   d) 11 × 64   e) 59 × 110   f) 91 × 120

10 × 80
= 800

    =   =   =   =   =

6. How many digits will the answer have? Write your answer in the box provided.

    a) (2 + 5) × 100: [   ] digits   b) (7 + 5) × 100: [   ] digits   c) (5 + 69) × 1000: [   ] digits

1. Nadia keeps track of how high or low her estimates are when she rounds.

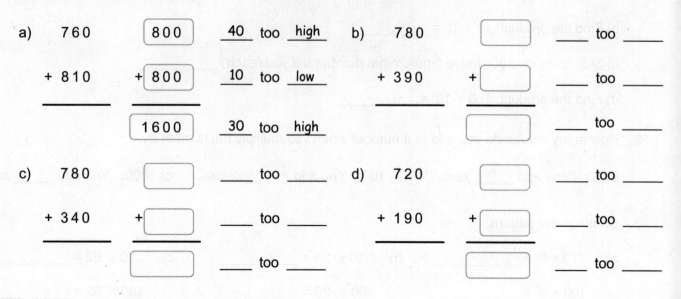

a)
```
    760        800      40  too  high      b)    780    ☐        ___ too ___
  + 810      + 800      10  too  low          + 390    + ☐      ___ too ___
  _____   _____                          _____
             1600       30  too  high                  ☐        ___ too ___
```

c)
```
    780        ☐        ___ too ___          d)    720    ☐       ___ too ___
  + 340      + ☐        ___ too ___             + 190    + ☐      ___ too ___
  _____   _____                            _____
             ☐         ___ too ___                      ☐        ___ too ___
```

2. Say whether you think the estimate is too high or too low. Then add to see if you are correct.

   a) 325 + 630   Estimate: 900

   b) 485 + 212   Estimate: 700

3. In **front end estimation**, you ignore all but the first digits of the number.

   $$(3)5\ 2\ +\ (4)1\ 0\ =\ (3)0\ 0\ +\ (4)0\ 0\ =\ (7)0\ 0$$

   Estimate using front end estimation:

   a) 385 + 204   b) 427 + 631   c) 782 + 541

4. Sometimes rounding one number up and one down will give a good estimate.

Example:	Actual answer	Rounding to nearest hundred	Front end estimate	Round one up and one down
763 + 751	1514	1 600	1400	1 500

   This method gives the best result.

   Which of the methods above gives the best result for the following sums and differences?

   a) 796 + 389   b) 648 + 639   c) 602 + 312   d) 687 − 235   e) 4 382 − 2 871

5. Make up a subtraction question where front end estimating is…

   a) better than rounding   b) worse than rounding   c) the same as rounding

Answer the following questions in your notebook.

1. Explain why 800 ÷ 20 = 80 ÷ 2.

2. Find the following products and quotients by rounding both numbers to the leading digit.

   Example: 572 ÷ 19
   ≈ 600 ÷ 20 = 30

   a) 537 ÷ 9   b) 2 341 ÷ 39   c) 571 × 27

   d) 934 ÷ 28   e) 387 × 19   f) 3 872 × 8

   g) 4 927 ÷ 48   h) 275 ÷ 32   i) 275 × 32

3. Find the quotients by rounding the first number to the nearest ten.

   Example: 476 ÷ 6
   ≈ 480 ÷ 6 = 80

   a) 357 ÷ 6   b) 242 ÷ 6   c) 747 ÷ 5

   d) 207 ÷ 3   e) 478 ÷ 8   f) 212 ÷ 7

   g) 275 ÷ 4   h) 539 ÷ 6   i) 361 ÷ 9

4. Double the number in the box and the number in the circle.

   20 ÷ (5) = 40 ÷ 10

   Explain why the quotient stays the same.
   (HINT: Compare the results when 5 people share $20 and 10 people share $40.)

5. Estimate by doubling both parts:

   Example: 142 ÷ 5
   = 284 ÷ 10 ≈ 28

   a) 234 ÷ 5   b) 425 ÷ 5   c) 2 312 ÷ 5

6. Estimate by finding pairs of numbers that add to about 100.

   Example: 2(3 5) + 3(4 8) + 2(6 2) + 4(5 3)
   = 200 + 300 + 200 + 400 + 100 + 100

   a) 341 + 120 + 679 + 258

   b) 254 + 318 + 348 + 583

7. Carla multiplied a 3 digit number by a 1 digit number.
   The result was about 1000.

   What might the numbers have been?

8. Explain how you could estimate the number of words in a book.

NS5-52: Counting Coins

1. Count by the first number given, then by the second number after the vertical line.

a) __5__ , ___ , ___ , ___ , ___ | ___ , ___ , ___

         Count by 5s   *Continue counting by 1s*

b) __5__ , ___ , ___ , ___ | ___ , ___ , ___

         Count by 5s   *Continue counting by 1s*

2. Complete each pattern.

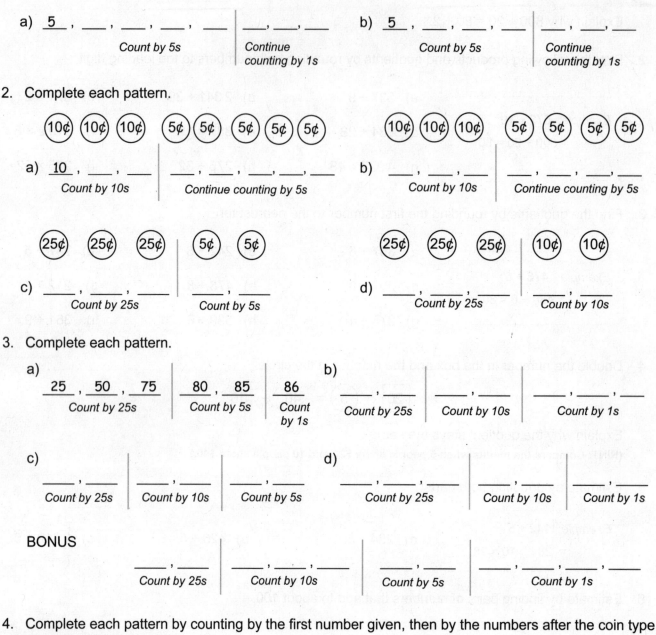

a) __10__ , ___ , ___ | ___ , ___ , ___ , ___ , ___

  Count by 10s   *Continue counting by 5s*

b) ___ , ___ , ___ | ___ , ___ , ___ , ___

  Count by 10s   *Continue counting by 5s*

c) ___ , ___ , ___ | ___ , ___

  Count by 25s   *Count by 5s*

d) ___ , ___ , ___ | ___ , ___

  Count by 25s   *Count by 10s*

3. Complete each pattern.

a) __25__ , __50__ , __75__ | __80__ , __85__ | __86__

  Count by 25s   *Count by 5s*   *Count by 1s*

b) ___ , ___ | ___ , ___ | ___ , ___ , ___

  Count by 25s   *Count by 10s*   *Count by 1s*

c) ___ , ___ | ___ , ___ | ___ , ___

  Count by 25s   *Count by 10s*   *Count by 5s*

d) ___ , ___ , ___ | ___ , ___ | ___ , ___ , ___

  Count by 25s   *Count by 10s*   *Count by 1s*

BONUS

___ , ___ | ___ , ___ , ___ | ___ , ___ | ___ , ___ , ___ , ___

  Count by 25s   *Count by 10s*   *Count by 5s*   *Count by 1s*

4. Complete each pattern by counting by the first number given, then by the numbers after the coin type changes.

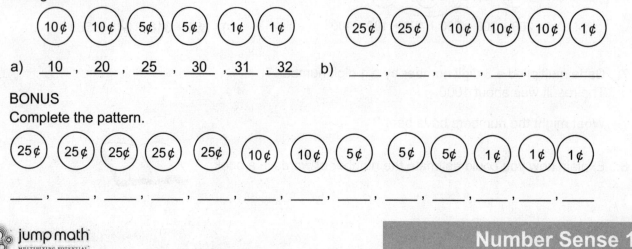

a) __10__ , __20__ , __25__ , __30__ , __31__ , __32__

b) ___ , ___ , ___ , ___ , ___ , ___

BONUS
Complete the pattern.

___ , ___ , ___ , ___ , ___ , ___ , ___ , ___ , ___ , ___ , ___ , ___ , ___

NS5-52: Counting Coins (continued)

5. Complete the pattern by counting each number given:

a)
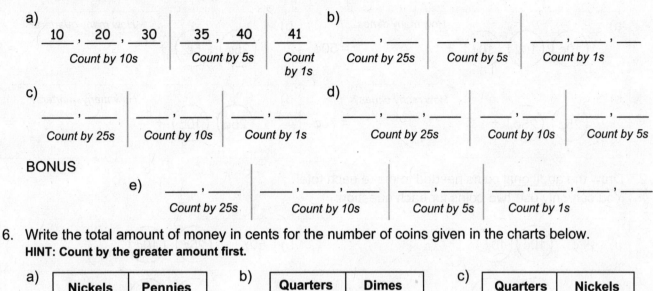

__10__ , __20__ , __30__ | __35__ , __40__ | __41__

Count by 10s | Count by 5s | Count by 1s

b)

____ , ____ | ____ , ____ | ____ , ____ , ____

Count by 25s | Count by 5s | Count by 1s

c)

____ , ____ | ____ , ____ | ____ , ____

Count by 25s | Count by 10s | Count by 1s

d)

____ , ____ , ____ | ____ , ____ | ____ , ____

Count by 25s | Count by 10s | Count by 5s

BONUS

e) ____ , ____ | ____ , ____ , ____ | ____ , ____ | ____ , ____ , ____ , ____

Count by 25s | Count by 10s | Count by 5s | Count by 1s

6. Write the total amount of money in cents for the number of coins given in the charts below.
HINT: Count by the greater amount first.

a)

Nickels	Pennies
6	7

Total amount = _____

b)

Quarters	Dimes
3	2

Total amount = _____

c)

Quarters	Nickels
5	5

Total amount = _____

d)

Quarters	Nickels	Pennies
4	2	4

Total amount = _____

e)

Quarters	Dimes	Nickels
6	3	7

Total amount = _____

f)

Quarters	Dimes	Nickels	Pennies
2	3	1	5

Total amount = _____

g)

Quarters	Dimes	Nickels	Pennies
5	2	2	2

Total amount = _____

7. Count the given coins and write the total amount:
HINT: Count by the greater amount first.

a) Total amount = _____

(25¢) (1¢) (1¢) (5¢) (5¢) (10¢) (1¢)

b) Total amount = _____

(10¢) (1¢) (10¢) (25¢) (25¢) (1¢) (25¢)

c) Total amount = _____

(10¢) (1¢) (25¢) (5¢) (10¢) (25¢) (10¢)

d) Total amount = _____

(5¢) (10¢) (25¢) (5¢) (1¢) (5¢) (25¢)

BONUS

e) Total amount = _____

(5¢) (1¢) (5¢) (1¢) (1¢) (5¢) (25¢) (5¢) (1¢) (10¢) (10¢) (25¢) (25¢)

 jump math
MULTIPLYING POTENTIAL

Number Sense 1

1. Draw the additional coins needed to make each total:

| a) How many dimes? 10¢ 10¢ 10¢ + = 50¢ | b) How many quarters? 25¢ 5¢ + = 80¢ |
| c) How many dimes? 25¢ 25¢ + = 70¢ | d) How many quarters? 25¢ 10¢ + = 85¢ |

2. Draw the **additional** coins needed to make each total.
    You can only use **two** coins for each question:

a) 26¢ 10¢ 10¢	b) 50¢ 25¢ 10¢
c) 45¢ 25¢ 10¢	d) 85¢ 25¢ 25¢
e) 31¢ 10¢ 1¢	f) 65¢ 25¢ 25¢
g) 105¢ 25¢ 25¢ 25¢	h) 95¢ 25¢ 25¢ 25¢
i) $5 $2	j) $7 $2 $2
k) $3 $1	l) $10 $2 $2 $2 $1
m) 131¢ $1 5¢	n) 340¢ $2 $1 25¢

3. Draw a picture to show the fewest extra coins the child will need to pay for the item:

    a) Ron has 25¢. He wants to buy an eraser for 55¢.

    b) Alan has 3 quarters, a dime, and a nickel. He wants to buy a notebook for 97¢.

    c) Jane has 2 toonies and 2 loonies. She wants to buy a plant for ten dollars.

    d) Raiz has 3 toonies and a loonie. He wants to buy a book for nine dollars and forty-five cents.

4. Show how to make 80¢ using only:

    a) dimes and quarters   b) nickels and quarters

5. Make up a problem like one of the problems in Question 3 and exchange it with a classmate to solve.

NS5-54: Least Number of Coins

1. What is the greatest amount you could pay in quarters without exceeding the amount?
   Draw the quarters to show your answer:

Amount	Greatest amount you could pay in quarters	Amount	Greatest amount you could pay in quarters
a) 45¢		b) 52¢	
c) 79¢		d) 83¢	
e) 63¢		f) 64¢	
g) 49¢		h) 31¢	
i) 82¢		j) 96¢	

2. Find the greatest amount you could pay in quarters.
   Represent the amount remaining using the least number of coins:

Amount	Amount paid in quarters	Amount remaining	Amount remaining in coins
a) 82¢	75¢	82¢ - 75¢ = 7¢	5¢ 1¢ 1¢
b) 57¢			
c) 85¢			
d) 95¢			

3. Trade coins to make each amount with the least amount of coins.
   Draw a picture in your notebook to show your final answer:

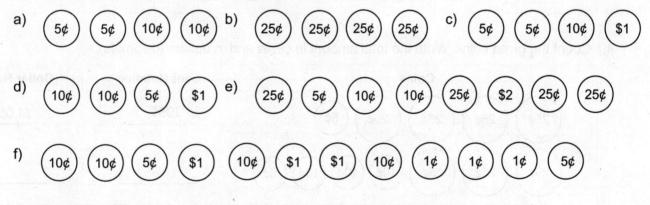

a) 5¢ 5¢ 10¢ 10¢   b) 25¢ 25¢ 25¢ 25¢   c) 5¢ 5¢ 10¢ $1

d) 10¢ 10¢ 5¢ $1   e) 25¢ 5¢ 10¢ 10¢ 25¢ $2 25¢ 25¢

f) 10¢ 10¢ 5¢ $1 10¢ $1 $1 10¢ 1¢ 1¢ 1¢ 5¢

4. Show how you could trade the amounts for the least number of coins:

   a) 6 quarters   b) 6 dimes and 2 nickels   c) 8 loonies

   d) 9 loonies and 5 dimes   e) 10 loonies, 6 dimes, 2 nickels and 5 pennies

NS5-55: Dollar and Cent Notation

1. Write the given amount in dollars, dimes and pennies, then in dollar notation.

	Dollars	Dimes	Pennies	Amount in $
a) 173¢	1	7	3	$ 1.73
c) 62¢				

	Dollars	Dimes	Pennies	Amount in $
b) 465¢				
d) 2¢				

2. Change the amount to cent notation, then dollar notation.

a) 7 pennies = __7¢__ = __$ .07__   b) 4 nickels = _____ = _____   c) 6 dimes = _____ = _____

d) 4 pennies = _____ = _____   e) 13 pennies = _____ = _____   f) 1 quarter = _____ = _____

g) 5 nickels = _____ = _____   h) 3 quarters = _____ = _____   i) 8 dimes = _____ = _____

j) 6 toonies = _____ = _____   k) 4 loonies = _____ = _____   l) 7 loonies = _____ = _____

3. Count the dollar amount and the cent amount. Write the total amount in dollar (decimal) notation.

Dollar Amount	Cent Amount	Total
a) $2 $2 $1 = _____	25¢ 25¢ 5¢ = _____	_____
b) 10 5 = _____	25¢ 10¢ 1¢ = _____	_____
c) 10 10 = _____	25¢ 25¢ 1¢ = _____	_____

4. Count the given coins. Write the total amount in cents and in dollars (decimals).

Coins	Cent Notation	Dollar Notation
a) 25¢ 25¢ 25¢ 25¢ 5¢	105¢	$1.05
b) 25¢ 25¢ 25¢ 10¢ 10¢ 10¢ 5¢	_____	_____

5. Write each number of cents in dollar notation.

a) 325¢ = _____   b) 20¢ = _____   c) 6¢ = _____   d) 283¢ = _____   e) 205¢ = _____

6. Write each amount of money in cents notation.

   a) $2.99 = _____   b) $3.43 = _____   c) $1.41 = _____   d) $0.08 = _____

7. Circle the greater amount of money in each pair:

   a)   193¢   or $1.96   b) $1.01   or   103¢   c)   840¢   or $8.04

8. Circle the larger amount of money in each pair:

   a) seven dollars and sixty-five cents   or   seven dollars and seventy cents

   b) nine dollars and eighty-three cents   or   978¢

   c) fifteen dollars and eighty cents   or $15.08

9. Tally the amount of each type of denomination then find the total.

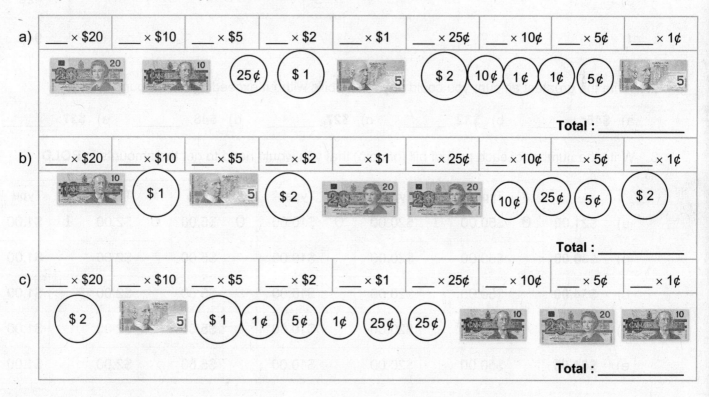

10. Which is a greater amount of money: 256¢ or $2.62? Explain how you know.

11. Alan bought a pack of markers for $3.50. He paid for it with 4 coins. Which coins did he use?

12. Tanya's weekly allowance is $5.25. Her mom gave her 6 coins. Which coins did she use? Can you find more than one answer?

13. Write words for the following amounts:

   a) $3.57   b) $12.23   c) $604.80   d) $327.25   e) $26.93   f) $766.03

NS5-56: Least Number of Coins and Bills

1. Find the number of coins you need to make the amount in the right hand column of the chart.

   HINT: Count up by quarters until you are as close to the amount as possible. Then count on by dimes, and so on.

	Number of Quarters	Subtotal	Number of Dimes	Subtotal	Number of Nickels	Subtotal	Number of Pennies	Total Amount
a)	3	75¢	0	75¢	1	80¢	3	83¢
b)								52¢
c)								97¢
d)								23¢
e)								42¢
f)								94¢

2. Write the greatest amount you could pay in $20 bills without exceeding the amount.

   a) **$45**: _____   b) **$32**: _____   c) **$27**: _____   d) **$48**: _____   e) **$37**: _____

3. Write the number of each type of bill (or coin) that you would need to get the amounts in **BOLD**:

		#	Type	#	Type	#	Type	#	Type	#	Type	#	Type
a)	**$21.00**	0	$50.00	1	$20.00	0	$10.00	0	$5.00	0	$2.00	1	$1.00
b)	**$30.00**		$50.00		$20.00		$10.00		$5.00		$2.00		$1.00
c)	**$54.00**		$50.00		$20.00		$10.00		$5.00		$2.00		$1.00
d)	**$85.00**		$50.00		$20.00		$10.00		$5.00		$2.00		$1.00
e)	**$64.00**		$50.00		$20.00		$10.00		$5.00		$2.00		$1.00

4. Draw the least number of coins you need to make the following amounts.

   a) 72¢   b) 93¢   c) 82¢   d) 52¢

5. Draw the least number of coins and bills you need to make the following amounts.

   a) $55.00   b) $67.00   c) $64.00   d) $123.00
   e) $62.35   f) $42.12   g) $57.61   h) $78.18
   i) $73.08   j) $157.50   k) $92.82   l) $85.23

NS5-57: Making Change Using Mental Math

1. Calculate the change owing for each purchase.

a) Price of a pencil = 44¢
   Amount paid = 50¢

   Change = _____

b) Price of an eraser = 41¢
   Amount paid = 50¢

   Change = _____

c) Price of a sharpener = 84¢
   Amount paid = 90¢

   Change = _____

d) Price of a ruler = 53¢
   Amount paid = 60¢

   Change = _____

e) Price of a marker = 76¢
   Amount paid = 80¢

   Change = _____

f) Price of a notebook = 65¢
   Amount paid = 70¢

   Change = _____

g) Price of a folder = 68¢
   Amount paid = 70¢

   Change = _____

h) Price of a juice box = 49¢
   Amount paid = 50¢

   Change = _____

i) Price of a freezie = 28¢
   Amount paid = 30¢

   Change = _____

2. Count up by 10s to find the change owing from a dollar (100¢):

Price Paid	Change	Price Paid	Change	Price Paid	Change
a) 90¢		d) 40¢		g) 20¢	
b) 70¢		e) 10¢		h) 60¢	
c) 50¢		f) 30¢		i) 80¢	

3. Find the change owing for each purchase:

a) Price of a binder = 80¢
   Amount paid = $1.00

   Change = _____

b) Price of an eraser = 70¢
   Amount paid = $1.00

   Change = _____

c) Price of an apple = 20¢
   Amount paid = $1.00

   Change = _____

d) Price of a marker = 60¢
   Amount paid = $1.00

   Change = _____

e) Price of a patty = 50¢
   Amount paid = $1.00

   Change = _____

f) Price of a pencil = 30¢
   Amount paid = $1.00

   Change = _____

g) Price of a sharpener = 10¢
   Amount paid = $1.00

   Change = _____

h) Price of juice = 40¢
   Amount paid = $1.00

   Change = _____

i) Price of a popsicle = 60¢
   Amount paid = $1.00

   Change = _____

4. Find the smallest two-digit number ending in zero (i.e. 10, 20, 30, …) <u>greater</u> than the number given.

a) 74 __80__   b) 56 _____   c) 43 _____   d) 28 _____   e) 57 _____   f) 4 _____

NS5-57: Making Change Using Mental Math *(continued)*

5. Make change for the number written below. Follow steps that are shown for 16¢:

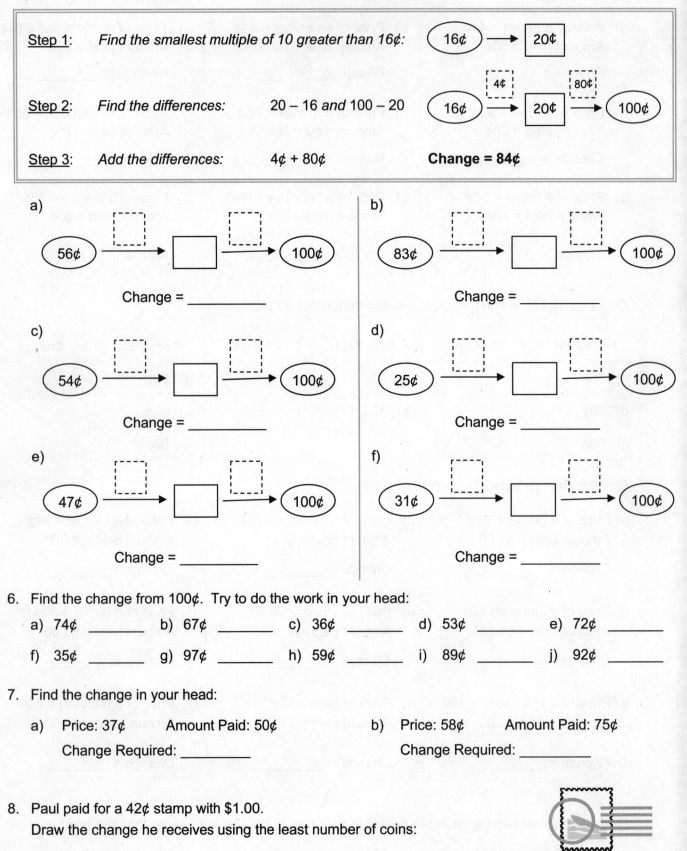

Step 1: *Find the smallest multiple of 10 greater than 16¢:*   16¢ → 20¢

Step 2: *Find the differences:*   20 – 16 *and* 100 – 20

Step 3: *Add the differences:*   4¢ + 80¢   **Change = 84¢**

a) 56¢ → ☐ → 100¢

Change = _____

b) 83¢ → ☐ → 100¢

Change = _____

c) 54¢ → ☐ → 100¢

Change = _____

d) 25¢ → ☐ → 100¢

Change = _____

e) 47¢ → ☐ → 100¢

Change = _____

f) 31¢ → ☐ → 100¢

Change = _____

6. Find the change from 100¢. Try to do the work in your head:

a) 74¢ _____   b) 67¢ _____   c) 36¢ _____   d) 53¢ _____   e) 72¢ _____

f) 35¢ _____   g) 97¢ _____   h) 59¢ _____   i) 89¢ _____   j) 92¢ _____

7. Find the change in your head:

a)   Price: 37¢   Amount Paid: 50¢

Change Required: _____

b)   Price: 58¢   Amount Paid: 75¢

Change Required: _____

8. Paul paid for a 42¢ stamp with $1.00.
    Draw the change he receives using the least number of coins:

9. Find the change:

Amount Paid	Price	Change	Amount Paid	Price	Change
a) $30.00	$22.00		b) $70.00	$64.00	
c) $40.00	$34.00		d) $90.00	$87.00	
e) $50.00	$46.00		f) $20.00	$13.00	

10. Follow the steps shown below for finding the change from $50.00 on a payment of $22.00:

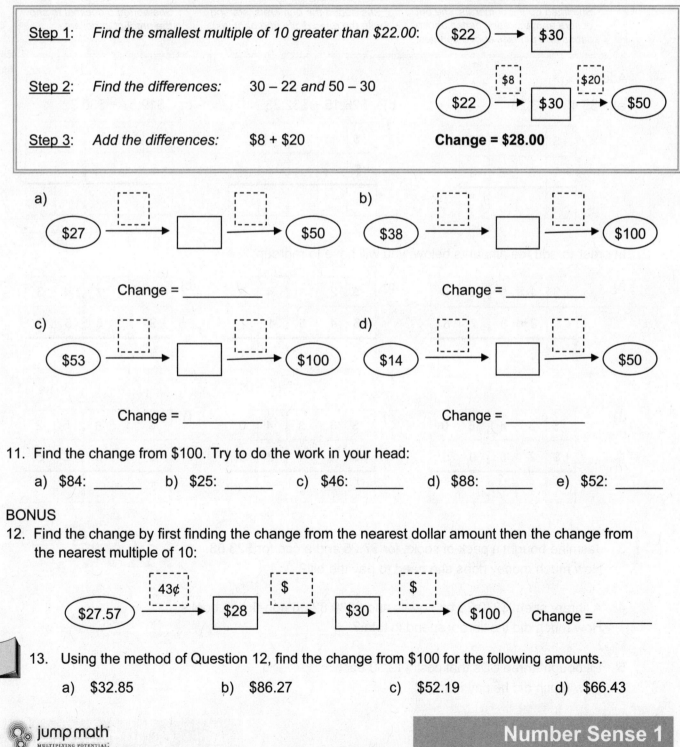

11. Find the change from $100. Try to do the work in your head:

a) $84: _____   b) $25: _____   c) $46: _____   d) $88: _____   e) $52: _____

BONUS

12. Find the change by first finding the change from the nearest dollar amount then the change from the nearest multiple of 10:

13. Using the method of Question 12, find the change from $100 for the following amounts.

a) $32.85   b) $86.27   c) $52.19   d) $66.43

NS5-58: Adding Money

1. Sara spent $14.42 on a plant and $3.53 on a vase.
   To find out how much she spent, she added the amounts using the following steps:

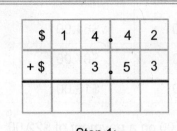

$	1	4 .	4	2
+ $		3 .	5	3

Step 1:
She lined up the numerals: she put dollars above dollars, dimes above dimes and pennies above pennies.

$	1	4 .	4	2
+ $		3 .	5	3
	1	7	9	5

Step 2:
She added the numerals, starting with the ones digits (the pennies).

$	1	4 .	4	2
+ $		3 .	5	3
$	1	7 .	9	5

Step 3:
She added a decimal to show the amount in dollars.

Add:

a) $5.45 + $3.23

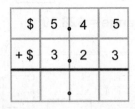

$	5 .	4	5
+ $	3 .	2	3

b) $26.15 + $32.23

$		.		
+ $		.		

c) $19.57 + $30.32

$		.		
+ $		.		

2. In order to add the amounts below, you will have to regroup:

a)

$	1	6 .	6	0
+ $	2	3 .	7	5

b)

$	2	7 .	4	5
+ $	4	5 .	1	2

c)

$	8	7 .	4	3
+ $		6 .	5	2
$				

d)

$	3	4 .	6	0
+ $	2	6 .	0	0

e)

$	3	8 .	4	0
+ $	4	4 .	2	5

f)

$	1	6 .	5	2
+ $	4	8 .	2	5
$				

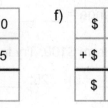

3. Jasmine bought a pack of socks for $7.25 and a cap for $23.53.
   How much money does she need to pay the bill?

4. A library spent $270.25 on novels and $389.82 on non-fiction books.
   How much did the library spend in total?

5. Eli bought three CDs that cost $12.30 each.
   How much did he pay in total?

Answer the following questions in your notebook.

6. Sakku has $25.

If he buys a chess game for $9.50 and a book for $10.35, will he have enough money left to buy a book which costs $5.10?

7. Find the amounts each child earned shovelling snow:

   a) Karen earned 3 twenty dollar bills, 1 toonie, 2 loonies, 2 quarters and 1 nickel.

   b) Jill earned 4 ten dollar bills, 6 toonies and 3 quarters.

   c) Sandor earned 2 twenty and 3 ten dollar bills, 2 loonies and 5 quarters.

   d) Tory earned 5 ten dollar bills, 6 toonies, 2 loonies and 6 dimes.

8. a) If you bought a watch and a soccer ball, how much would you pay?

   b) Which costs more: a watch and a cap or a pair of pants and a soccer ball?

   c) Could you buy a soccer ball, a pair of tennis rackets and a pair of pants for $100?

   d) What is the total cost of the three most expensive things in the picture?

   e) Make up your own problem using the items.

$12.30

$49.95

$15.64

$35.47

$28.50

$42.89

9. Try to find the answer mentally.

   a) How much do 4 loaves of bread cost at $2.30 each?

   b) How many apples, costing 40¢, could you buy with $3.00?

   c) Permanent markers cost $3.10.

      How many could you buy if you had $25.00?

   d) Is $10.00 enough to pay for a book costing $4.75 and a pen costing $5.34?

   e) Which costs more, 4 apples at 32¢ an apple, or 3 oranges at 45¢ an orange?

1. Find the remaining amount by subtracting:

a)
	4 . 6	2
– $	2 . 3	0

b)
$	8 . 6	5
– $	4 . 2	3

c)
$	7 . 8	9
– $	3 . 6	8

d)
$	9 . 8	2
– $	7 . 8	1

e)
$	6 . 8	2
– $	5 . 2	1

2. Subtract the given money amounts by regrouping once or twice:

Example:

Step 1:
          6   10
$	7̶ . 0̶	0
– $	2 . 4	3

Step 2:
              9
          6 1̶0̶
$	7 . 0	0
– $	2 . 4	3
$	4 . 5	7

a)
$	4 . 0	0
– $	2 . 2	9

b)
$	9 . 0	0
– $	6 . 2	4

c)
$	7 . 0	0
– $	5 . 7	2

d)
$	4	6 . 0	0
– $	2	3 . 4	5

e)
$	5	8 . 4	5
– $	2	7 . 7	8

f)
$	6	7 . 2	3
– $	3	4 . 6	4

3. Andrew spent $3.67 on his breakfast.

   He paid for it with a five dollar bill.

   Calculate his change.

4. Mera has $12.16 and Wendy has $13.47.

   How much more money does Wendy have than Mera?

5. Rita has $20.00. She wants to buy vegetables for $7.70, juice for $3.45 and dairy products for $9.75.

   Does she have enough money to buy all these items?

   If not, by how much is she short?

6. Mark has $30.00.

   He wants to buy a pair of shoes for $18.35 and pants for $14.53.

   How much more money does he need?

NS5-60: Estimating with Money

1. Estimate the amount of money to the nearest dollar and then count the precise amount:

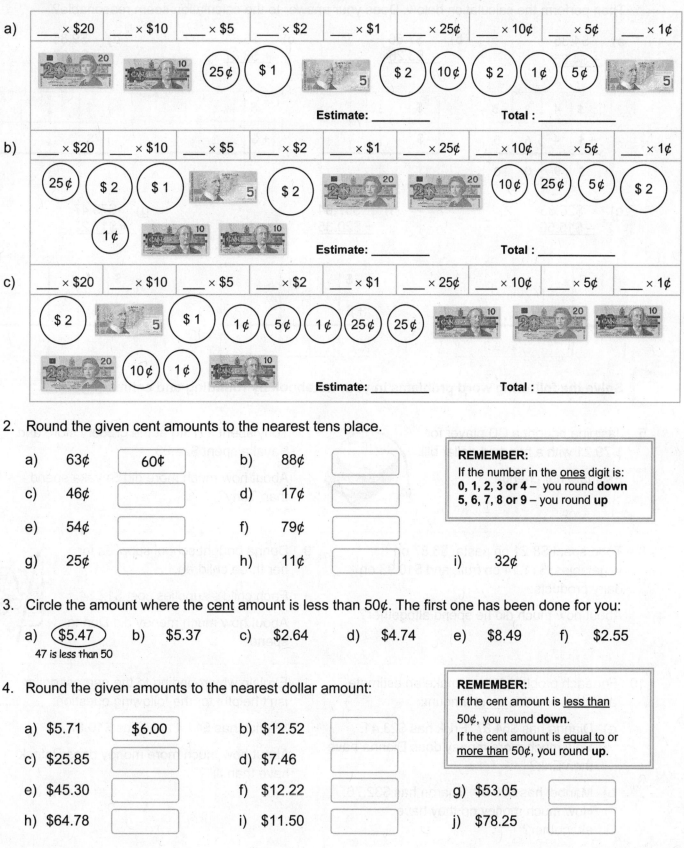

a) ___ × $20 ___ × $10 ___ × $5 ___ × $2 ___ × $1 ___ × 25¢ ___ × 10¢ ___ × 5¢ ___ × 1¢

Estimate: _____ Total : _____

b) ___ × $20 ___ × $10 ___ × $5 ___ × $2 ___ × $1 ___ × 25¢ ___ × 10¢ ___ × 5¢ ___ × 1¢

Estimate: _____ Total : _____

c) ___ × $20 ___ × $10 ___ × $5 ___ × $2 ___ × $1 ___ × 25¢ ___ × 10¢ ___ × 5¢ ___ × 1¢

Estimate: _____ Total : _____

2. Round the given cent amounts to the nearest tens place.

a) 63¢   60¢
b) 88¢
c) 46¢
d) 17¢
e) 54¢
f) 79¢
g) 25¢
h) 11¢
i) 32¢

REMEMBER:
If the number in the <u>ones</u> digit is:
0, 1, 2, 3 or 4 – you round **down**
5, 6, 7, 8 or 9 – you round **up**

3. Circle the amount where the <u>cent</u> amount is less than 50¢. The first one has been done for you:

a) ($5.47)   b) $5.37   c) $2.64   d) $4.74   e) $8.49   f) $2.55
  47 is less than 50

4. Round the given amounts to the nearest dollar amount:

a) $5.71 $6.00
b) $12.52
c) $25.85
d) $7.46
e) $45.30
f) $12.22
g) $53.05
h) $64.78
i) $11.50
j) $78.25

REMEMBER:
If the cent amount is <u>less than</u> 50¢, you round **down**.
If the cent amount is <u>equal to</u> or <u>more than</u> 50¢, you round **up**.

5. Estimate the following sums and differences by rounding each amount to the nearest dollar amount. Then perform the calculation below. Does your answer to the calculation seem reasonable?

a) $4.35
+ $4.65

b) $7.66
− $3.26

c) $5.81
+ $3.37

d) $9.85
− $2.67

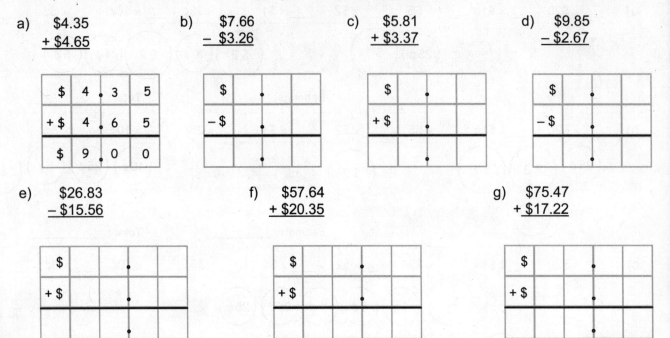

$	4 . 3	5
+ $	4 . 6	5
$	9 . 0	0

e) $26.83
− $15.56

f) $57.64
+ $20.35

g) $75.47
+ $17.22

Solve the following word problems in your notebook by rounding and estimating.

6. Jasmine bought a CD player for $ 79.21 with a hundred dollar bill.

Estimate her change.

7. Tony spent $17.46 at the grocery store and Sayaka spent $24.93.

About how much more did Sayaka spend than Tony?

8. Todd spent $8.21 on pasta, $6.87 on vegetables, $11.14 on fruit, and $10.93 on dairy products.

About how much did he spend altogether?

9. Donna bought school supplies for her three children.

Each child's supplies cost $12.34.

About how much money did Donna spend?

10. For each problem below, make an estimate and then find the <u>exact</u> amount:

a) Dianna has $54.37. Erick has $23.41. How much more money does Dianna have than Erik?

b) Maribel has $29.04. Sharon has $32.76. How much money do they have altogether?

11. Explain why rounding to the nearest dollar isn't helpful for the following question:

"Patrick has $11.41. Jill has $10.87.

About how much more money does Patrick have than Jill?"

1. How many minutes is it past the hour? Count by 5s around the clock, filling in the boxes as you go.

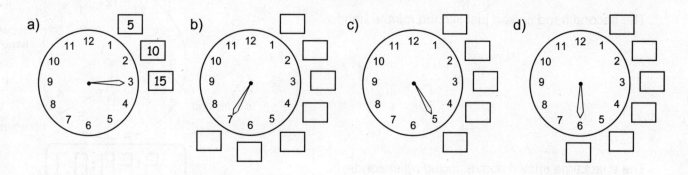

2. Under each clock, write the time in two ways – digitally and in words:

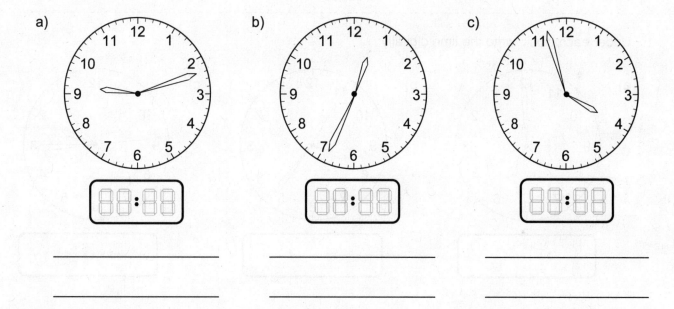

3. Draw the hands on the following clocks to show the time given:

a)   11:21   b)   8:46   c)   3:19

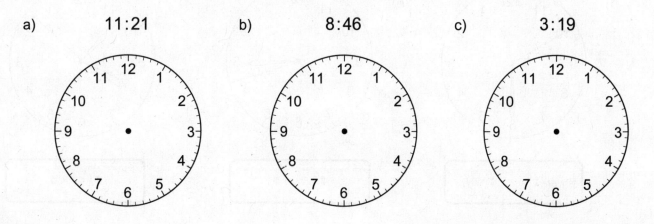

The second hand is longer and thinner than both the minute and hour hands.

The second hand is read just like the minute hand.

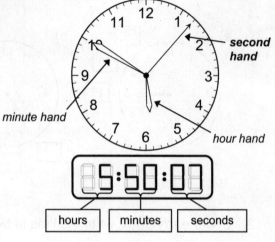

The exact time shown above, including seconds, is:

1. Under each clock, write the time digitally:

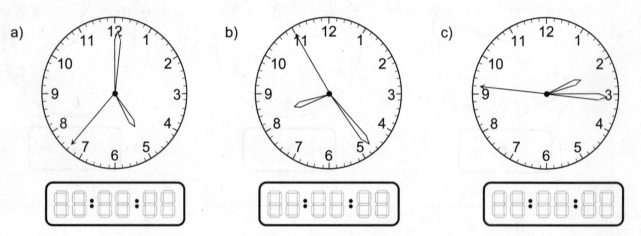

a)

b)

c)

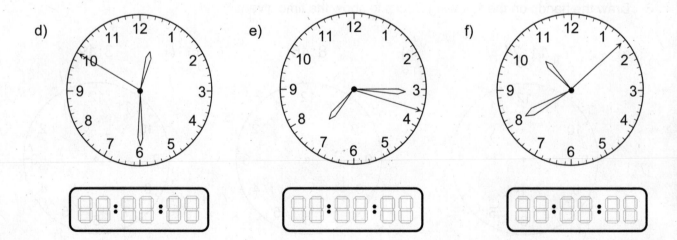

d)

e)

f)

Measurement 1

2. Find the difference in the times on the two clocks:
> in minutes and seconds
> in seconds only

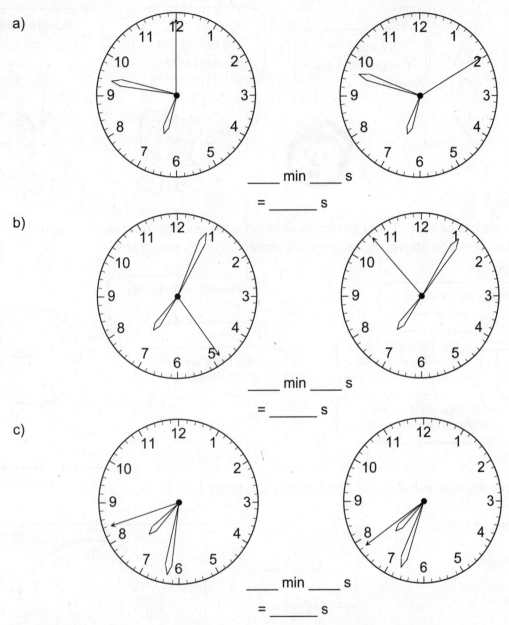

a)

_____ min _____ s

= _____ s

b)

_____ min _____ s

= _____ s

c)

_____ min _____ s

= _____ s

3. Using the clock in your classroom, do the following tasks with a partner.
   Fill in the chart carefully and be sure to *do all your estimations first*!
   Don't forget to include units:

Task	Estimated Time	Actual Time
Write out the alphabet on a piece of paper		
Count by 5s to 200		
Name all the students in your class		
Count backwards from 100 to 1		

jump math
MULTIPLYING POTENTIAL

Measurement 1

What time is it?

Actually all three people are correct. There are many different ways you can read clocks – you've probably heard all the variations above. Here are a few more you might recognize:

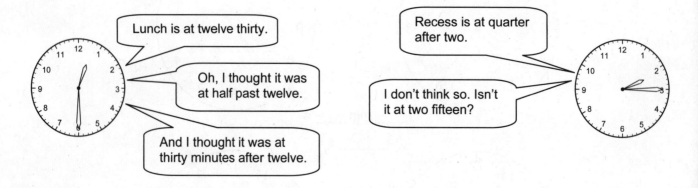

---

1. In each case, write the time in numbers. The first one has been done for you:

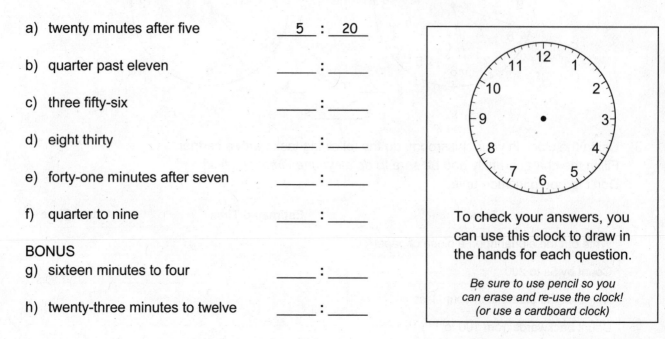

a) twenty minutes after five   __5__ : __20__

b) quarter past eleven   _____ : _____

c) three fifty-six   _____ : _____

d) eight thirty   _____ : _____

e) forty-one minutes after seven   _____ : _____

f) quarter to nine   _____ : _____

BONUS

g) sixteen minutes to four   _____ : _____

h) twenty-three minutes to twelve   _____ : _____

To check your answers, you can use this clock to draw in the hands for each question.

Be sure to use pencil so you can erase and re-use the clock! (or use a cardboard clock)

2. For each question below, use words to write the time in two different ways.
   Look at a clock face to help you see the answers.

   EXAMPLE: 6:42 can be written "42 minutes after 6" or "18 minutes to 7."

   a)   **11:35**   b)   **7:40**

   _____   _____

   _____   _____

   c)   **4:57**   d)   **1:34**

   _____   _____

   _____   _____

   BONUS
   e) Can you think of **three** different ways of writing the following time?

   i) _____

   ii) _____

   iii) _____

3. For each question, the time should be given in **four** ways:

   - In digital form
   - In analog form
   - In written form – **two** different ways

   a) **9:48**   b) **4:32**

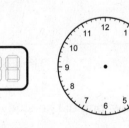      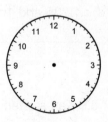

   _____   _____

   _____   _____

ME5-4: Elapsed Time

1. By counting by 5s, find out how much time elapsed from…

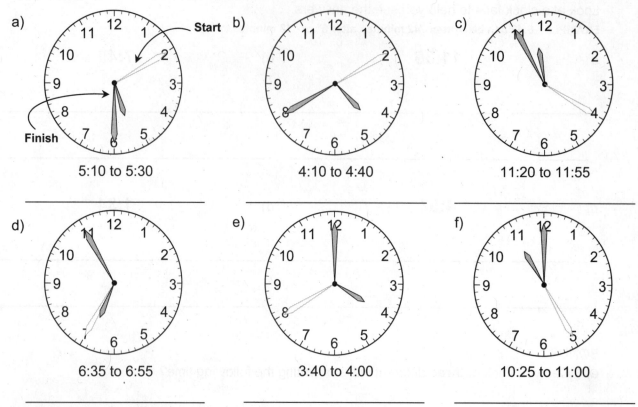

a) 5:10 to 5:30

b) 4:10 to 4:40

c) 11:20 to 11:55

d) 6:35 to 6:55

e) 3:40 to 4:00

f) 10:25 to 11:00

2. Count by 5s to show how much time has elapsed between …

a) 8:45 and 9:20.

_____, _____, _____, _____, _____, _____, _____, _____, _____
   0   5   10   15

Time elapsed: _____

b) 3:40 and 4:10.

_____, _____, _____, _____, _____, _____, _____, _____, _____

Time elapsed: _____

c) 11:25 and 12:05.

_____, _____, _____, _____, _____, _____, _____, _____, _____

Time elapsed: _____

d) 12:35 and 1:15.

_____, _____, _____, _____, _____, _____, _____, _____, _____

Time elapsed: _____

3. Karl started studying at 7:25 and finished at 8:10. How long did he study?

4. Briana left for school at 7:45. Amil left half an hour later. When did Amil leave?

5. Tom put a loaf of bread in the oven at 3:50. It should bake for 45 minutes. At what time should he take the loaf out?

ME5-4: Elapsed Time (continued)

6. Find how much time has passed between the times in bold (intervals are not shown to scale).

a)

20 minutes   **2 hours**   **5 minutes**

1:40 1:45 1:50 1:55 2:00   3:00   4:00 **4:05**

Time elapsed: _____

b)

10:50 10:55 11:00   12:00   1:00   2:00 2:05 **2:10**

Time elapsed: _____

c)

12:45 12:50 12:55 1:00   2:00   3:00 3:05 3:10 **3:15**

Time elapsed: _____

7. Count on by 5-minute and by 1-hour intervals to find out how much time has elapsed between ...

a) 9:40 and 12:05.

___9:40___ , ___9:45___ , ___9:50___ , _____, _____, _____, _____, _____ Time elapsed: _____

b) 4:50 and 7:10.

_____, _____, _____, _____, _____, _____, _____, _____ Time elapsed: _____

c) 6:55 and 11:10.

_____, _____, _____, _____, _____, _____, _____, _____ Time elapsed: _____

8. Find how much time has elapsed by subtracting the times.

a) 3:43
    3:20
    ____

b) 8:22
    7:21
    ____

c) 11:48
    5:30
    ____

d) 6:40
    2:25
    ____

e) 3:42
    1:05
    ____

9. Draw a time line to find out how much time has elapsed between ...

a) 9:30 and 11:05.   b) 2:35 and 4:05.   c) 1:50 and 4:15.

ME5-5: The 24-Hour Clock

1. Complete the following table using the pattern.

12-hr Clock	24-hr Clock
12:00 a.m.	00:00
1:00 a.m.	01:00
2:00 a.m.	02:00

12-hr Clock	24-hr Clock
9:00 a.m.	09:00
10:00 a.m.	
12:00 p.m.	12:00
1 p.m.	13:00

12-hr Clock	24-hr Clock
5:00 p.m.	17:00
6:00 p.m.	

2. a) What number must you add to 1:00 p.m. to change it to 24-hour clock notation? _____

   b) List three other times that change this way: _____

3. For each a.m./p.m. time, write the corresponding 24-hour clock notation.
   HINT: Only look at the chart above if you need help.

   a) 6:00 a.m. = _____   b) 7:00 p.m. = _____   c) 4:00 p.m. = _____

   d) 8:00 p.m. = _____   e) 9:00 p.m. = _____   f) 12:00 a.m. = _____

   g) 12:00 p.m. = _____   h) 5:00 p.m. = _____   i) 10:00 a.m. = _____

4. For each 24-hour clock notation, write the corresponding a.m./p.m. time.

   a) 8:00 = _____   b) 14:00 = _____   c) 12:00 = _____   d) 00:00 = _____

   e) 19:00 = _____   f) 16:00 = _____   g) 05:00 = _____   h) 22:00 = _____

5. David went to see the reptiles at 10:30. Complete the chart to show when David left each part of the zoo (using 24-hour time).

	Start	Reptiles	Monkeys	Lunch	Polar Bears	Lions
Time Spent		2 hr	1 hr 30 minutes	30 minutes	45 minutes	20 minutes
Time Finished	10:30					

6. Describe any differences between the way time is written for a 24-hr and a 12-hr clock …

   a) in the morning (a.m.)   b) in the afternoon or evening (p.m.)

ME5-6: Topics in Time

1. Fill in the charts.

a)

Days	Hours
1	24
2	48
3	

b)

Weeks	Days
1	7
2	
3	

c)

Years	Weeks
1	52
2	
3	

d)

Years	Days
1	365
2	
3	

2. A decade is 10 years. A century is 100 years. Fill in the blanks.

a) 40 years = _____ decades

b) 60 years = _____ decades

c) 90 years = _____ decades

d) 200 years = _____ centuries

e) 800 years = _____ centuries

f) 1500 years = _____ centuries

g) 2 decades = _____ years

h) 3 centuries = _____ years

i) 40 decades = _____ centuries

3. Columbus discovered the New World in 1492.
   About how many centuries ago was this?

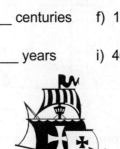

4. Which interval is longer? Explain.

a) 70 minutes   OR   1 hour 20 minutes

b) 3 hours 10 minutes   OR   170 minutes

5. A cheetah can run 30 metres each second.
   The fastest human can run about 600 metres in a minute.
   How much further can a cheetah run in a minute?

6. Tom worked for 1 hour and 55 minutes. Clara worked 20 minutes longer.
   How long did Clara work?

7. Boat B left the Vancouver harbour one hour later than boat A.
   Both boats traveled at a steady speed in the same direction.

	Time	14:00	15:00	16:00	17:00	18:00	19:00	20:00
Distance from Harbour	**Boat A**	0 km	4 km					
	Boat B	0 km	0 km					25 km

a) How far apart were the boats at 17:00?
b) At what time did boat B catch boat A?

ME5-7: Temperature

Degree Celsius is a unit of measurement for temperature. It is written: °C

Water freezes at 0°C. Water boils at 100°C. The normal temperature of the human body is 37°C.

---

1. Read the thermometers and record the temperature:

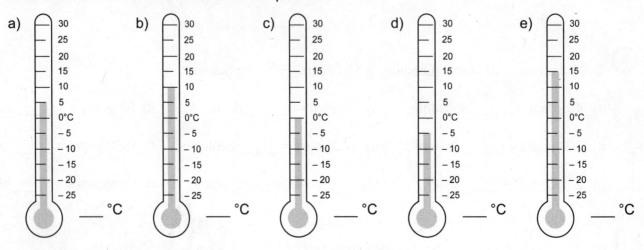

a) ___ °C   b) ___ °C   c) ___ °C   d) ___ °C   e) ___ °C

2. What is the normal temperature range of each season where you live?
    (Ask your teacher for help with this.)

    a) Winter –
        between _____ °C and _____ °C

    b) Spring –
        between _____ °C and _____ °C

    c) Summer –
        between _____ °C and _____ °C

    d) Fall –
        between _____ °C and _____ °C

3. Kyle's temperature is 36°C. How much lower is his temperature than normal?

4.
Animal	Body Temperature
Dog	39°C
Pigeon	41°C
Lizard	31°C - 35°C
Salmon	5°C - 17°C
Rattlesnake	15°C - 37°C

a) How much higher is the body temperature of the pigeon than that of the dog?

b) Which animal has the greatest range of body temperatures?

c) The temperature of cold blooded animals changes with the temperature of the air.

    Which animals are cold-blooded?

BONUS

5. Pam measured the temperature one day and found it was – 10°C.
    The next day, the temperature was 10°C.
    How many degrees did the temperature rise?

PDM5-1: Classifying Data

Data is facts or information. For example, your age is a piece of data, and so is your name.

Data can be organized into **categories.** We use attributes to sort data, such as ...

• Gender (boy or girl)   • Age (age 11 or age 10)   • Length of Hair (long hair or short hair)

- -

1. Count how many objects are in each category. Read all the categories first:

   a) *Objects:*   coin   tree   telephone pole

      staple   window   gold necklace

      Categories: Wood ____   Glass ____   Metal ____

   b) *Objects:*   raspberries   sky   grass   lips

      fire truck   lime   pickle   stop sign

      Categories: Green ____   Blue ____   Red ____

In math, we sometimes use circles to show which objects have a property.
Objects inside a circle have the property and objects outside the circle do not.

---

2. Which shapes go inside the circle and which go outside?
   Write their letters in the right place. (**NOTE: Polygons have straight sides.**)

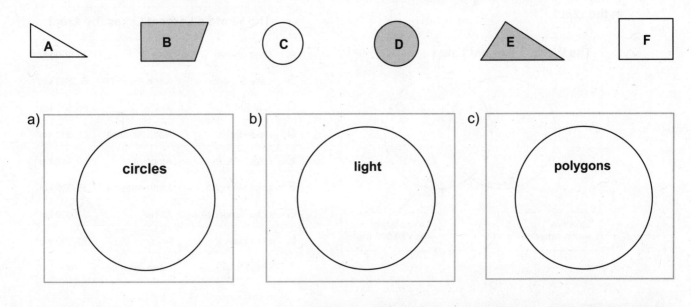

PDM5-1: Classifying Data (continued)

Venn diagrams are a way to use circles to show which objects have a property.

Objects inside a circle have the property and objects outside the circle do not.

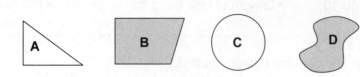

3. a) Which shape has both properties?
Put its letter inside both circles.

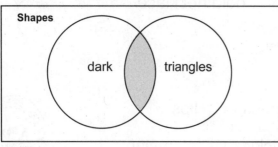

b) Which shape has neither property?
Put its letter outside both circles.

4. Complete the Venn diagrams. (**NOTE: A polygon has straight sides.**)

a)

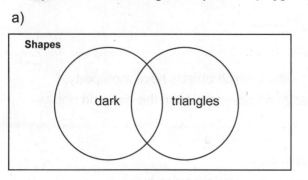

b)

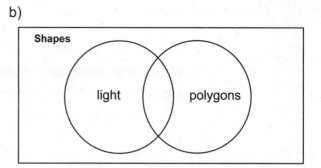

5. Complete the Venn diagram using the letters in the chart.

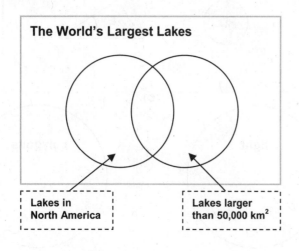

The World's Largest Lakes (by Area)			
A	Caspian Sea	Asia	371,000 km^2
B	Lake Superior	North America	84,500 km^2
C	Aral Sea	Asia	64,500 km^2
D	Lake Huron	North America	63,500 km^2
E	Lake Victoria	Africa	62,940 km^2
F	Lake Michigan	North America	58,020 km^2
G	Lake Tanganyika	Africa	32,000 km^2
H	Lake Baykal	Asia	31,500 km^2
I	Great Bear Lake	North America	31,400 km^2

PDM5-2: Venn Diagrams (Advanced)

1.

Sam collected the following information about the planets in our solar system:

Planet	Number of Moons	Days Needed to Orbit the Sun
Mercury (A)	0	88
Venus (B)	0	225
Earth (C)	1	365
Mars (D)	2	687
Jupiter (E)	62	4 344
Saturn (F)	33	10 768
Uranus (G)	27	30 660
Neptune (H)	13	60 152

Data from spacetoday.org

a) Which planets have more than 15 moons?

List their letters here: _____

b) Which planets orbit the sun in fewer than 10 000 days?

List their letters here: _____

c) Are any planets on **both** lists? If so, write the planet's letter: _____

d) Are there any planets on **neither** list? If so, write the planet's letter: _____

e) Now place **all** the planets – by letter – into the following Venn diagram.

Pay particular attention to the planet on both lists. Where will it go?
Where will the planet on neither list go?

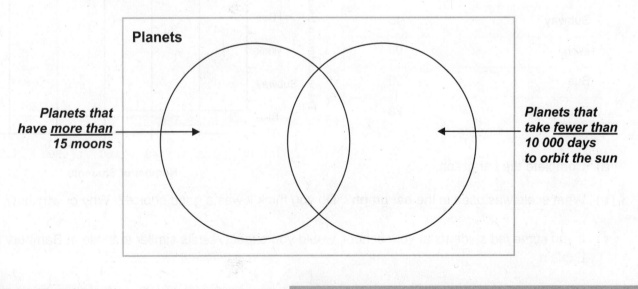

PDM5-3: Choosing a Scale for a Bar Graph

A **bar graph** has 4 parts:

- a vertical and horizontal **axis**,
- a **scale**,
- **labels** (including a title),
- **data** (given by the bars).

The bars in a bar graph can either be vertical or horizontal.

The scale tells how much each marking on the axis represents.

The labels indicate what the data in the bars is.

---

1. Find the scale on each bar graph.

a)

start at: _____

count by: _____

stop at: _____

b)

start at: _____

count by: _____

stop at: _____

c)

start at: _____

count by: _____

stop at: _____

2.

Transportation Used to Get to School	Number of Students
Bike	51
Subway	46
Walk	90
Bus	95
Car	28

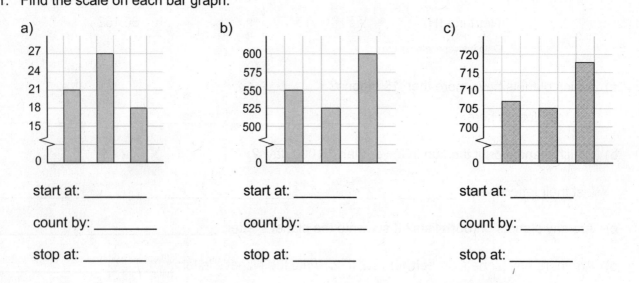

How Students at Bambury PS Get to School

a) Complete the bar graph.

b) What scale was used in the bar graph? Do you think it was a good choice? Why or why not?

c) If you surveyed students at your school, would you expect results similar to those at Bambury PS? Explain.

Probability & Data Management 1

3.

Items Sold at Bake Sale		# Sold
(B)	Brownies	12
(C)	Cookies	15
(D)	Date Squares	7
(F)	Fruit Pastries	10
(M)	Muffins	5

Items Sold at Bake Sale

Items Sold at Bake Sale

a) Draw two bar graphs for the same data on the graphs above.

b) Which graph makes the bake sale look more successful?
Why do you think that is?

4. From the bar graph, recreate Karen's original tally of the wildlife she saw.

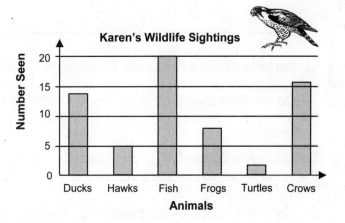

Karen's Wildlife Sightings

5.

Election Results

Election Results

a) Which graph makes it easier to tell the difference in votes for each candidate? Explain.

b) Who won the election?

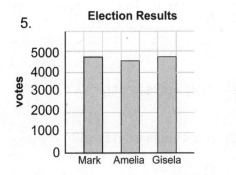

6. Choose a scale and draw a bar graph that …

A. doesn't have too many or too few markings and

B. makes it easy to see the data.

Life Span of Animals

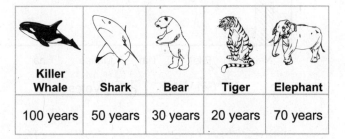

Killer Whale	Shark	Bear	Tiger	Elephant
100 years	50 years	30 years	20 years	70 years

PDM5-4: Double Bar Graphs

1. A **double bar graph** compares two sets of data.

    Student's Favourite Snack

    a) How many students chose potato chips in October?

    _____

    b) What was the most popular snack in December?

    _____

    c) Which snack had the same number of votes in October as in December?

    _____

    d) How many students are in the class?

    _____

    e) Sometime before Christmas the students did a project on nutrition.

        Do you think their project was in September or November? Explain.

2. Sonia made a double bar graph to record the votes in her school election.

Name	Naoko	Bilal	Tim	Matias	Tina
Girl Votes	65	43	60	3	50
Boy Votes	18	41	11	95	10

    a) Copy and complete her graph on grid paper.

    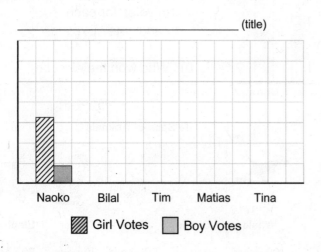

    _____ (title)

    b) Who had the most votes from girls?

    c) Who had the most votes from boys?

    d) How many people had more votes from boys than votes from girls?

        How does your graph show this?

    e) How many girls voted for the person who won?

        How did you find that data?

PDM5-5: Broken Line Graphs – An Introduction

On a **broken line graph** individual points are connected by a line.

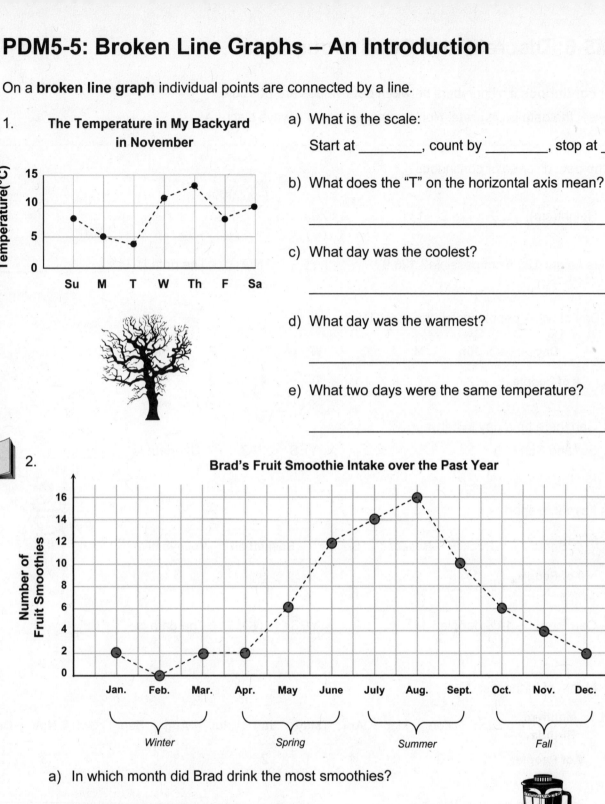

1. **The Temperature in My Backyard in November**

a) What is the scale:

Start at _____, count by _____, stop at _____.

b) What does the "T" on the horizontal axis mean?

_____.

c) What day was the coolest?

_____.

d) What day was the warmest?

_____.

e) What two days were the same temperature?

_____.

2. **Brad's Fruit Smoothie Intake over the Past Year**

a) In which month did Brad drink the most smoothies?

b) How many smoothies did Brad drink:

i) in May?   ii) in July?

c) In which months did Brad drink more than 5 smoothies?

d) List the seasons in order, starting with the one in which Brad drank the most fruit smoothies.

jump math
MULTIPLYING POTENTIAL.

Probability & Data Management 1

PDM5-6: Discrete and Continuous Data

Data is **continuous** if all numbers between data values are possible.

Otherwise, the data is **discrete**. Non-numerical data is always discrete.

----

1. Is the data discrete or continuous?

    a) Height(cm): 120   128.2   131   132   140.6

        Is height 128.5 cm possible? 128.9?   YES   NO   The data is _____

    b) Day of week people watch the most TV:

Day	Sun	M	T	W	Th	F	Sat
# of People	2	2	1	0	4	2	5

        Can there be a day in between
        Sat and Sun?   YES   NO   The data is _____

    c) Favourite sport:

Sport	Hockey	Baseball	Soccer	Basketball	Volleyball
# of People	17	3	14	9	6

        Can there be 14½ people? 14¾?   YES   NO   The data is _____

    d) Month of birthdays:

Month of Birthday	Jan	Feb	Mar	Apr	May	Jun	Jul	Aug	Sep	Oct	Nov	Dec
# of People	2	3	0	4	1	2	5	3	2	4	3	2

        Can there be a month between
        January and February?   YES   NO   The data is _____

    e) Temperature: 23°C   22.5°C   37°C   0°C

        Is temperature 32.3°C possible? 17.1 °C?   YES   NO   The data is _____

PDM5-6: Discrete and Continuous Data (continued)

2. Is the data **continuous** or **discrete**?

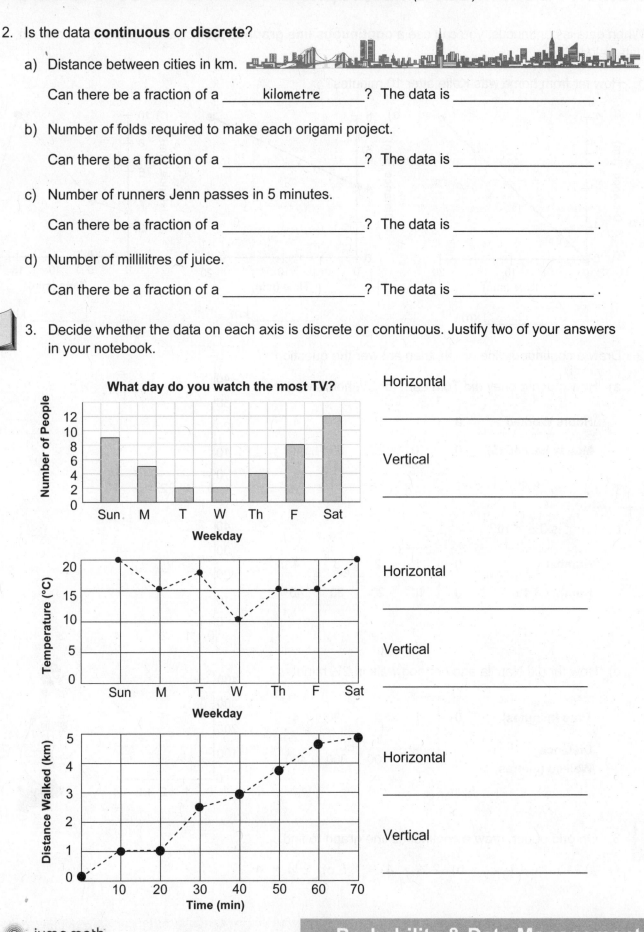

a) Distance between cities in km.

Can there be a fraction of a _____kilometre_____? The data is _____ .

b) Number of folds required to make each origami project.

Can there be a fraction of a _____? The data is _____ .

c) Number of runners Jenn passes in 5 minutes.

Can there be a fraction of a _____? The data is _____ .

d) Number of millilitres of juice.

Can there be a fraction of a _____? The data is _____ .

3. Decide whether the data on each axis is discrete or continuous. Justify two of your answers in your notebook.

What day do you watch the most TV?

Horizontal

_____

Vertical

_____

Horizontal

_____

Vertical

_____

Horizontal

_____

Vertical

_____

PDM5-7: Continuous Line Graphs

When data is continuous, you can use a **continuous line graph** to predict what happens in between data values.

1. How far from home was Katie after 10 minutes?

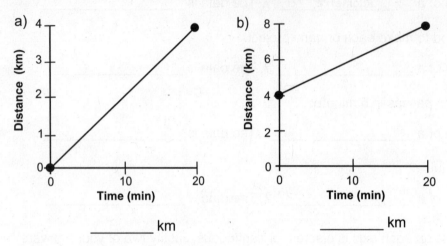

a)

_____ km

b)

_____ km

c)

_____ km

2. Draw a continuous line graph, then answer the question.

a) How much money did Tom earn for 3½ hours work?

Hours Worked	0	1	2	3	4
Money Earned ($)	0	10	20	30	40

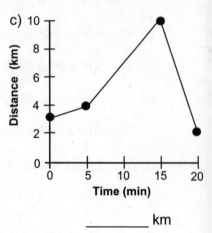

b) What is 3½ × 10?

Number	0	1	2	3	4
Number × 10	0	10	20	30	40

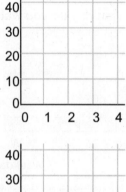

c) How far did Natalia and her dog walk in 2½ minutes?

Time (minutes)	0	1	2	3	4
Distance Walked (metres)	0	100	200	300	400

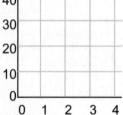

3. On grid paper, draw a continuous line graph to find …

a) 1 ½ × 10   b) 2 ½ × 4   c) 2 ¼ × 4

jump math
MULTIPLYING POTENTIAL

Probability & Data Management 1

1. If the data on **both** axes are continuous, join the dots with a continuous line (————).
   Otherwise, join the dots with a broken line (- - - - -) as in a).

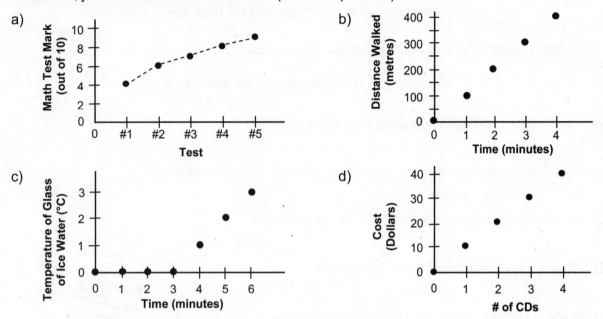

2. Sometimes graphs are drawn with solid lines (to show **trends**) even when the data is not continuous.

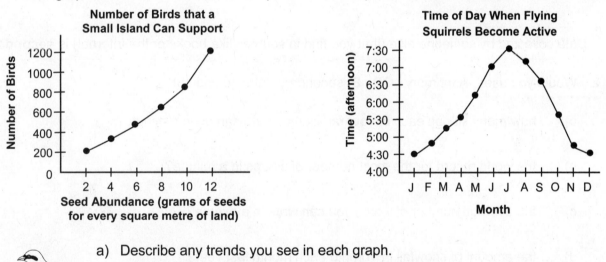

a) Describe any trends you see in each graph.

b) Which data in the graphs are not continuous? Explain.

c) Compare the times flying squirrels become active in January and July.
   Why do you think there is a difference?

3. Would you use a line graph or a bar graph to display the data? Explain your choice.

a)

Child	Sonia	Natalia	Soren	Bilal
Number of muffins sold	38	47	25	42

b)

# of CDs	1	2	3	4	5
Cost ($)	20	40	55	70	80

Explain your responses to the questions below in your notebook.

Data you collect yourself is called **primary (or first-hand) data.**

1. How would you collect primary data to answer each question?

    A. survey   **B.** observation   **C.** measurement

    a) What fraction of bikers wear white clothing at night?

    b) How does the temperature of a cup of heated water change over time?

    c) Are more people born in the winter or in the summer?

    d) What are my classmates' favourite movies?

    e) In which subjects do I have the thickest textbooks?

Data collected by someone else (that you find in sources like books or the Internet) is **secondary**.

2. Would you use   **A.** primary **OR** **B.** secondary data   to find out…

    a) … how many sit-ups each of your family members can do in a minute?

    b) … the world record for the most number of sit-ups in a minute?

    c) … the average number of words you can write in a minute?

    d) … the amount of snowfall in Toronto each month last year?

3. Make up a question you would answer using:

    a) first-hand data.

    b) second-hand data.

4. Watch the weather report on the news.
   What examples of second-hand data can you find?

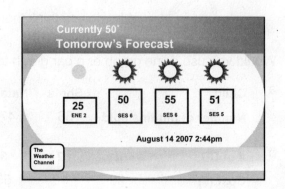

Currently 50°
Tomorrow's Forecast

| 25 | 50 | 55 | 51 |
| ENE 2 | SES 6 | SES 6 | SES 5 |

August 14 2007 2:44pm

The Weather Channel

Answer the following questions in your notebook.

1. Tasha wants to estimate how many of the pea pods in her garden are ripe.
   There are 100 pea plants in the garden. Here is her data:

	In the first plant	In the first 20 plants
# of ripe pods	5	40
# of pods	10	160

   a) What fraction of the pods on the first plant are ripe?

   b) What fraction of the pods on the first twenty plants are ripe?

   c) Can Tasha predict what fraction of pods in the garden are ripe just from looking at 1 plant?

   d) Which gives a better estimate: looking at one plant or 20 plants? Explain.

   e) Use the data in the first 20 plants to estimate …

   i) the total number of pods in the garden   ii) the number of **ripe** pods in the garden

2. Would you survey the whole population or only a sample if you want to find …

   a) …the average height of grade 5 students in Ontario

   b) …the average height of grade 5 students in your class

   c) …what movie your friends want to see tonight

   d) …how many people watched the Super Bowl

Answer the following questions in your notebook.

1. Which question (A, B, C, or D) would you use to find out if girls or boys like to read more? Explain.

A. Gender   F ☐   M ☐

Do you like to read for fun?

     YES ☐   NO ☐

B. Gender   F ☐   M ☐

How many books have you read in the last year for fun? _____

C. Gender   F ☐   M ☐

How often do you like to read for fun?

Any chance I get ☐   Sometimes ☐

Not very often ☐   Never ☐

D. Gender   F ☐   M ☐

How many books have you read in the last year for fun?

     0 ☐   1-5 ☐

6-10 ☐   11 or more ☐

2. Write a survey question for each topic below. To find out …

   i) …the most common shoe size among grade 5 girls.

   ii) …how many pets students in your school have.

   iii) …what kind of fruit juice students like best.

3. Who would you survey for each survey in question 2?
   Choose a sample that represents the group you want to find out about.

4. Now do your own survey. Record all of your ideas, data, observation and conclusions.

   a) Decide what question you want to ask. What answers do you expect?

How do you get to school?	Tally
Walk	
Take the bus	
Ride my bike	

   b) Who should you survey? Is the sample representative?
      Are you including enough people?

   c) What type of graph should you use?

   d) Summarize your conclusions. Did people respond as expected?

 jump math
MULTIPLYING POTENTIAL

Answer the following questions in your notebook.

1. *Do ice cubes made from the same amount of water but different shaped containers melt at the same rate?*

    a) Draw 3 different containers you could use to do the experiment.

    b) How would you make sure the same amount of water is put into each container?

    c) How would you measure the rate of melting?

    d) What other equipment do you need?

    e) What will happen to the results of your experiment, if you place one container in the open sun and another in the shade?

    f) Predict your results. Do you think the shape of the container will affect how fast the ice melts?

    g) What type of graph would you use to display your results?

2. Now design your own experiment.

   a) Decide on your question. You can use one of the examples below or make up your own question.

      A. Choose 3 paper rectangles with the same area but different perimeters to build paper airplanes.

      Which rectangle makes an airplane that flies the furthest?

      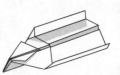

      B. How does adding sugar to strawberries affect how long the strawberries stay good for?

      C. How does adding salt to ice affect how fast it melts?

   b) What do you need to measure?

   c) How will you measure your results?

   d) How will you make sure your experiment gives reliable results? (You will need to keep everything except what you want to measure constant).

   e) Predict your results.

   f) Draw the table you will use to record your results.

   g) Choose and draw an appropriate type of graph to display your data.

   h) Summarize your conclusions.

G5-1: Sides and Vertices of 2-D Figures

Polygons have **sides** (or 'edges') and **vertices** (the 'corners' where the sides meet):

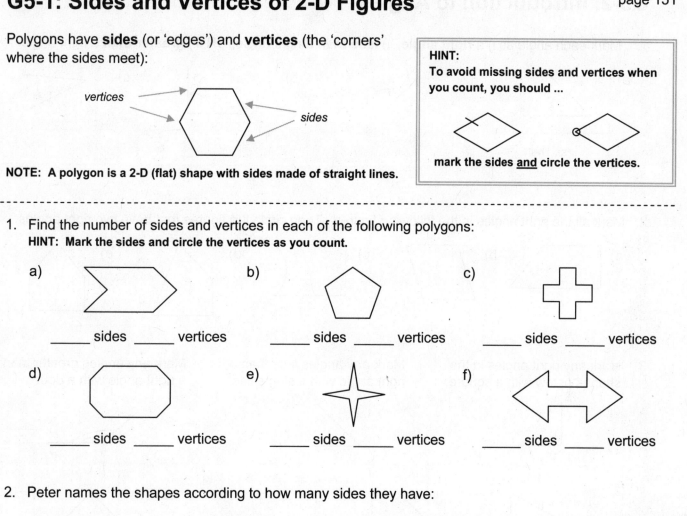

vertices → → *sides*

NOTE: A polygon is a 2-D (flat) shape with sides made of straight lines.

HINT:
To avoid missing sides and vertices when you count, you should ...

mark the sides <u>and</u> circle the vertices.

---

1. Find the number of sides and vertices in each of the following polygons:
   HINT: Mark the sides and circle the vertices as you count.

   a)

   _____ sides _____ vertices

   b)

   _____ sides _____ vertices

   c)

   _____ sides _____ vertices

   d)

   _____ sides _____ vertices

   e)

   _____ sides _____ vertices

   f)

   _____ sides _____ vertices

2. Peter names the shapes according to how many sides they have:

   a) _____ sides
   triangle

   b) _____ sides
   quadrilateral

   c) _____ sides
   pentagon

   d) _____ sides
   hexagon

3. Complete the chart. Find as many shapes as you can for each shape name:

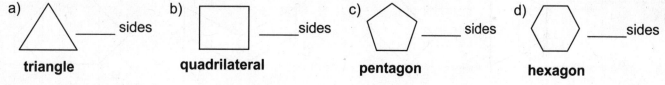

A B C D E F G H I

Shapes	Letters
Triangles	
Quadrilaterals	

Shapes	Letters
Pentagons	
Hexagons	

4. On grid paper, draw a polygon with: a) 4 sides   b) 6 sides

5. How many sides do three quadrilaterals and five pentagons have altogether? Explain.

G5-2: Introduction to Angles

1. Mark each angle as i) a **right angle**; ii) **less than** a right angle; OR iii) **greater than** a right angle.

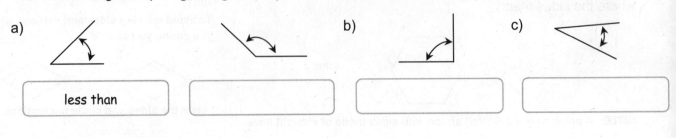

a)   b)   c)

less than			

2. Mark all the right angles in the following figures. Then circle the figures that have <u>two</u> right angles:

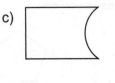

a)   b)   c)   d)   e)

3.
Mark any right angles in the shapes below with a square.	Mark any angles less than a right angle with a single line.	Mark any angles greater than a right angle with a double line.

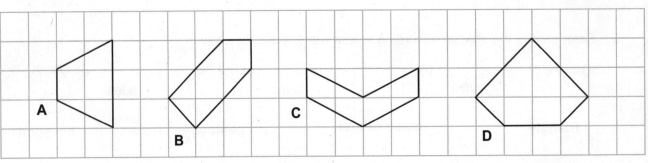

A   B   C   D

4. a) Draw 5 letters with at least one right angle.
      Mark all the right angles with a square.

   b) Which letter of the alphabet do you think has the most right angles?

5. Angles that are less than a right angle are called <u>acute</u> angles.
   Angles that are greater than a right angle are called <u>obtuse</u> angles.

   a) Draw 3 letters with acute angles and 3 with obtuse angles.

   b) Can you find a letter that has both a right angle and an acute angle?

F

M

M has 3 acute angles

A

A has 2 obtuse angles

Geometry 1

G5-3: Measuring Angles

To measure an angle, you use a **protractor**. A protractor has 180 subdivisions around its circumference. The subdivisions are called degrees. 45° is a short form for "forty-five degrees."

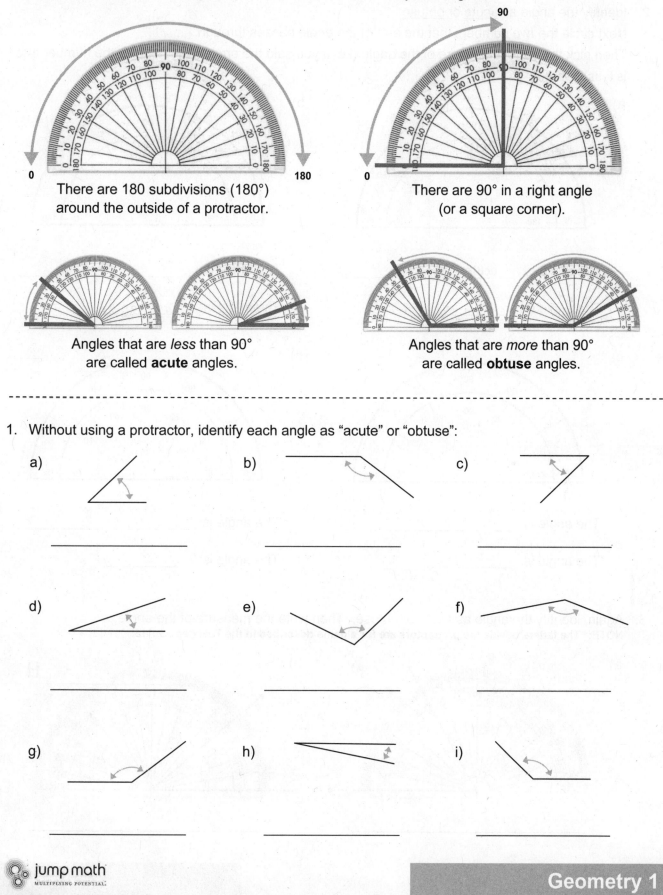

There are 180 subdivisions (180°) around the outside of a protractor.

There are 90° in a right angle (or a square corner).

Angles that are *less* than 90° are called **acute** angles.

Angles that are *more* than 90° are called **obtuse** angles.

---

1. Without using a protractor, identify each angle as "acute" or "obtuse":

   a)

   b)

   c)

   d)

   e)

   f)

   g)

   h)

   i)

A protractor has two scales. The exercise below will help you decide which scale to use:

2. Identify the angle as <u>acute</u> or <u>obtuse</u>.

   Next circle the *two* numbers that the arm of the angle passes through.

   Then pick the correct measure of the angle (i.e. if you said the angle is acute, pick the number that is less than 90):

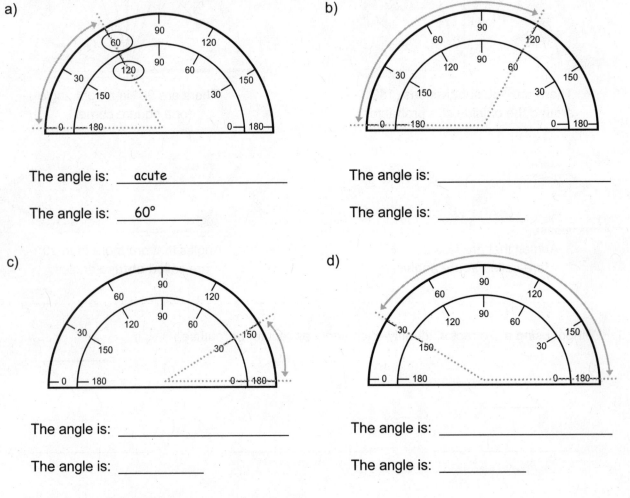

a)

The angle is: ___acute___

The angle is: ___60°___

b)

The angle is: _____

The angle is: _____

c)

The angle is: _____

The angle is: _____

d)

The angle is: _____

The angle is: _____

3. Again, identify the angle as acute or obtuse. Then write the measure of the angle:

   NOTE: The letters beside the protractors are for a game described in the Teachers Guide.

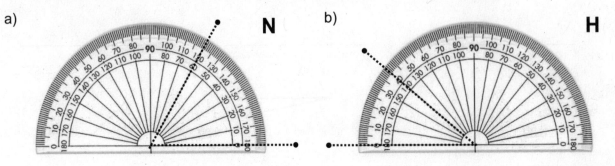

a)   **N**

_____

b)   **H**

_____

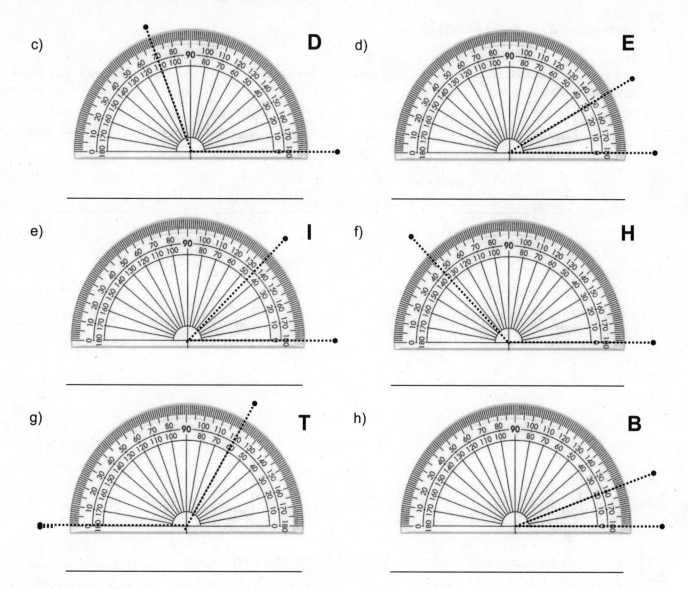

c) **D**

d) **E**

e) **I**

f) **H**

g) **T**

h) **B**

4. Measure the angles using a protractor. Then write the answer in the boxes provided – don't forget units!

   HINT: Use a ruler to extend the lines in d) and e).

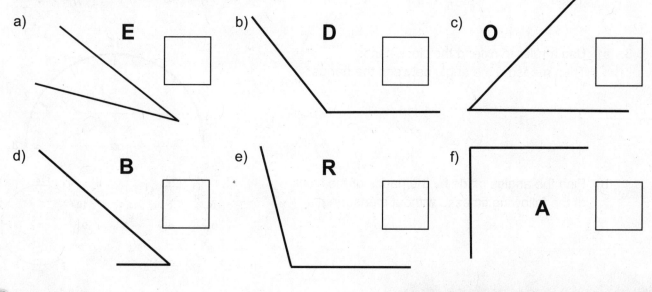

a) **E**

b) **D**

c) **O**

d) **B**

e) **R**

f) **A**

Clare makes a 60° angle as follows:

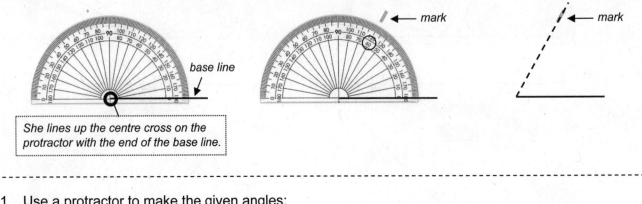

Step 1:
She draws a base line and places the protractor on the base line as shown:

Step 2:
She makes a mark at 60°:

← mark

Step 3:
Using a ruler, she joins the end point of the base line to her mark:

← mark

base line

She lines up the centre cross on the protractor with the end of the base line.

----

1. Use a protractor to make the given angles:

    a)

    b)

    150°

    120°   60°

2. In your notebook, use a protractor to construct the following angles:

    a) 45°   b) 80°   c) 50°   d) 35°   e) 62°

    f) 90°   g) 125°   h) 75°   i) 145°   j) 168°

3. a) Use a ruler to extend the clock hands.
        Then measure the angle between the hands.

    b) Find the angles made by the hands of the clock
        at the following times ... without measuring!

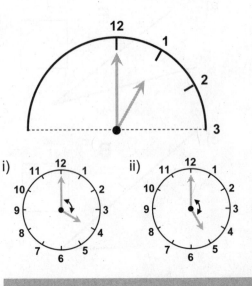

i)   ii)

G5-5: Angles in Triangles and Polygons

An <u>acute</u> angle is less than 90°, an <u>obtuse</u> angle is greater than 90° and a <u>right</u> angle is exactly 90°.

  i) An **acute-angled triangle** has all acute angles.

  ii) An **obtuse-angled triangle** has an obtuse angle.

  iii) A **right-angled triangle** has a 90° angle.

If you measure the angles in a triangle accurately, you will find that they always add up to 180°.

----

1. Classify each triangle as <u>acute-angled</u>, <u>obtuse-angled</u> or <u>right-angled</u>.
  For short, you can just write acute, obtuse or right.

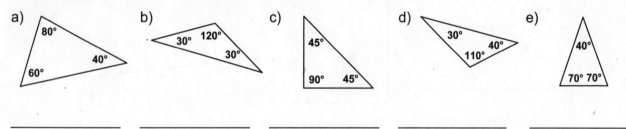

a)   b)   c)   d)   e)

_____ _____ _____ _____ _____

2. Measure all of the angles in each triangle and write your measurement in the triangle. Then say what type of triangle it is:

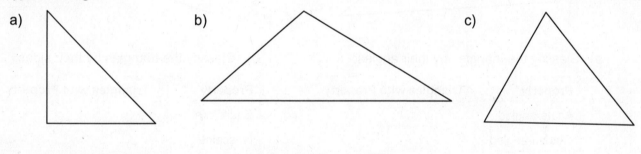

a)   b)   c)

_____   _____   _____

3. A **regular** polygon has all angles and sides equal.

  a) Measure one angle in each of the regular polygons below. Then fill in the chart:

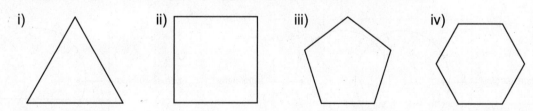

    i)   ii)   iii)   iv)

Polygons	i) Equilateral Triangle	ii) Square	iii) Regular Pentagon	iv) Regular Hexagon
Measure of Angles				

  b) Do you think the angles in a regular octagon will be greater or less than 120°? Explain.

jump math
MULTIPLYING POTENTIAL.

Triangles can be classified by the size of their angles, but they can also be classified by the length of their sides:

    i)   In an **equilateral triangle**, all three sides are of equal length.

    ii)   In an **isosceles triangle**, two sides are of equal length.

    iii)   In a **scalene triangle**, no two sides are of equal length.

----

1. Measure the <u>angles</u> and <u>sides</u> (in cm – or mm if necessary) of each triangle, and write your measurements on the triangles. Then use the charts to classify the triangles:

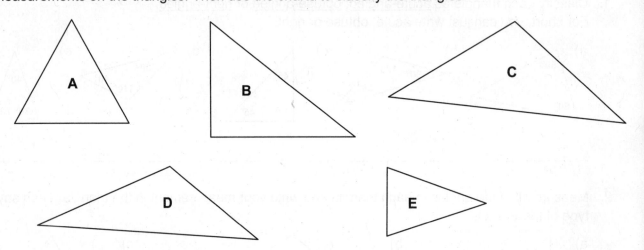

  a) Classify the triangles by their angles:

Property	Triangles with Property
Acute-angled	
Obtuse-angled	
Right-angled	

  b) Classify the triangles by their sides:

Property	Triangles with Property
Equilateral	
Isosceles	
Scalene	

2. Sort the triangles above by their properties:

  a)

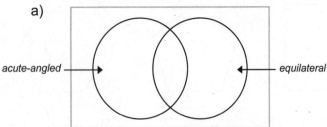

acute-angled   equilateral

  b)

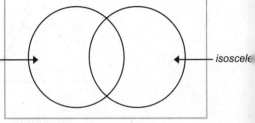

obtuse-angled   isoscele

3. Pick one property from each list below. Draw a rough sketch of a triangle that has both properties. If you can't sketch the triangle, write "impossible":

    List 1: acute-angled, obtuse-angled, right-angled   **List 2:** equilateral, isosceles, scalene

G5-7: Constructing Triangles and Polygons

To construct a triangle from a given base line:

i) Using a protractor, construct an angle at each end of the base:

ii) Extend the arms of your angles until they meet:

base

1. Construct triangles using the bases and base angles given below.

    a)

    b)

    40°   70°   50°   40°

2. Construct triangles with the following measurements:

    a) Base = 5 cm; Base angles = 45° and 50°

    b) Sides = 5 cm and 7 cm; Angle between these two sides = 40°

3. a) Construct three triangles, each with a 5 cm base and the given base angles:

    i)   40° and 40°   ii)   50° and 50°   iii) 60° and 60°

    b) Measure the sides of the triangles you drew.
        What do you notice about the lengths of the sides?

    c) What kind of triangles did you draw?

4. Draw free hand sketches of ...

    a) a right-angled triangle   b) an acute-angled triangle   c) an obtuse-angled triangle

5. Draw a square on grid paper and draw the diagonals of the square.
    Measure all the angles around the point P where the diagonals meet.
    What do you notice?

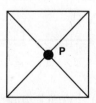

G5-8: Parallel Lines

Parallel lines are like straight sections of railway tracks – that is, they are:

- ✓ Straight
- ✓ Always the same distance apart

No matter how long they are - parallel lines will <u>never</u> meet.

NOTE:
Lines of different lengths can still be parallel (as long as they are both straight and are always the same distance apart).

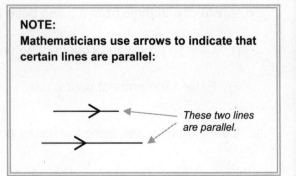

NOTE:
Mathematicians use arrows to indicate that certain lines are parallel:

These two lines are parallel.

---

1. Mark any pairs of lines that are parallel with arrows (see note above):

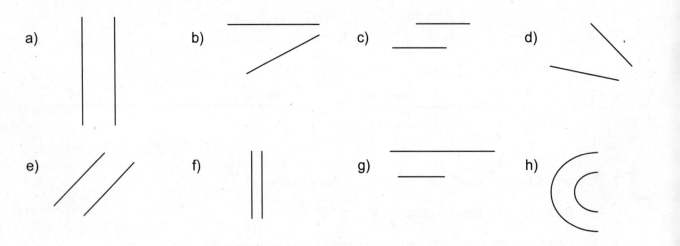

a)   b)   c)   d)

e)   f)   g)   h)

BONUS

i) Select one pair of lines above that <u>are not</u> parallel. Put the corresponding letter here: _____

j) How do you know these lines aren't parallel?

2. The following pairs of lines are parallel. In each case, join the dots to make a quadrilateral. The first one has been done for you:

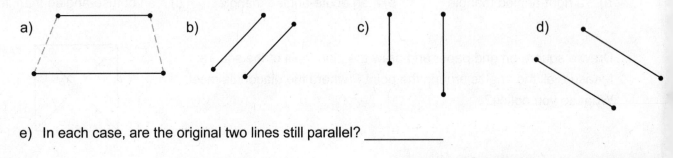

a)   b)   c)   d)

e) In each case, are the original two lines still parallel? _____

3. Each of the shapes below has **one pair** of parallel sides. Mark opposite sides that are <u>not</u> parallel. The first one has been done for you:

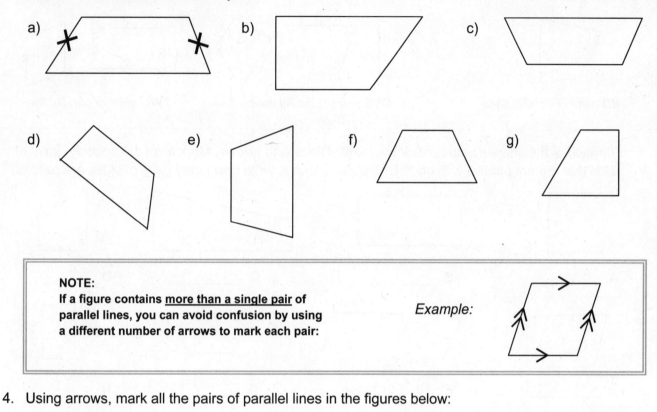

NOTE:
If a figure contains <u>more than a single pair</u> of parallel lines, you can avoid confusion by using a different number of arrows to mark each pair:

Example:

4. Using arrows, mark all the pairs of parallel lines in the figures below:

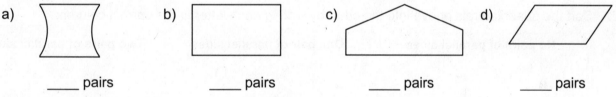

a) ____ pairs   b) ____ pairs   c) ____ pairs   d) ____ pairs

5. On the grid, draw ...

a) ... a pair of horizontal lines that are parallel and 3 units apart

b) ... a pair of vertical lines that are parallel and that have different lengths

c) ... a figure with 1 pair of parallel sides

6. The letter F has two parallel lines in it.
Choose 5 letters of the alphabet and mark any parallel lines.
Which letter of the alphabet do you think has the greatest number of lines that are all parallel?

Some quadrilaterals have no pairs of parallel lines. Trapezoids have <u>one</u> pair of parallel lines. **Parallelograms** have <u>two</u> pairs of parallel lines:

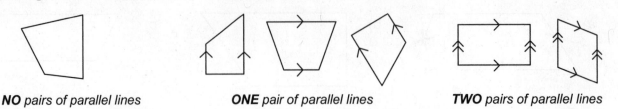

NO *pairs of parallel lines*   **ONE** *pair of parallel lines*   **TWO** *pairs of parallel lines*

1. For each of the shapes below, mark the parallel lines with arrows. Mark all of the opposite pairs of sides that are not parallel with an X. Under each shape, write how many <u>pairs</u> of sides are parallel:

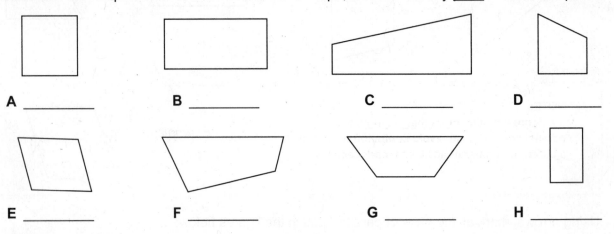

A _____   B _____   C _____   D _____

E _____   F _____   G _____   H _____

2. Sort the quadrilaterals above into the chart by writing each letter in the correct column:

No pairs of parallel sides	One pair of parallel sides	Two pairs of parallel sides

3. Using the figures below, complete the two charts. Start by marking the right angles and parallel lines in each figure:

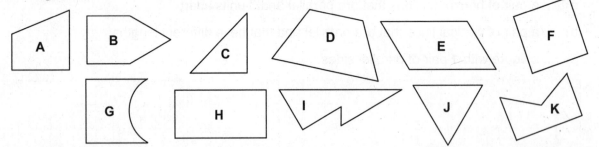

a)

Property	Shapes with Property
No right angles	
1 right angle	
2 right angles	
4 right angles	

b)

Property	Shapes with Property
No parallel lines	
1 pair	
2 pairs	

4. Use a ruler to measure the sides of the shapes below. Circle the shapes that are equilateral:

   NOTE: A shape with all sides the same length is called <u>equilateral</u>. ("Equi" comes from a Latin word meaning "equal" and "lateral" means "sides".)

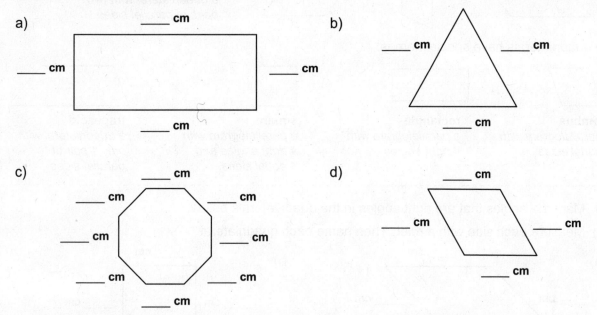

a)

b)

c)

d)

5. Complete the charts below. Start by marking the right angles and parallel lines in each figure. If you are not sure if a figure is equilateral, measure its sides with a ruler:

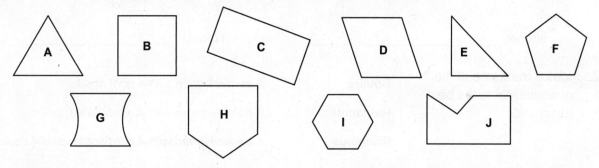

a)

Property	Shapes with Property
Equilateral	
Not equilateral	

b)

Property	Shapes with Property
No right angles	
1 right angle	
2 right angles	
3 right angles	
4 right angles	

c)

Property	Shapes with Property
No obtuse angles	
1 or more obtuse angles	

d)

Property	Shapes with Property
No parallel sides	
1 pair of parallel sides	
2 pairs of parallel sides	
3 pairs of parallel sides	

e)

Polygon Name	Shapes
Triangles	
Quadrilaterals	
Pentagons	
Hexagons	

NOTE: Polygons must have <u>straight</u> sides.

G5-10: Special Quadrilaterals

A **quadrilateral** (shape with 4 sides) with two pairs of parallel sides is called a **parallelogram**:

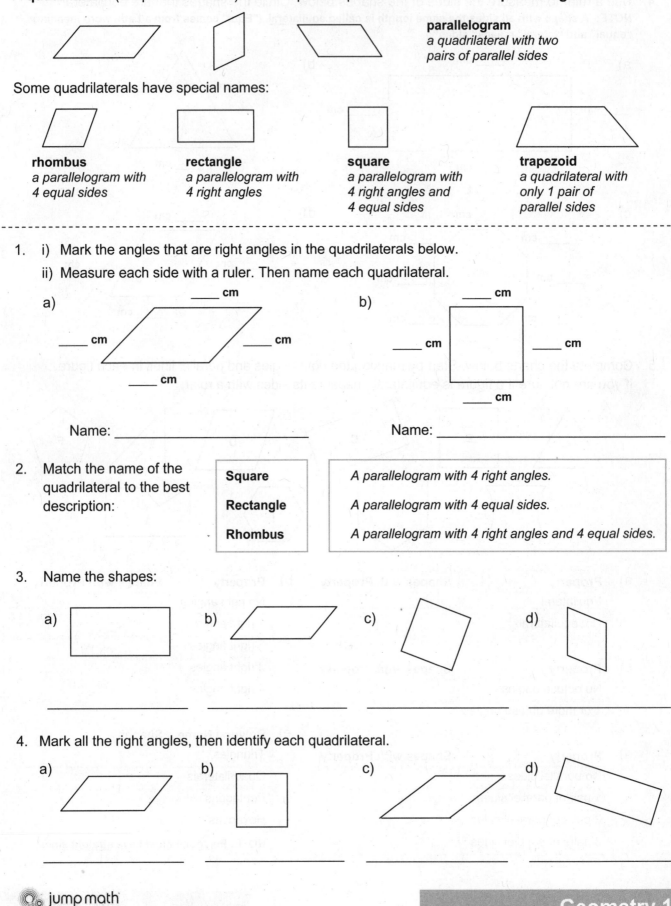

parallelogram
a quadrilateral with two
pairs of parallel sides

Some quadrilaterals have special names:

rhombus
a parallelogram with
4 equal sides

rectangle
a parallelogram with
4 right angles

square
a parallelogram with
4 right angles and
4 equal sides

trapezoid
a quadrilateral with
only 1 pair of
parallel sides

- -

1. i) Mark the angles that are right angles in the quadrilaterals below.

   ii) Measure each side with a ruler. Then name each quadrilateral.

   a) _____ cm

   _____ cm   _____ cm

   _____ cm

   Name: _____

   b) _____ cm

   _____ cm   _____ cm

   _____ cm

   Name: _____

2. Match the name of the quadrilateral to the best description:

Square	A parallelogram with 4 right angles.
Rectangle	A parallelogram with 4 equal sides.
Rhombus	A parallelogram with 4 right angles and 4 equal sides.

3. Name the shapes:

   a) _____   b) _____   c) _____   d) _____

4. Mark all the right angles, then identify each quadrilateral.

   a) _____   b) _____   c) _____   d) _____

5. Say how many <u>pairs</u> of sides are parallel, then identify each quadrilateral.

   a)

   _____

   _____

   b)

   _____

   _____

   c)

   _____

   _____

6. The shape on the grid is a trapezoid.
   On the grid, draw a second trapezoid
   that has <u>no</u> right angles:

7. Use the words "all", "some", or "no" for each statement:

   a) _____ squares are rectangles

   b) _____ trapezoids are parallelograms

   c) _____ parallelograms are trapezoids

   d) _____ parallelograms are rectangles

8. a) I have 4 equal sides, but no right angles. What am I? _____

   b) I have 4 right angles, but my sides are not all equal. What am I? _____

   c) I have exactly 2 right angles. Which special quadrilateral could I be? _____

9. A shape has 4 right angles.

   Which two special quadrilaterals might it be?

   _____

   _____

10. A quadrilateral has all equal sides.

    Which two special quadrilaterals might it be?

    _____

    _____

11. Write 3 different names for a square.

12. On grid paper (or on a geoboard), construct a quadrilateral with:

    a) no right angles   b) one right angle   c) two right angles   d) no parallel sides

    e) one pair of parallel sides   f) two pairs of parallel sides and no right angles

13. Describe any similarities or differences between…

    a) a rhombus and a square

    b) a trapezoid and a parallelogram

G5-11: Exploring Congruency

Shapes are **congruent** if they are **the same size** and **the same shape**. Congruent shapes can have different colours and patterns, and can be facing different directions:

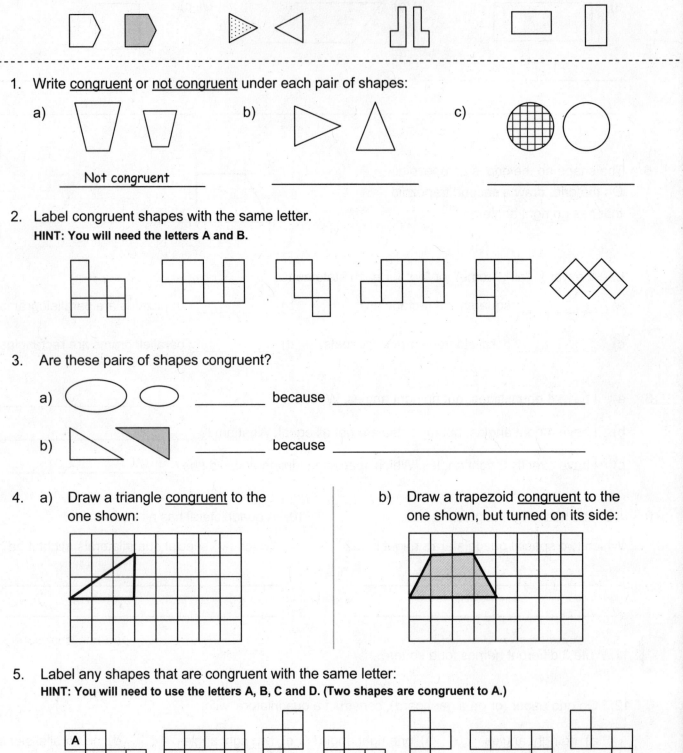

1. Write <u>congruent</u> or <u>not congruent</u> under each pair of shapes:

   a)

   Not congruent

   b)

   c)

2. Label congruent shapes with the same letter.

   HINT: You will need the letters A and B.

3. Are these pairs of shapes congruent?

   a) _____ because _____

   b) _____ because _____

4. a) Draw a triangle <u>congruent</u> to the one shown:

   b) Draw a trapezoid <u>congruent</u> to the one shown, but turned on its side:

5. Label any shapes that are congruent with the same letter:

   HINT: You will need to use the letters A, B, C and D. (Two shapes are congruent to A.)

   A

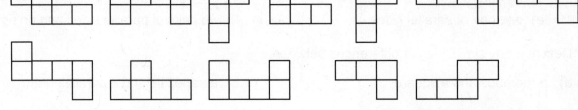

G5-12: Exploring Congruency (Advanced)

1. Look at the shapes from left to right. If you find a shape that is congruent to a shape you have already looked at, cross it out.
   How many non-congruent shapes are left? The first one is done for you:

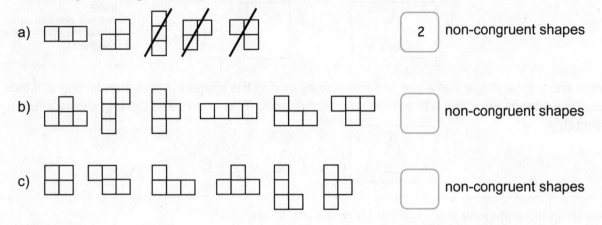

   a)   **2**   non-congruent shapes

   b)   non-congruent shapes

   c)   non-congruent shapes

2. Starting with the shape on the left, add a square to each shape in the position shown by the arrow.
   If you create a shape that is congruent to a shape you have already made, cross it out.
   How many non-congruent shapes did you make?

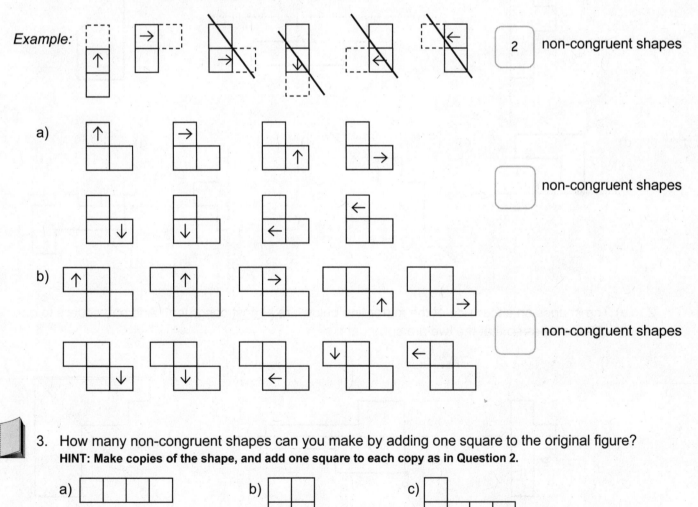

   Example: **2**   non-congruent shapes

   a)   non-congruent shapes

   b)   non-congruent shapes

3. How many non-congruent shapes can you make by adding one square to the original figure?
   HINT: Make copies of the shape, and add one square to each copy as in Question 2.

   a)   b)   c)

Some shapes have lines of **symmetry**. Tina places a mirror across half the shape. If the half reflected in the mirror makes the shape 'whole' again, the shape is symmetrical.

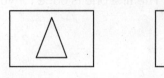

mirror

NOTE:
The two sides on either side of the mirror line are congruent.

Tina also checks if a shape has a line of symmetry by cutting the shape out and then folding it. If the halves of the shapes on either side of the fold match exactly, Tina knows that the fold shows a **line of symmetry**:

1. Complete the picture so that the dotted line is a line of symmetry:

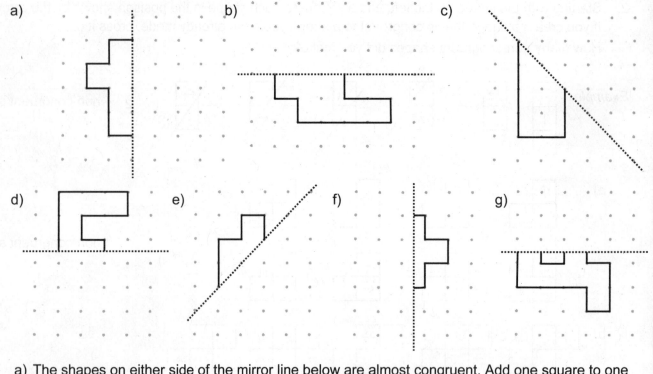

a) b) c)

d) e) f) g)

2. a) The shapes on either side of the mirror line below are <u>almost</u> congruent. Add one square to one of the shapes so that the two are congruent:

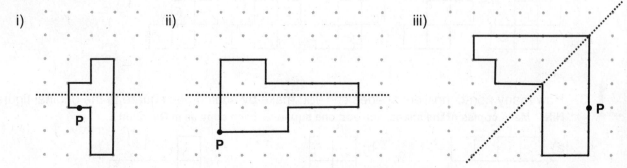

i) ii) iii)

b) On each shape above, show the image of point P after a reflection through the mirror line.

3. Quilts are often made from triangles of fabric that are sewn together.

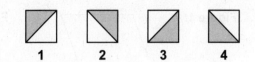

a) Make some designs for quilts using half shaded squares.
   Draw any lines of symmetry you see (vertical, horizontal, and diagonal).

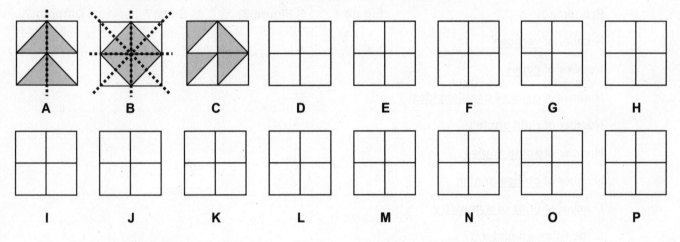

b) Complete the following chart based on the number of lines of symmetry you found:

Number of Lines of Symmetry	0	1	2	4
Letter beneath Grid	C,	A,		B,

4. a) Draw at least 5 letters of the alphabet and show their lines of symmetry.

   b) Can you find a letter with 2 or more lines of symmetry?

5.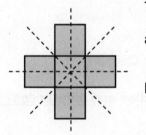

   The figure shown has four lines of symmetry.

   a) Show how you could move one square so the resulting figure has no lines of symmetry.

   b) Show two different ways to move a square so the resulting figure has one line of symmetry. **NOTE: You are allowed to move the centre square.**

6. Use a ruler and a protractor to construct a triangle with the dimensions shown.

   Then construct its reflection in the mirror line.

   What kind of triangle do the two smaller triangles make?

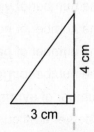

1.   Figure 1:   Figure 2:

a) Compare the two shapes above by completing the following chart:

Property	Figure 1	Figure 2	Same?	Different?
Number of **vertices**				
Number of **edges**				
Number of **pairs of parallel sides**				
Number of **right angles**				
Number of **acute angles**				
Number of **obtuse angles**				
Number of **lines of symmetry**				
Is the figure **equilateral**?				

b) By simply looking at Figures 1 and 2 below, can you say how they are the same and different?

Figure 1:

Figure 2:

Property	Same?	Different?
Number of **vertices**		
Number of **edges**		
Number of **pairs of parallel sides**		
Number of **right angles**		
Number of **acute angles**		
Number of **obtuse angles**		
Number of lines of **symmetry**		
Is the figure **equilateral**?		

2. Draw two figures and compare them using a chart (similar to that in Question 1).

3. Looking at the following figures, can you comment on their **similarities** and **differences**? Be sure to mention the following properties:

   ✓ The number of **vertices**
   ✓ The number of **edges**
   ✓ The number of **pairs of parallel sides**
   ✓ The number of **right angles**
   ✓ Number of **symmetries**
   ✓ Whether the figure is **equilateral**

Figure 1:   Figure 2:

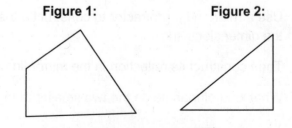

1. The following figures can be sorted by their properties using a Venn diagram:

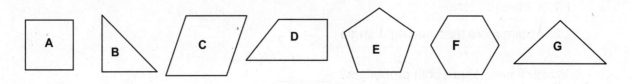

a)

Property	Figures with This Property
1. I am a quadrilateral	A, C, D
2. I am equilateral	A, C, E, F

Which figures share both properties? _____

Using the information in the chart above, complete the following Venn diagram:

NOTE: If a shape does not have either property, write its letter inside the box, but outside both circles.

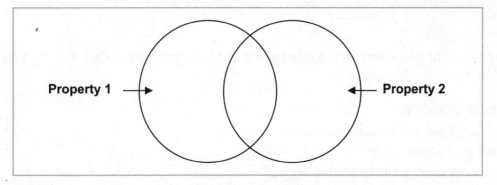

Using figures A through G above, complete the charts and the Venn diagrams below:

b)

Property	Figures with This Property
1. I have <u>no</u> right angles	
2. I have four or more sides	

Which figures share both properties? _____

Using the information in the chart above, complete the following Venn diagram:

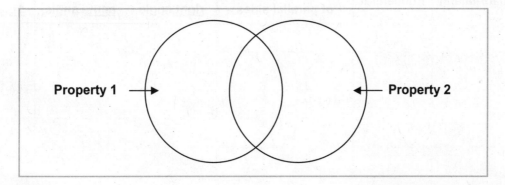

Geometry 1

c)

Property	Figures with This Property
1. I am equilateral	
2. I have more than one right angle	

Which figures share both properties? _____

Using the information in the chart above, complete the following Venn diagram:

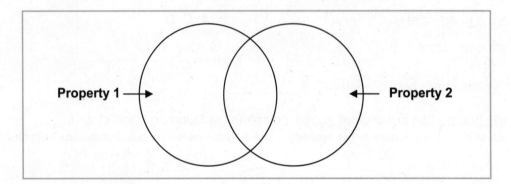

Property 1 →   ← Property 2

2. Using two properties of your own make a chart and a Venn diagram (as in Question 1). You may want to choose from the following:

- ✓ Number of vertices
- ✓ Number of pairs of parallel sides
- ✓ Number of edges
- ✓ Number of right, acute or obtuse angles
- ✓ Lines of symmetry
- ✓ Equilateral

3. Record the properties of each shape. Write "yes" in the column if the shape has the given property. Otherwise, write "no":

A   B   C   D   E

Shape	Quadrilateral	Equilateral	Two or more pairs of parallel sides	At least one <u>right</u> angle	At least one <u>acute</u> angle	At least one <u>obtuse</u> angle
A						
B						
C						
D						
E						

jump math
MULTIPLYING POTENTIAL.

1. Write T (for true) or F (for false). The figure has ...

a) 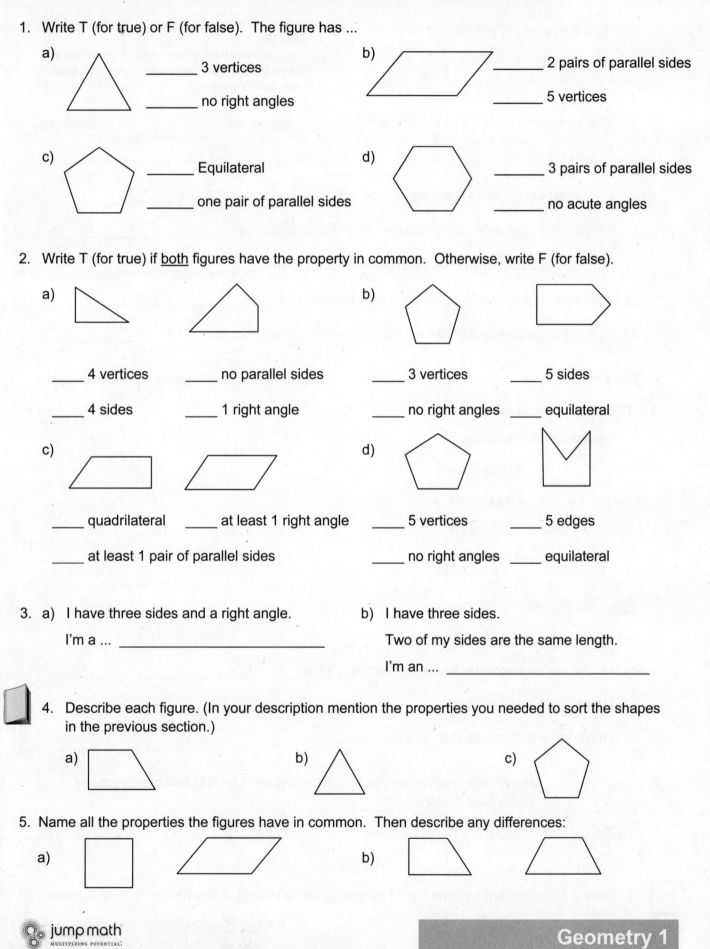 _____ 3 vertices

_____ no right angles

b) _____ 2 pairs of parallel sides

_____ 5 vertices

c) _____ Equilateral

_____ one pair of parallel sides

d) _____ 3 pairs of parallel sides

_____ no acute angles

2. Write T (for true) if <u>both</u> figures have the property in common. Otherwise, write F (for false).

a) _____ 4 vertices   _____ no parallel sides

_____ 4 sides   _____ 1 right angle

b) _____ 3 vertices   _____ 5 sides

_____ no right angles   _____ equilateral

c) _____ quadrilateral   _____ at least 1 right angle

_____ at least 1 pair of parallel sides

d) _____ 5 vertices   _____ 5 edges

_____ no right angles   _____ equilateral

3. a) I have three sides and a right angle.

I'm a ... _____

b) I have three sides.

Two of my sides are the same length.

I'm an ... _____

4. Describe each figure. (In your description mention the properties you needed to sort the shapes in the previous section.)

a)   b)   c)

5. Name all the properties the figures have in common. Then describe any differences:

a)   b)

G5-17: Puzzles and Problems

1. Measure the sides of the following parallelograms:

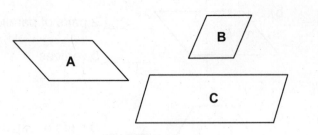

> **NOTE:**
> In a quadrilateral, a pair of sides that meet at a vertex are called <u>adjacent</u>. Otherwise, they are called <u>opposite</u>:
>
> <u>adjacent</u> sides →   ← <u>opposite</u> sides

a) Are all pairs of opposite sides equal in all of the parallelograms? _____

b) Are all pairs of adjacent sides equal in all of the parallelograms? _____

c) How many acute angles does each parallelogram have? _____

d) How many obtuse angles does each parallelogram have? _____

e) One of the parallelograms has another name. Which parallelogram is it? _____

2. Complete the chart:

	Square	Rectangle	Rhombus	Parallelogram
Opposite pairs of sides equal	Yes			
Adjacent pairs of sides equal				
4 sides equal				
4 right angles				
Number of pairs of parallel sides	2			
Number of lines of symmetry				

3. Name the triangles:

a) I have three equal sides. I am an ... _____

b) I have one angle greater than a right angle. I am an _____

c) I have one right angle. I am a ... _____

d) I have three angles less than 90°. I am an ... _____

4. How many shapes can you find in the hexagon (at left) that are <u>congruent</u> to the ones below?

     a) _____   b) _____

5. Draw a trapezoid that has one line of symmetry and a trapezoid that has no lines of symmetry.